AF600064

THE CATHOLIC UNIVERSITY OF AMERICA
CANON LAW STUDIES
No. 275

TIME AND PLACE FOR THE CELEBRATION OF MASS

HISTORICAL SYNOPSIS AND COMMENTARY

by the

REVEREND JAMES GODLEY, J.C.L.
Priest of the Diocese of Cheyenne.

A DISSERTATION

Submitted to the Faculty of the School of Canon Law of the Catholic University of America in Partial Fulfillment of the Requirements for the Degree of Doctor of Canon Law

THE CATHOLIC UNIVERSITY OF AMERICA
WASHINGTON, D. C.
1948

Nihil Obstat:

Eduardus G. Roelker, S.T.D., J.C.D.,
Censor Deputatus.

Imprimatur:

✠ Patrick A. McGovern, D.D.,
Bishop of Cheyenne, Wyoming.

Printed by
The Paulist Press
401 West 59th Street
New York 19, N. Y.

51

TABLE OF CONTENTS

CHAPTER III

CHAPTER IV

FOREWORD

THE Holy Sacrifice of the Mass, the central act of worship of the Catholic Church, was instituted by Christ on the first Holy Thursday night. The church was the upper room in Jerusalem, the altar was the dining table, and the time was in the evening. These were the circumstances attendant on the scene of the Last Supper, hence, the legal institutes of time and place in reference to the Holy Sacrifice had small beginnings. Thus, the Church in accordance with its meager beginnings and inexperienced members had little or no legislation on the Mass for some time after the death of Christ.

It is the purpose of this work to trace the development of the law in reference to the time and place for the celebration of Mass. In this treatment two main divisions are observed—the first containing a historical synopsis of the development of the legislation before the Code of Canon Law, the second containing a commentary on the currently existing law.

The first part of the work falls under four divisions: (1) The history of the Mass in regard to the time and place of celebration from the first Holy Thursday to the Edict of Milan (313), which brought an end to the persecutions of the Christians; (2) the development of the law from the Edict of Milan to Gratian (ca. 1140); (3) the treatment of the legislation from the time of Gratian to the Council of Trent; and (4) from the Council of Trent to the Code of Canon Law.

The second part of the work consists of the canonical commentary on the present law. This falls under two principal divisions, namely, the first, treating of the time for the celebration of Mass in reference to days and hours, and the second, dealing with the place, which involves a review of the church and oratory, the altar, and finally the use of a portable altar outside the church or oratory.

The writer wishes to express his sincere gratitude to the Most Reverend Patrick A. McGovern, Bishop of Cheyenne, Wyoming, for the opportunity to pursue advanced studies at The Catholic University of America, Washington, D. C.; to the members of the Faculty of the School of Canon Law for their assistance and direction in the preparation of this work; and to all others who contributed towards the completion of this dissertation.

CHAPTER I

THE FIRST HOLY THURSDAY TO THE EDICT OF MILAN (313)

ARTICLE 1. THE FIRST HOLY MASS

LEGISLATION on the time for the celebration of Mass points to the days on which, and the hours of the day at which Mass may be offered. Legislation on the place for the celebration of Mass is concerned with the altar on which and the church in which the Holy Sacrifice may be offered.[1]

On all these points Sacred Scripture furnishes the account of the first Mass.[2] On the first day of the unleavened bread,[3] the fourteenth of Nisan,[4] the first Holy Thursday, in the evening,[5] Christ and the Apostles gathered together in the large upper room [6] and reclined at table.[7] There the first Holy Mass was offered by Christ.

ARTICLE 2. THE MASS IN APOSTOLIC TIMES

It is commonly thought that probably no other Mass was offered by the Apostles after Holy Thursday until Pentecost,[8] when the

[1] Blat, *Commentarium Textus Codicis Iuris Canonici* (5 vols. in 7, Lib. III, pars I, *De Sacramentis*, 2. ed., 1938), Lib. III, pars I, n. 128 (hereafter cited *De Sacramentis*).

[2] Matt., XXVI, 17-28; Mark, XIV, 12-26; Luke, XXII, 7-20; I Cor., XI, 23-27.

[3] Luke, XXII, 7; Matt., XXVI, 17; Mark, XIV, 12.

[4] De Puniet, *The Mass, Its Origin and History*, translated by the Benedictines of Stanbrook (London: Burns, Oates & Washbourne, Ltd., 1931), p. 6 (hereafter cited *The Mass*).

[5] Mark, XIV, 17; Matt., XXVI, 20; I Cor., XI, 23.

[6] Mark, XIV, 15; Luke, XXII, 12.

[7] Matt., XXVI, 20; Mark, XVI, 18; Luke, XXII, 14.

[8] Cf. Bona, *Rerum Liturgicarum Libri Duo* (2 vols., Taurini, 1749), Lib. I, c. V, n. 1; O'Brien, *History of the Mass and Its Ceremonies* (14. revised ed., New York: Catholic Publication Society Co., 1891), pp. 18 ff.

Holy Ghost came upon them after the third hour.[9] Then the scene of the first Mass was duplicated by the Apostles gathered together in the upper room.[10] Thenceforward the Mass was offered more frequently among the Christians of the Apostolic age. According to St. Paul it was offered daily.[11] In explaining the statement of St. Paul as contained in the *Acts of the Apostles* Eisenhofer (+1942) stated that the word "daily" as used in the text cannot be adduced as proof that daily Mass was the practice at that early period.[12] Mass was offered particularly on Sunday, the first day of the week.[13]

In conformity with its institution at the Last Supper the Holy Sacrifice was originally celebrated in the evening,[14] after the *Agape*.[15] The faithful who were gathered together for common prayer and the reading of the Scriptures partook of a common meal called the *Agape*, after which usually followed the celebration of the Holy Sacrifice.[16]

The altar for the "breaking of bread" was the wooden dining table in imitation of Christ's use of such a table at the Last Supper.[17]

9 Acts, II, 15.

10 Acts, I, 13; II, 1.

11 Acts, II, 46.

12 Eisenhofer, "Aus dieser Stelle auf eine taegliche Opferfeier im Urchristentum schliessen zu wollen, ginge zu weit. Es kann des 'taeglich' sich auch lediglich beziehen auf den Besuch des Tempels und das Brotbrechen nur auf die Agape, die ja mit dem Brotbrechungsritus eingeleitet wurde."—*Handbuch der katholischen Liturgik* (2 vols., Freiburg im Breisgau, 1931-1933), II, 21, a.

13 Acts, X, 7; Fortescue, *The Mass, A Study of the Roman Liturgy*, with additions by Herbert Thurston (new edition, London: Longmans, Green & Co., 1937), p. 3 (hereafter cited *The Mass*).

14 Acts, XX, 7-11.

15 I Cor., XI, 20-34; Funk, *A Manual of Church History* (second impression of the authorized translation from the fifth German edition by Luigi Cappadelta, 2 vols., St. Louis: Herder Book Co., 1910), I, 65; Fortescue, *The Mass*, p. 5.

16 De Puniet, *The Mass*, p. 33.

17 Gihr, *The Holy Sacrifice of the Mass*, translated from the sixth German edition (12. ed., St. Louis: Herder Book Co., 1937), p. 236. Cf. I Cor., X, 21: "You cannot be partakers of the table [*mensa*] of the Lord and of the table of devils." (Conc. Trident., sess. XXII, c. 1)—Schroeder, *Canons and Decrees of the Council of Trent, Original Text with English Translation* (St. Louis: Herder Book Co., 1941), pp. 145, 418.

The church was neither the Temple nor the Synagogue where the Apostles often went to pray,[18] but the first churches were the houses of the faithful.[19] Thus St. Paul broke bread in the third story room at Troas,[20] and tradition has it that St. Peter offered the first Mass in the house of Senator Pudens.[21]

This is a short synopsis of historical facts regarding the Mass of the Apostles, as gleaned from their own accounts in the Sacred Scripture, when they went about on their missionary labors.

ARTICLE 3. THE MASS AFTER THE TIME OF THE APOSTLES AND DURING THE PERSECUTIONS UNTIL 313.

During the first centuries there was no explicit legislation regarding the time and place for the celebration of Mass. A similar absence of regulation obtained with reference to most of the liturgical practices which did not involve the validity of the sacraments. It was custom and the exigencies of the times that determined the practice. Hence the writings of the Fathers must be consulted to show what the practice was with regard to the time and place for the celebration of Mass.

(*a*) *Time of Mass*

It is commonly agreed that solemn Mass was not celebrated daily.[22] The *Didache* or *Teaching of the Apostles* (ca. 90) refers to the meeting of the faithful every Sunday for the "breaking of bread." [23]

[18] Acts, II, 46.

[19] Acts, II, 46; Rom., XVI, 5; I Cor., XVI, 19; Col., IV, 15; Philemon, 2; Schuster, *The Sacramentary,* translated from the Italian by Arthur Levilis-Marke (5 vols., London: Burns, Oates & Washbourne, Ltd., 1924), I, 57.

[20] Acts, XX, 9.

[21] Gihr, *The Holy Sacrifice of the Mass,* p. 236; Benedictus XIV, *Commentarius de Sacrosancto Missae Sacrificio* (2 vols., cum appendicibus, Lovanii: Typographia Academica, 1762), Tom. I, c. 14 (hereafter cited as *De Missae Sacrificio*).

[22] Martène, *De Antiquis Ecclesiae Ritibus* (3 vols., Editio Novissima, Venetiis, 1783), Lib. I, c. II, art. III, n. 1.

[23] C. CIV, n. 1. "Die autem dominica congregati frangite panem et gratias agite, postquam confessi eritis peccata vestra, ut mundum sit sacrificium vestrum." —Quasten, *Monumenta Eucharistica et Liturgica Vetustissima* (Bonnae, 1935),

St. Justin the Martyr (ca. 100-ca. 166)[24] and Pliny the Younger (62-113) also intimated that as a rule Mass was celebrated only on Sunday in that early period.[25] Hence the Holy Sacrifice of the Mass was offered in common for all at least on Sunday.[26]

Other days were soon added for the public celebration of Mass. At first Wednesday and Friday were added, as appears from the testimony of Epiphanius of Salamis (+403)[27] and Tertullian (ca. 240).[28] Then Saturday was further added as a day for public Mass, at least in the East, according to the testimony of St. Basil (+379),[29]

pars I, p. 12, based on the Funk-Bihlmeyer edition of the *Didache,* 1924 (hereafter this work will be cited as *Monumenta*); De Puniet, *The Mass,* p. 41; Fortescue, *The Mass,* p. 8; cf. also *Constitutiones Apostolicae,* Lib. VII, c. 30: "Dominica, convenite assidue . . . ut sacrificium vestrum. . . ."—Migne, *Patrologiae Cursus Completus, Series Graeca* (161 vols., Parisiis, 1856-1866), I, 1022 (hereafter cited as *MPG*).

24 *Apologia,* I, c. 67: "Et die qui dicitur solis omnium qui in urbibus et in agris habitant, in unum fit conventus . . . panis adfertur et vinum et aqua . . .," Quasten, *Monumenta,* pars I, p. 19 (an emendation of the Goodspeed-Otto edition of the *Apologia*); *MPG,* VI, 429; Duchesne, *Christian Worship, Its Origin and Evolution,* translated from the third French edition (London: Society for Promoting Christian Knowledge, 1903), p. 50 (hereafter cited *Christian Worship*); Fortescue, *The Mass,* pp. 20, 185.

25 *Epistolae,* Lib. X, n. 97, *Plinius Trajano Imperatori De Christianorum Rebus Accurate Praescribit*—J. M. Gesneri, *Epistolae* (2 vols., Venetiis, 1786), II, 146; Fortescue, *The Mass,* pp. 16, 17, 185.

26 Cf. Hippolytus, *Traditio Apostolica* (ca. 220), c. LXVIII, n. 1, "de die dominica."—Quasten, *Monumenta,* pars I, p. 27; Duchesne, *Christian Worship,* p. 229; Fortescue, *The Mass,* pp. 56, 185.

27 *Expositio Fidei,* n. 22—*MPG,* XLII, 825.

28 *De Oratione,* c. XIX, Tertullian reprimanded those of the faithful who refrained from Holy Communion under the pretext of not breaking their fast in the morning on fast days—Migne, *Patrologiae Cursus Completus, Series Latina* (221 vols., Parisiis, 1844-1864), I, 1181 (hereafter this will be cited as *MPL*); *Corpus Scriptorum Ecclesiasticorum Latinorum,* Vol. XX, pars I (Ex recensione Augusti Reifferscheid et Georgii Wissowa, Pragae, Lipsiae, 1890), p. 192.

29 *Epistola XCIII* (Ad Caesariam Patriciam)—*MPG,* XXXII, 484; cf. also Funk (*A Manual of Church History,* I, 67), who adverted to the testimony of the *Apostolic Constitutions* (VIII, n. 33) in this regard in Antioch and Jerusalem—*MPG,* I, 1133.

of Sozomen (4.—5. century)[30] and of Socrates (ca. 380- ca. 450).[31] The Church of Alexandria however reflected a notable exception to this practice, and continued to have Mass only on Sunday, though the faithful met for the reading of the Scriptures and for common prayer on Wednesday and Friday.[32] Rome also had in this matter a custom similar to that of the Church of Alexandria.[33] Martène (1654-1739)[34] concluded that the fifth century epistle of Pope Innocent I (401-417) offers an indication of this custom.[35] On the other hand, in Africa there was already a daily offering of Mass, according to the testimony of Tertullian (+ca. 420),[36] of St. Cyprian (+258)[37] and of St. Augustine (+430).[38] Thus St. Augustine wrote in his own day: "Some offer every day, some on Saturday and Sunday only, and some on Sunday only." [39]

As a result of the persecutions, Mass had to be said when its celebration would be least detected.[40] Hence the celebration took

30 *Historia Ecclesiastica,* Lib. VII, c. 19—*MPG,* LXVII, 1478.

31 *Historia Ecclesiastica,* Lib. V, c. 22—*MPG,* LXVII, 635.

32 Socrates, *Historia Ecclesiastica,* Lib. V, c. 22—*MPG,* LXVII, 638; Martène, *De Antiquis Ecclesiae Ritibus,* Lib. I, c. II, art. III, n. 1.

33 Duchesne, *Christian Worship,* p. 230.

34 *De Antiquis Ecclesiae Ritibus,* Lib. I, c. II, art. III, n. 1.

35 *Epistola* XXV (Decentio)—*MPL,* XX, 555; Jaffé, *Regesta Pontificum Romanorum ab condita Ecclesia ad annum post Christum MCXLVIII* (2. ed., 2 vols. in 1, Lipsiae, 1885-1888), n. 311 (hereafter cited Jaffé). On the other hand, Bona (1609-1634) at an earlier time had contended that the epistle of Pope Innocent I (417) referred chiefly to the non-observance of the fast on those days, and not to the lack of Mass. However, good foundation for the negative practice in Rome is found in Sozomen, *Historia Ecclesiastica,* Lib. VII, c. 19—*MPG,* LXVII, 1478.

36 *Adversus Marcionem,* Lib. IV, c. 26—*MPL,* II, 425; *Liber de Corona Militis,* c. III—*MPL,* II, 79.

37 *De Oratione Dominica,* c. XVIII—*MPL,* IV, 531; *Epistola,* LVII, c. 3—*MPL,* III, 857; *Epistola,* LXIII, cc. 15, 16—*MPL,* IV, 387.

38 *Sermo* XVIII, *De Oratione Dominica*—*MPL,* XXXVIII, 395; *Epistola XCVII,* n. 9—*MPL,* XXXIII, 364.

39 *Epistola LIV* (Ad Januarium), c. 2—*MPL,* XXIII, 200; cf. also Martène, *De Antiquis Ecclesiae Ritibus,* Lib. I, c. II, art. III, n. 2.

40 Chardon, *Histoire des Sacrements* (4 vols., Paris, 1745), II, 199.

place in the early hours of the morning around daybreak,[41] according to Pliny the Younger, who as governor of Bithynia and Pontus wrote to Emperor Trajan (98-117) about the year 111.[42] This change from the Apostolic custom of saying Mass in the evening may have been occasioned in part by the abuses which St. Paul referred to in the celebration of the *Agape* feast,[43] or it may have resulted from Trajan's decree against the *Hetaeriae,* or unlawful nocturnal gatherings.[44] St. Cyprian (+258), when writing about the custom in Africa, stated that Mass was celebrated very early in the morning,[45] but Tertullian, when writing for Africa in the third century, had referred to the celebration of Mass as taking place in the evening.[46] When it was possible, the solemn Mass on the fast days took place after the breaking of the fast in mid-afternoon.[47]

Duchesne (1843-1922) gave a short synopsis of the custom in regard to the time for the celebration of Mass in the early centuries in the following words: "On Sunday there were two meetings, one for the vigil and a later one very early in the morning for Mass. On Wednesday, too, services were held in Rome and Alexandria, but they did not include Mass, as they did in the East, where Saturday also became a day on which the Synaxis was celebrated." [48] Hence up to the time when St. Augustine wrote to Januarius (400) there was no universal practice in regard to the time for the celebration of Mass.[49]

41 Martène, *De Antiquis Ecclesiae Ritibus,* Lib. I, c. III, art. IV, n. 2; Duchesne, *Christian Worship,* p. 229.

42 *Epistola,* Lib. X, n. 97—Gesneri edition, II, 146; Fortescue, *The Mass,* p. 16.

43 I Cor., XI, 20 ff.

44 Funk, *A Manual of Church History,* I, 65; Ramsay, *The Church in the Roman Empire* (New York, 1893), pp. 219 ff.

45 *Epistola LXIII,* n. 16—*MPL,* IV, 389.

46 *Liber de Corona Militis,* c. III—*MPL,* II, 79; *Adversus Marcionem,* Lib. IV, c. 26—*MPL,* II, 426; cf. also Socrates (*Historia Ecclesiastica,* Lib. V, c. 22—*MPG,* LXVII, 635) and Sozomen (*Historia Ecclesiastica,* Lib. VII, c. 19—*MPG,* LXVII, 1478), who testify that evening sacrifice was still the custom in Egypt in the fifth century.

47 Tertullianus, *De Oratione,* c. XIX—*MPL,* I, 1181.

48 *Christian Worship,* p. 230.

49 Martène, *De Antiquis Ecclesiae Ritibus,* Lib. I, c. II, art. III, n. 2.

(*b*) *Place of Mass*

Celsus (ca. 170-185) in his attacks upon the Christians accused them of having neither temples nor altars. After a fashion this statement seems confirmed in the words of Tertullian, (+ca. 240), of Origen (+ca. 254), or of Lactantius (+ca. 317). But the Fathers of the second and third centuries, when they contrasted the spiritual faith of the Christians with the beliefs of the pagan materialism, denied the possession of temples, of altars, and of idols in the heathen sense. Their declaration simply implied a rejection of the sum and substance of the pagan religion.[50] Even though there was on the side of the Christians an apparent denial of the possession of temples and altars, Mass was definitely celebrated in special places during the early centuries as in every other period.[51] The custom of using private dwellings as places for divine worship continued more or less throughout the post-Apostolic age,[52] though gradually certain places were set apart as the *"Domus Dei."*[53]

All efforts to stabilize a practice in regard to the requisite place for the celebration of Mass proved futile in consequence of the persecutions. The Christians were not safe either in private houses or in public churches, so they gathered in subterranean crypts, the catacombs, which served as the burial places for the martyrs, and also in their other cemeteries.[54] In these catacombs one can still find

[50] Schuster, *The Sacramentary*, I, 136, 137.

[51] Benedictus XIV, *De Missae Sacrificio*, Tom. I, c. 5.

[52] Duchesne, *Christian Worship*, p. 389; Martène, *De Antiquis Ecclesiae Ritibus*, Lib. I, c. III, art. V, n. 2; Funk, *A Manual of Church History*, I, 66; cf. also the *Gesta apud Zenophilum*, concerning the Church of Certa in 303—*MPL*, VII, 731.

[53] Martène *(loc. cit.)* refers to the *Acts of St. Cecilia the Martyr* as revealing an example of this change. Cf. also Gattico, *De Oratoriis Domesticis et Usu Altaris Portatilis* (Romae, 1746), pars I, c. IV, n. 4 (hereafter cited *De Oratoriis Domesticis*).

[54] *Const. Apost.*, Lib. VI, c. 30: "Eucharistiam offerte in ecclesiis vestris et in coemeteriis."—*MPG*, I, 987; Eusebius, *Hist. Eccles.*, Lib. VII, c. 11—*MPG*, XX, 666. Cabrol (1855-1937) described one of these meetings at the beginning of the third century in the cemetery of Domitilla on the Via Ardeatina—*Liturgical Prayer, Its History and Spirit*, translated by the Benedictines of Stanbrook (London: Burns, Oates & Washbourne, Ltd., 1925), pp. 64 ff.

ample evidence that they served as a place for the celebration of Mass. St. Dionysius of Alexandria (+ca. 264) testified that during the days of trial and tribulation Mass was offered in any place: in the field, in the desert, in stables, on ships, and in prisons.[55]

However, even during lulls in the intensity of the persecution the Christians erected churches for divine worship, as St. Gregory of Nyssa (ca. 336-ca. 394)[56] and Eusebius (263-339) testify.[57] But most probably these churches were not much used because of their early destruction during the last violent persecution of Diocletian (284-305).[58]

Martène remarked that there was never a sacrifice without an altar.[59] It was during the early period of Christianity that some changes were introduced with regard to the platform or stand on which Mass was offered. The earliest altars were wooden tables, similar to the ones employed for dining purposes.[60] But in consequence of the persecutions which necessitated the celebration of Mass in the catacombs, the practice of using the stone sarcophagus of a martyr was introduced, although this type of altar did not then come into universal use, and did not entirely supplant the traditional wooden table for some time.[61]

[55] Eusebius, *Hist. Eccles.*, Lib. VII, c. 22—*MPG,* XX, 688; St. Cyprian (*Epistola IV* [*Ad Presbyteros et Diaconos*]) likewise referred to celebration of Mass in prisons—*MPL,* IV, 230.

[56] *De Vita S. Greg. Thaumaturgi*—*MPG,* XLVI, 893.

[57] *Hist. Eccles.,* Lib. VIII, c. 1—*MPG,* XX, 741. In the *Didascalia* (Lib. II, n. 57, *Ordo Synaxis Christianae*) one may note a description of the seating arrangements in the early church edifice—Quasten, *Monumenta,* pars I, p. 34.

[58] Lactantius, *Institutiones Divinae,* Lib. VII, c. 48—*MPG,* VI, 553.

[59] *De Antiquis Ecclesiae Ritibus,* Lib. I, c. III, art. VI, n. 1.

[60] An example is the one regarding which it is claimed that St. Peter used it in the house of Praxedes in Rome. Cf. Benedictus XIV, *De Missae Sacrificio,* Tom. I, c. 14; Schuster, *The Sacramentary,* I, 137, 138; Gasparri, *Tractatus Canonicus de Sanctissima Eucharistia* (2 vols., Lugduni: Delhomme & Briguet, 1897, I, n. 289 (hereafter cited *De Sanctissima Eucharistia*). Gattico (*De Oratoriis Domesticis,* Pars II, c. I, n. 4) explained with much detail that the table on which the Mass was offered was never a common table, but rather was one especially set aside for that purpose.

[61] Cf. St. Optatus, *De Schismate Donatistarum,* Lib. VI, n. 1—*MPL,* XI, 1068; St. Augustinus, *Epistola CLXXXV,* c. VI, n. 27—*MPL,* XXXIII, 805;

In the *Liber Pontificalis* the origin of the custom of celebrating Mass on the tomb of a martyr is attributed to Pope Felix I (269-274),[62] but this declaration of the Pope seems to point to the confirmation of a custom already existing for some time.[63] It was this custom, also referred to by St. Augustine when he wrote about the altar of St. Cyprian,[64] and by the poet Prudentius (348-ca. 405) when he wrote of the altar-tomb of St. Hippolytus,[65] that finally led to the universal practice of the altar stone which contained the relics of one or more of the saints.

Two notable exceptions to the general rule which required an altar for the celebration of Mass were the case of St. Lucian (+312), priest and martyr of Antioch, who in prison offered Mass while lying on his back in order that his breast might serve as the altar,[66] and the case of Bishop Theodoret of Cyprus (+ca. 458), who celebrated on the hands of the deacons in the cell of a hermit.[67] However, Pope Benedict XIV (1740-1758) stated that these exceptions served rather for edification than as an expression of the regular practice, since the traditional discipline of the Church had always required that Mass be celebrated on an altar.[68]

St. Athanasius, *Historia Arianorum ad Monachos,* c. LVI,—*MPG,* XXV, 760. Bona stated that during the persecutions it was the use of wooden altars that certainly proved the most convenient—*Rerum Liturgicarum Libri Duo,* Lib. I, c. XX.

62 *Liber Pontificalis,* pars prior, c. XXVII, Felix I: "Hic constituit supra sepulcra martyrum missas celebrari."—*Monumenta Germaniae Historica, Gesta Pontificum Romanorum,* I (ed. T. Mommsen, Berlin, 1898), 37 (hereafter cited *MGH*).

63 Schuster, *The Sacramentary,* I, 138.

64 *Sermo CCCX* (*In Natali Cypriani Martyris*), Lib. II, c. II, n. 2—*MPL,* XXXVIII, 1413.

65 *Peristephanon Hymn.,* c. XI, 1, 169-174—*MPL,* LX, 548.

66 Philostorgius, *Hist. Eccles.,* Lib. II, c. 13—*MPG,* LXV, 476.

67 *Religiosa Historia,* c. XX—*MPG,* LXXXII, 1430.

68 *De Missae Sacrificio,* Tom. I, c. 13.

CHAPTER II

FROM THE EDICT OF MILAN (313) TO GRATIAN (CA. 1140)

THE peace of Constantine, initiated with the Edict of Milan (313) which granted religious freedom, marks a new era in liturgical developments.[1] The freedom of the Church in liturgical matters as manifested through the individual initiative in Christian worship during the primitive times had a tendency to go to extremes. In order to forestall disorders, the Church of Rome began to legislate on these matters. Outstanding in this field of legislation was the work of Pope Gregory the Great (590-604).[2] But even during his time many of the details in liturgical worship were left to the regulation of the local bishops.

ARTICLE 1. DIFFERENCE BETWEEN SOLEMN AND PRIVATE MASS

The difference between solemn and private Mass must be considered before a clear study can be made of the law regulating the time for the celebration of Mass during the period when the different orders among the clergy became more or less stabilized.[3] Much of the legislation and many of the customary usages referred exclusively to the solemn Masses celebrated on Sundays and on the major feasts in the episcopal city by the bishop when he was assisted by the assembled priests and clergy.[4] Besides the solemn Mass private Masses were celebrated whenever it proved convenient, though they were to be said at such a time and place as not to distract the congregation during the solemn services.[5]

[1] Fortescue, *The Mass,* p. 76.

[2] Schuster, *The Sacramentary,* I, 38.

[3] Martène, *De Antiquis Ecclesiae Ritibus,* Lib. I, c. III, art. IV, n. 10.

[4] Thomassinus, *Vetus et Nova Ecclesiae Disciplina circa Beneficia et Beneficiarios* (10 vols., Moguntiaci, 1787), Pars I, Lib. II, c. XXV, n. 1 (hereafter this work will be cited *Disciplina circa Beneficia*).

[5] There is a difference of opinion as to when exactly the custom of the private celebration of Mass began. Fortescue (*The Mass,* pp. 187 ff.) stated that the older practice of one solemn Mass a day, with the clergy assisting, as is still the custom in the East, was gradually replaced in the early middle ages by separate private Masses said by the individual priests. Some cases of the

Cardinal Bona (1609-1674) attempted to furnish a very thorough study of the different types of Masses. He listed no less than sixteen such types, several of which implied further subdivisions or yielded to added designations.[6] Admittedly from the beginning the Mass was instituted principally that it be offered publicly and solemnly with the clerics and the assembled people participating in their various roles and communicating with the principal minister.[7]

Despite this fact private Masses, not intended especially for the participation by a large congregation of the faithful, were in constant use.[8] This type of Mass was offered on any day,[9] for its celebration

daily celebration of private Mass are found as early as the sixth century. Fortescue contended that from very early times there were only isolated cases of the private celebration with a simplified service. On the other hand, Cardinal Bona (*Rerum Liturgicarum Libri Duo,* Lib. I, c. XIII, n. 4) very definitely maintained that the private celebration of Mass had its origin, not from the monks as was commonly stated, but rather from the early Fathers of the Church. He offered an abundance of references (*ibid.*, c. XIV) to show that the celebration of private Masses was in constant use from the very beginning. De Puniet (*The Mass,* p. 77) designated the celebration of private Mass as a very early practice. Magani (*L'Antica Liturgia Romana,* 3 vols., Milano, 1897-1899, pars I, p. 296) asserted that the private Mass dated from Apostolic times, for the Mass said at that time in the cemeteries and on the tombs of the martyrs did not lend itself to all the ceremonies of the solemn Mass. Gasparri (*De Sanctissima Eucharistia,* I, n. 66) taught that in view of the lack of evidence concerning early private Masses nothing of a definite character can be said about them.

[6] *Rerum Liturgicarum Libri Duo,* Lib. I, c. XIII, sqq.: Solemn, conventual, canonical, capitular, principal, major, daily, public, private; with relation to the time or place of their celebration, to attendance, or to the faithful who received Holy Communion; legitimate, solitary, general, special, Mass of the season, Mass of the saint; ferial Mass, votive Mass, Mass of the living, Mass of the dead, Mass of the Presanctified, and the dry Mass.

[7] Bona, *ibid.*, n. 2. Cf. the Council of Antioch (341), c. 2, which declared that if the faithful refused to receive Holy Communion they were to be ejected —Mansi, *Sacrorum Conciliorum Nova et Amplissima Collectio* (53 vols. in 60, Parisiis, 1901-1927), II, 1319 (hereafter this work will be cited as Mansi). Cf. also the Council of Coyanza (1050), c. 6—Mansi, XIX, 788.

[8] Bona, *op. cit.*, c. XIV. Cf. Tertullianus, *De Fuga,* c. XIV—*MPL,* II, 119; Eusebius, *De Vita Constantini,* Lib. IX, c. 17, 45—*MPG,* XX, 1165, 1196; Sozomenus, *Hist. Eccles.*, Lib. I, c. 8—*MPG,* LXVII, 880.

[9] Cf. Hippolytus (*Fragmentum, in illud Prov.*, c. IX, n. 1, 2), who stated

was not restricted to Sundays, feasts and other designated days as were the solemn services. Thus one reason for the name "private" was the fact that these Masses were offered on private days to which no special Mass was assigned.[10] Hence, when it is said that up to the fourth century there were many different customs as regards the days on which Mass was offered, this refers primarily to the solemn public Mass.

Article 2. Time of Mass

(*a*) *Days*

By the fourth century there is evidence that the practice of daily solemn Mass began to spread. It was already the custom in Africa as St. Augustine,[11] St. Cyprian,[12] and Tertullian testified.[13] The custom also existed in Spain when the I Council of Toledo was held in the year 400, for this Council required that every cleric attend the public sacrifice daily in the place where he happened to be.[14] In the East, St. John Chrysostom (+407) [15] and St. Basil (+379) [16] referred to the same practice.

This custom of daily Mass became more and more widespread, at least in the urban churches,[17] as the liturgy gradually developed into a complete unit having a special Mass for every day of the year.[18]

that every day Christ's Immaculate Body and Blood are offered on the divine table—*MPG,* X, 628.

[10] Bona, *loc. cit.,* c. XIV.

[11] *Epist. XCVIII,* n. 9—*MPL,* XXXIII, 364.

[12] *Epistola Synodica,* LVII, c. 3—*MPL,* III, 857.

[13] *Liber de Corona Militis,* c. III—*MPL,* II, 79.

[14] C. 5: ". . . ad ecclesiam ad sacrificium quotidianum . . ."—Mansi, III, 999; Burchardus, *Decretum,* Lib. III, c. 152—*MPL,* CXL, 650.

[15] *Homilia III in Epist. ad Ephesios,* c. 1—*MPG,* LXII, 29; Martène, *De Antiquis Ecclesiae Ritibus,* Lib. I, c. II, art. III, n. 2.

[16] *Epistola XCIII,*—*MPG,* XXXII, 484.

[17] The Council of Lerida (666), c. 3, decreed that daily Mass should be offered for the King and the army—Mansi, XI, 78; the XVI Council of Toledo (693), c. 8, referred to the celebration of Mass every day in the Cathedral church, except on Good Friday—Mansi, XII, 76; the Council of Tarragona (516), c. 7, testified that in the rural churches in the sixth century daily Mass was not yet the custom—Mansi, VIII, 542.

[18] Fortescue (*The Mass,* p. 186) stated that this became the practice in

Thus a council in 1056 declared that all priests should offer Holy Mass daily, and invited those who could not celebrate at least to attend the daily Mass.[19] However, already in the ninth century there is evidence of priests who celebrated several times in one day. Walafrid Strabo (+849) related that Pope Leo III (795-816) said nine Masses on one day,[20] and the Council of Seligenstadt (1022) legislated that a priest could say no more than three Masses on any one day.[21]

During this period the number of liturgical days did not increase in the East the same as in Rome, although in the beginning the number in the Oriental Rite exceeded those of the Western Church. For example, during Lent in the East only the Mass of the Presanctified was celebrated except on Saturday, Sunday, and the Feast of the Annunciation, and on Good Friday there was no Eucharistic service at all.[22]

(*b*) *Hours*

The persecutions in the earlier centuries were major factors in determining the hours for the celebration of Mass, but with the restoration of peace to the Church definite hours of the day became more clearly established for the solemn offering of the Holy Sacrifice.

Rome some time after the sixth century. Cf. also Thomassinus, *Disciplina circa Beneficia,* Pars III, lib. I, c. CLXIX, n. 3. A complete study of this development can be made from the different Sacramentaries (538-574) and from the Roman Ordo (770—ca. 1400). The latter regulated the papal liturgy and the former were the forerunners of the modern Missal, which was first drawn up primarily for the accommodation of the priest who said a low Mass. The three best known Sacramentaries are the Leonine, the oldest and most complete, which exhibits the rite for the celebration of the Mass in the fifth and sixth centuries; the Gelasian, which reflects the liturgy of the Mass during the sixth and seventh centuries; and finally the Gregorian, which obtained force in the eighth century. These were edited by Muratori in a work entitled *Liturgia Romana Vetus* (2 vols., Neopoli, 1776).

19 The Council of Compostella (1065), c. 1—Mansi, XIX, 855.

20 *De Rebus Ecclesiasticis,* c. XXI—*MPL,* CXIV, 943.

21 C. 5—Mansi, XIX, 397.

22 The Council of Laodicea (343-381), c. 49—Mansi, II, 571; the Council of Trullo (Quinisextum, 692), c. 52: "In omnibus sanctae quadragesimae ieiunii diebus praeterquam sabbato et dominica et sancto annuntiationis die, fiat sacrum praesanctificatorum"—Mansi, XI, 968.

Amalarius of Metz (+850) indicated that the hours determined for the Sacrifice were the third, sixth, and ninth,[23] that is, mid-morning, noon, and mid-afternoon. Honorius of Autun in the early twelfth century,[24] and three centuries earlier Walafrid Strabo (+849),[25] related in closer detail that on Sundays and on feasts the Mass was said at the third hour, on private days at the sixth hour, on fast days at the ninth hour, during Lent at the vesperal hour, and on certain privileged days even at night.

Thus several councils[26] and Theodulph of Orleans (+821) in his capitulary[27] referred to the Mass as being celebrated at nine o'clock in the morning on Sundays and on solemn feasts. The tradition of celebrating only after nine o'clock was attributed to Pope Telesphorus (c. 125-136) by the *Liber Pontificalis*,[28] and a corresponding decree fabricated by the pseudo-Isidorian collectors was contained in all the collections of that period.[29] Regino of Prüm (+915), in the list of questions which the visiting bishop was to ask the pastor, included the question whether the latter celebrated Mass before nine o'clock.[30] In line with the general warning that the priest was to fast until noon in order that he could offer Mass for any travelers who came late, Burchard, Bishop of Worms (1002-1025),[31] and Ivo, Bishop of

[23] *De Ecclesiasticis Officiis ad Ludovicum Pium,* Lib. III, c. 42—*MPL,* CV, 1160.

[24] *De Gemma Animae,* Lib. I, c. 113—*MPL,* CLXVII, 581.

[25] *De Rebus Ecclesiasticis,* c. XXIII—*MPL,* CXIV, 951.

[26] Cf. the IV Council of Rome (392), c. 5—Mansi, III, 642; the Council of Orleans (538), c. 15 (14)—*MGH,* Legum Sectio III, *Concilia* (3 vols., ed. F. Maassen, A. Werminghoff, H. Bastgen, Hannoverae, 1893-1924), I, 78.

[27] C. 45—*MPL,* CV, 205; Mansi, XIII, 1006.

[28] N. IX: ". . . omni tempore ante horae tertiae cursum nullus praesumeret missas celebrare."—*MGH, Gesta Pontificum Romanorum,* I, 12.

[29] *Decretales Pseudo-Isidorianae et Capitula Angelramni,* ed. P. Hinschius (Lipsiae, 1836), p. 110, n. 2; Regino of Prüm, *Libri Duo de Synodalibus Causis et Disciplinis Ecclesiasticis,* Lib. I, c. 186—*MPL,* CXXXII, 224; Burchardus, *Decretum,* Lib. III, c. 63—*MPL,* CXL, 686; Ivo, *Decretum,* Lib. III, c. 65—*MPL,* CLXI, 212.

[30] *Libri Duo de Synodalibus Causis et Disciplinis Ecclesiasticis,* Lib. I, qq. 29, 33—*MPL,* CXXXII, 188.

[31] *Decretum,* Lib. III, c. 228—*MPL,* CXL, 722.

Chartres (1090-1117),[32] included in their collections an excerpt from a letter of Pope St. Leo I (445),[33] in which a second Mass was contemplated after the one offered in the earlier part of the day on solemn feasts, in order to accommodate the large congregations.

On fast days, however, the time of Mass was different, so that no celebration took place until the fast was ended.[34] Mass therefore was said at vespers or at sun-down during Lent,[35] and in mid-afternoon, at three o'clock, on other fast days, for example on the ember days.[36] The III Council of Carthage (397)[37] and the II of Braga (563),[38] in condemning the celebration of Mass by one who was not fasting, referred however to the custom of holding funeral Masses before the actual burial, which usually took place on the same day as the death of the party. Accordingly the Mass was said in the afternoon or evening for the deceased. This custom was still in existence in the thirteenth century.[39]

But this legislation again concerned only the public Masses. Private Masses, on the other hand, were celebrated at any hour of the day, in the morning, in the afternoon, in the evening, or even at compline.[40] The only restriction of the law was that care should

[32] *Decretum,* Lib. III, 268; lib. II, c. 87—*MPL,* CLXI, 260, 181.

[33] *Epist. IX* (Ad Dioscorum Alexandrinum Episcopum), c. 2—*MPL,* LIV, 626; Jaffé, n. 406.

[34] The I Council Vaison (442), c. 2; II (529), c. 3: ". . . missis seu in matutinis, seu in quadragesimalibus, seu in illis quae pro defunctis commmoratione fiunt . . ." thus implying that there was a difference between the ordinary morning Mass and the Masses in Lent—Mansi, III, 175; VIII, 727.

[35] The III Council of Orleans (538), c. 29—*MGH,* Legum Sectio III, *Concilia,* I, 78; Mansi, IX, 19; Capitulare Theodulphi Aurelianensis (797), n. 39—*MPL,* CV, 204; Mansi, XIII, 1005; Burchard (*Decretum,* Lib. XIII, c. 12), ascribing the canon to Pope St. Sylvester I (314-335), stated that in Lent the fast was not to be broken at the ninth hour, but that the faithful were to come to Mass and vespers first—*MPL,* CXL, 887.

[36] The Council of Mainz (813), c. 34—Mansi, XIV, 73; Regino of Prüm, *Libri Duo de Synodalibus Causis et Disciplinis Ecclesiasticis,* Lib. I, c. 227—*MPL,* CXXXII, 243; Ivo, *Decretum,* Lib. IV, c. 35—*MPL,* CLXI, 272.

[37] C. 29—Mansi, III, 885.

[38] C. 16—Mansi, IX, 776; cf. also the III Council of Braga (572), c. 10—Mansi, IX, 841; Bona, *Rerum Liturgicarum Libri Duo,* Lib. I, c. XXL, n. 2.

[39] Many, *Praelectiones de Missa* (Paris: Letouzey et Ané, 1903), n. 173 (2).

[40] Martène, *De Antiquis Ecclesiae Ritibus,* Lib. I, c. III, art. IV, n. 10.

be taken that the people be not attracted away from the public Mass through the celebration of the private Mass.[41]

Thus there is evidence that the Mass was celebrated at many different times of the day.[42] As a result it must be concluded that as yet there was no definite legislation regarding the time of the day for the celebration of Mass, especially in regard to private Masses, and that it was left to the devotion of the individual and to the disposition of local custom to determine at what hour Mass would be celebrated.

Article 3. Special Days

In the consideration regarding the time for the celebration of Mass one must also advert to the special feast days which were gradually introduced into the liturgy of the Western Church. The introduction of these feasts in Church's calendar occasioned further regulations in reference to the celebration of Mass.

In the Latin rite private Masses could lawfully be said every day except on Good Friday and on Holy Saturday. But also all the Fridays of Lent were excepted in Milan;[43] on the other hand, the Greeks did not celebrate Mass during Lent except on Saturdays,

Cf. Humbert of Silva Candida (*Libri III adversus Simoniacas* [156-1058], nn. 13, 23, 24), who raised an accusation against the Greeks in this matter—*MPL,* CXLIII, 980, 994, 995.

[41] The Capitulary of Theodulph (c. 45) proposed that priests celebrate privately before the second hour so as to fulfill this injunction—*MPL,* CV, 205; Mansi, XIII, 1006.

[42] Cf. Socrates, *Hist. Eccles.*, Lib. V, c. 22—*MPG,* LXVII, 635. Sozomen (*Hist. Eccles.,* Lib. VII, c. 19), while relating events which occurred towards the end of the fourth century, spoke of some in Egypt who celebrated in the evening—*MPL,* LXVII, 1478. Cf. the Council Vaison (442), c. 2—Mansi, III, 175; the III Council of Orleans (538), c. 29—Mansi, IX, 19; Hincmar advised the clergy to sing Nones, then to say Mass, and afterwards to visit the sick—*Capitula presbyteris data,* c. I, n. 19—Mansi, XV, 477. *The Life of St. Gerald of Aurillac* (Lib. III, c.7), written by Abbot Odo of Cluny (+942), testified to the celebration of Mass after compline as a means whereby the reception of Holy Viaticum could be assured for the dying—*MPL,* CXXXIII, 694.

[43] Martène, *De Antiquis Ecclesiae Ritibus,* Lib. I, c. II, art. III, n. 4; Bona, *Rerum Liturgicarum Libri Duo,* Lib. c. XVIII, n. 4.

on Sundays, and on the Feast of the Annunciation.[44] On Good Friday there was no liturgical celebration of the Eucharist anywhere.[45]

Holy Saturday and also the Saturdays of ember weeks were days of strict fast. At the end of these days there was celebrated the Ordination Mass, which continued into Sunday morning.[46] So on these five Saturdays the Mass merged with that of Sunday morning. In fact, the old Sacramentaries had only a single Mass assigned for these days.[47]

By the eighth century, on every day except Good Friday, a different Mass was said in the Roman Rite. There was Sunday, feast day, vigil, station, ferial and votive Masses.[48] As regards the vigil Masses, probably in the earlier centuries a nocturnal Mass was celebrated before every great feast. In time the practice of the celebration of these vigil Masses disappeared, or their celebration was moved up to an earlier time of the day.[49]

[44] The Council of Laodicea (343-381), c. 49: "Non oportet in Quadragesima panem offere, nisi sabbato et solis dominicis."—Mansi, II, 571; Bona, *op. cit.*, Lib. I, c. XVIII, n. 4.

[45] Duchesne, *Christian Worship*, p. 248.

[46] It may be noted here that the prayers and indeed the whole liturgy of our present Holy Saturday morning service and Mass point to the fact that this Mass was celebrated at night in anticipation of the Resurrection. For example, in the prayer for the blessing of the incense, the celebrant speaks of "the sacrifice that is offered this night . . ."; the deacon chants the *Exultet*: "This therefore is the night . . ."; and the celebrant in the oration of the Mass: "This most sacred night . . ."; and in the preface: ". . . most especially on this night. . . ."

[47] On Holy Saturday the ceremonies of the vigil, which consisted of lessons, of chants and of prayers, began in the afternoon in the eighth century, and the Mass began with the first signs of dawn—Duchesne, *Christian Worship*, pp. 229, 232, 233, 247, 257.

[48] Bona, *Rerum Liturgicarum Libri Duo*, Lib. I, c. XVIII, nn. 2, 4.

[49] These Masses always belonged to the vigil day, and not to the feast. Thus they differed from the nocturnal Mass celebrated on the five aliturgical Saturdays. The feast of St. John the Baptist, for example, still retains this vigil celebration with its proper Mass, and the feast of Pentecost also has a vigil ceremony, the liturgy of which clearly shows that this ceremony was formerly celebrated at night. Cf. Martène, *De Antiquis Ecclesiae Ritibus*, Lib. I, c. III, art. III, n. 14; Duchesne, *Christian Worship*, pp. 229, 289, 515; Schuster, *The Sacramentary*, II, 383; Many, *Praelectiones de Missa*, n. 19.

But the Feast of Christmas remained unique in its development in this matter. This feast grew in prominence after the Council of Ephesus (431), and gradually, as its vigil Mass came to be celebrated the day before, the actual feast day had assigned to it another Mass celebrated at mid-night,[50] together with its regular Mass of the day and the one at dawn, which latter originally served in celebration of the Feast of St. Anastasia, Martyr (+ca. 304).[51]

In view of the custom which modelled the annual commemoration of the Last Supper on the succession of events as they had occurred on the first Holy Thursday, the Mass on Holy Thursday was said in the evening after the *Agape* feast. So when the III Council of Carthage (397) legislated on the Eucharistic fast, an exception was explicitly indicated for this day.[52] In Spain this custom was revoked by the II Council of Braga (563);[53] however, the custom apparently continued in many places for several centuries.[54]

[50] Cf. Pope Telesphorus: "Hic fecit, ut natalem domini nostri Jesu Christi noctu Missas celebrarentur."—*MGH, Gesta Pontificum Romanorum,* I, 12; Ivo, *Decretum,* Lib. II, c. 71—*MPL,* CLXI, 175.

[51] Schuster (*The Sacramentary,* I, 361-365) says that Pope Gregory the Great (c. 600) bore witness to the midnight Mass on Christmas, but that it was probably of an earlier origin. Martène (*De Antiquis Ecclesiae Ritibus,* Lib. I, c. III, art. IV, n. 3) referred to the similar custom of saying Mass at night on the Feast of St. John the Baptist.

[52] C. 29—Mansi, III, 885. In the collection compiled by Dionysius Exiguus (+ ca. 540) this legislation is identified with c. 41 of the Council—*MPL,* LXVII, 194. Cf. the II Council of Mâcon (585), c. 6—Mansi, IX, 952; St. Augustinus, *Epist. LIV* (*Ad Januarium*), c. 1—*MPL,* XXXIII, 204.

[53] C. 16—Mansi, IX, 776.

[54] Walafrid Strabo, *De Rebus Ecclesiasticis,* c. XIX—*MPL,* CXIV, 940. This canon of the Council of Carthage was included in the *Anselmi Episcopi Lucensis Collectio Canonum una cum Collectione Minore* (ed. F. Thaner, Oeniponte, 1906-1915), Lib. IX, c. 3. It is strange that Gratian (c. 49, D. I. *de cons.*) also included this canon from the Council of Carthage which pointed to an exemption from the law of the Eucharistic fast on Holy Thursday. Rufinus (+ 1190), while commenting in his *Summa Decretorum* (1157-1159) on this text in Gratian, declared that this exception was no longer valid, for it was contrary to the practice of the Church, and also not in harmony with other canons in Gratian's *Decree,* e.g., c. 16, C. VII, q. 1, and c. 54, D. II, *de cons.*—ed. Singer, *Die Summa Decretorum des Magister Rufinus* (Paderborn, 1902), p. 547.

In the first centuries three Masses were celebrated on Holy Thursday: one in the morning, for the reconciliation of penitents; the second for the blessing of the oils; and the third, at the close of the day, in commemoration of the institution of the Holy Eucharist. But under Pope St. Gregory the Great (590-604) these three functions were reduced to one, and the unified function was to be celebrated by the highest ranking ecclesiastic of each church.[55]

Article 4. Place of Mass

(*a*) *The Church*

After the Edict of Milan (313) many magnificent churches were erected throughout the Christian world.[56] It was then that legislation against the celebration of Mass in private houses was instituted. The first such legislation was enacted in the Council of Laodicea (343-381.) This Council decreed:

> "Non oportet in domibus oblationes celebrari ab episcopis vel presbyteris." [57]

The Council ruled that the Mass be offered in churches, and not in private houses. However, the legislation was so worded that it did not constitute an absolute prohibition,[58] and there is evidence that in the early period Mass continued quite frequently to be celebrated in private houses, and especially in oratories set aside for religious services.[59] This difference in practice is probably ex-

[55] Martène, *De Antiquis Ecclesiae Ritibus,* Lib. I, c. III, art. III, n. 8.

[56] Eusebius, *Vita Constantini,* Lib. IV, c. 58—*MPG,* XX, 1209.

[57] C. 58—Mansi, II, 574; n. LIX, c. 161, in the *Collectio Dionysiana—MPL,* LXVII, 170.

[58] Gattico, *De Oratoriis Domesticis,* Pars I, c. I, art. IV, n. 8.

[59] St. John Chrysostom, patriarch of Constantinople (398-407), urged the wealthy to erect oratories in their rural homes in order to have Mass celebrated there (*In Actus Apostolorum Homiliae,* XVIII, n. 5)—*MPG,* LX, 147; St. Ambrose (+397) offered Mass in the house of an important layman—Martène, *De Antiquis Ecclesiae Ritibus,* Lib. I, c. III, Art. IV, n. 7; Benedictus XIV, *De Missae Sacrificio,* Tom. I, c. 10. The so-called Gelasian Sacramentary somewhat later contained a special oration for the Mass which was to be offered in private houses—Muratori, *Liturgia Romana Vetus, Sacramentarium Gelasianum,*

plained by the fact that the law referred especially to conditions in the city, where churches were available, and not to rural sections, where churches were few and far between.[60] After the Council of Laodicea this restriction on the celebration in private houses was repeated by numerous councils.[61] The VIII Council of Paris (829) condemned priests who neglected to avail themselves of the basilicas dedicated to God and accordingly said Mass in their houses and gardens, contrary to the canonical ordinance.[62] The civil law relative to this point was contained in the *Novellae* of Justinian (573),[63] and the same restrictive legislation was repeated in the capitularies of the kings of France.[64]

Among the reasons for this legislation was the fact that there was no longer any need for secrecy in the celebration of Mass, and also the fact that priests began to be ordained for a certain church. The law regarding the place for the celebration of Mass was enacted for the sake of forestalling all possible danger of abuses in the performance of the sacred functions, and with a view to combating the

Lib. III, n. 73. Cf. the Council of Agde (506), c. 21: "Clerici, si qui in festivitatibus in oratoribus, nisi iubente aut permittente episcopo, Missas facere aut tenere voluerint, a communione pellantur."—Mansi, VIII, 328; the I Council of Orleans (511), c. 25—Mansi, VIII, 355; Burchardus, *Decretum,* Lib. II, c. 70—*MPL,* CXL, 638.

60 Thomassinus, *Disciplina circa Beneficia,* Pars I, lib. II, c. XCII, nn. 8, 9.

61 The Council of Epaôn (517) c. 52 (inter addita)—Mansi, VIII, 565; the III Council of Chalon-sur-Saône (813), c. 49—*MGH,* Legum Sectio III, *Concilia,* Tom. II, pars I (4°H), p. 283; the Council of Aachen (816), c. 84—*MGH, ibid.,* p. 368; the I Council of Orleans (511), c. 86 (inter addita)—Mansi, VIII, 364; Burchardus, *Decretum,* Lib. II, c. 61—*MPL,* CXL, 686; the Council of Mainz (888), c. 9: "Missarum solemnia non ubique, sed in locis ab episcopo consecratis, vel ubi permiserit, celebranda esse censemus"—Mansi, XVIII A, 67.

62 Lib. I, c. 47; lib. III, c. 6—*MGH,* Legum Sectio III, *Concilia,* Tom. II, pars 2, p. 641, 672.

63 N. 58: "Omnibus . . . interdicimus . . . in domibus suis habere quasdam quasi orationum domos et in his sacra celebrare mysteria."—*Corpus Iuris Civilis* (3 vols., Vol. III, *Novellae,* quas recognovit Rudolphus Schoell, absolvit Guilielmus Kroll, editio stereotypa quinta, Berolini: Apud Weidmannos, 1928), III, 314.

64 *Capitularia,* n. 23, *Duplex Legationis Edictum* (789), c. 25—*MGH,* Legum Sectio II, *Capitularia* (in 4°H), Tom. I, p. 64.

heretical sects of the time, namely, the Eustathians, who had been condemned in the Council of Gangra (340), and the Anomoeans, who had been condemned in the II General Council (Constantinople, 381), for both of these sects repudiated public worship and insisted on performing their rites in the privacy of their homes.[65]

(1) Consecrated Churches

It became necessary to have the permission of the bishop to erect a church or an oratory in which Mass could be celebrated, and then that place remained under his jurisdiction.[66] Besides the obtaining of permission for the erection of the church or oratory it was also necessary to have these buildings consecrated or blessed before Mass was to be celebrated there.[67]

[65] Gattico, *De Oratoriis Domesticis,* Pars I, c. IV, n. 4.

[66] The II Council of Carthage (390), c. 9—Mansi, III, 695; the General Council of Chalcedon (451), c. 4—Mansi, VII, 394. The latter canon referred especially to the erection of a monastery or a "house of prayer." Cf. the Council of Orleans (566), c. 17: ". . . ut in eius Episcopi, in cuius positae sunt territorio, potestate consistant"—Mansi, VIII, 354; *Novellae,* 67 (538); the Council of Chalon-sur-Saône (650), c. 14—Mansi, X, 1192; Capitulare Wormatiense (829), c. 3—*MGH,* Legum Sectio II, *Capitularia* (in 4° H), Tom. II, pars prior, p. 12; the Council of London (1138), c. 12: "Apostolica auctoritate prohibemus, ne quis absque licentia episcopi sui ecclesiam vel oratorium constituat"—Mansi, XXI, 513; cf. also Eidenschink, "Dedication of sacred places in the early sources and in the letters of Gregory the Great"—*The Jurist* (Washington, 1941—), V (1945), 181-215; 323-358.

[67] The IV Council of Carthage (398), c. 6, ordered the reconsecration in a case of doubt—Mansi, III, 969. Cf. the I Council of Orange (441), c. 10—Mansi, VI, 437; the III Council of Braga (572), c. 5—Mansi, IX, 839; the III Council of Saragossa (691), c. c. 1—Mansi, XII, 42; *Epistolae Zachariae Papae* (741), n. VII (ad Pipinum)—Mansi, XII, 331; *Capitularia Regum Francorum Spuria Benedicti,* Lib. VI (II), cc. 201, 208; Lib. VII (III), c. 431—*MGH, Leges,* Tom. II (in folio), pars altera, pp. 83, 84, 129; the Council of Mâcon (888), c. 9: ". . . in locis ab episcopo consecratis . . ."—Mansi, XVIII A, 67; Buchardus, *Decretum,* Lib. III, cc. 56, 57, 59—*MPL,* CXL, 683, 684, 685; the Council of Winchester (1076), c. 8: "Ut in ecclesiis nisi ab episcopis consecratis missae non celebrentur."—Mansi, XX, 460. It may be noted here that there is positive evidence of the consecration of churches already in the fourth century. Cf. Eusebius, *Hist. Eccles.,* Lib. III, c. 5—*MPG,* LXVII, 1042; Vigilius, *Epist. I,* c. 4—Jaffé, n. 907.

Thus the churches and oratories were under the jurisdiction of the bishop, and he could therefore put certain restrictions on them, especially the oratories, by permitting Masses there only on certain days and at specified hours.[68] The general principle in these regulations was that on major feasts Mass should not be celebrated in domestic oratories.[69] The bishop, however, had the power to dispense from the regulation which called for the celebration of Mass in the church.[70] Certain cases of necessity too were recognized as valid excuses for not celebrating Mass in a church: for example, sickness,[71] war,[72] a journey through districts where there was no church,[73] or the destruction or the reparation of the church.[74]

[68] The I Council of Agde (506), c. 21—Mansi, VIII, 328; the Council of Clermont (535), c. 15—Mansi, VIII, 862; the IV Council of Orleans (541), c. 7—Mansi, IX, 114; the Council of Chalon-sur-Saône (650), c. 14—Mansi, X, 1192; The Trullan Synod (692), c. 31—Mansi, XI, 956; Zacharias Papa, *Epistola VII* (ad Pipinum)—Mansi, XII, 331; the Council of Verneuil-sur-Oise (755), c. 8: "Omnes presbyteri, qui in parochia sunt, sub potestate episcopi esse debeant de eorum ordine, ut nullus presbyter praesumat in illa parochia nec baptizare, nec missas celebrare sine iussione episcopi in cuius parochia est."—*MGH,* Legum Sectio II, *Capitularia* (in 4° H), I, 34.

[69] The Council of Agde (506), c. 21, listed Easter, Ascension, Pentecost, the Nativity of St. John the Baptist, Christmas and Epiphany as forbidden days—Mansi, VIII, 328; the Council of Lyons (583), c. 5, declared that the bishop himself was not to celebrate outside the church on Christmas and Easter unless he was sick—Mansi, IX, 943.

[70] The II Council of Carthage (390), c. 9—Mansi, III, 695; the Council of Pontigny (876), c. 7—Mansi, XVII A, 67. Cf. Duranti, *De Ritibus Ecclesiae Catholicae* (Romae, 1591), Lib. II, c. 6, n. 3.

[71] Martène (*De Antiquis Ecclesiae Ritibus,* Lib. I, c. VII, art. IV, Ordo XI (V)) listed a Mass oration taken from a Sacramentary of around 800, which reads: "Missa pro Infirmo, Coll., . . . qui famulum tuum in hac domo consistentem . . ." Cf. also Many, *Praelectiones de Missa,* n. 2.

[72] *Capitularia Regum Francorum Spuria Benedicti,* Lib. VI (II), c. 208; lib. VII (III), c. 396—*MGH, Leges,* Tom. II, (in folio), pars altera, pp. 84, 128.

[73] The VIII Council of Paris (829), Lib. I, c. 47—*MGH,* Legum Sectio III, *Concilia,* Tom. II, pars 2, p. 641; the Council of Mainz (888), c. 9—Mansi, XVIII A, 67; the IV Council of Metz (888), c. 8—Mansi, XVIII A, 80; Burchardus, *Decretum,* Lib. III, c. 61—*MPL,* CXL, 686.

[74] The Council of Mainz, *loc. cit.,* ". . . in capellis . . . liceat celebrare, donec ipsae ecclesiae restaurari queant"—Mansi, XVIII A, 67; Burchardus, *Decretum,* Lib. III, c. 56—*MPL,* CXL, 683.

(2) Violated Churches

In addition to the positive precept which required that a church be consecrated in order that Mass be celebrated there, evidence is also had of the negative precept which prohibited Mass in desecrated and violated churches. In the strict sense desecration implied the loss of the consecration or blessing of a church. It thereby lost its sacred character and had to be reconsecrated before Mass was again permitted there. Violation, on the other hand, implied the temporary suspension of the effects of consecration or blessing through certain acts contrary to its sacredness. The violated church then was unfit for divine service until the blemish was removed by means of reconciliation.[75] During the centuries here considered these two factors were not so clearly distinguished, though the foundation for the distinction did exist. A church was violated through the burial of an infidel therein, and Mass was prohibited there until the body was removed and the place purified.[76]

A church was violated in consequence of an act of homicide or of the shedding of human blood therein,[77] of an act of adultery[78] and of the removal of the altar.[79] A church suffered desecration through the act of its destruction.[80] In each of these cases the church had to be reconsecrated before Mass could again be celebrated in it.

(*b*) *The Altar*

There was never any essential change regarding the requirement of an altar, for from the time of Christ some kind of table was always

[75] Schmalzgrueber, *Ius Ecclesiasticum Universum* (5 vols., in 12, Romae, 1843-1845), Lib. III, tit. 40, n. 63.

[76] *Poenitentiale Theodori* (c. 673), Lib. II, cc. 4, 5—*Councils and Ecclesiastical Documents relating to Great Britain and Ireland* (3 vols. in 5, ed. Haddan & Stubbs, Oxford: Clarendon Press, 1869-1873), III, 190, 211 (hereafter cited *Councils and Ecclesiastical Documents*); Burchardus, *Decretum*, Lib. III, c. 38—*MPL*, CXL, 697; Ivo, *Decretum*, Lib. III, c. 43—*MPL*, CLXI, 207.

[77] *Historia Francorum* (590), Lib. IX, n. 12—*MPL*, LXXI, 491.

[78] Ivo, *Panormia*, Lib. II, c. 21 (Ex decretis Eugenii papae, c. 6)—*MPL*, CLXI, 1087.

[79] *Excerptiones Egberti* (749), c. 139—Mansi, XII, 426.

[80] Vigilius Papa, *Epist. I*, c. 4—*MPL*, LXIX, 18; Jaffé, n. 907.

required for the celebration of Mass. Bishops could permit Mass to be offered outside of a sacred place, but never without an altar.[81]

After the persecutions, however, the universal use of stone altars for Mass became the custom. The first known legislation against the use of wooden altars for Mass derives from the Council of Epaôn in France in 517. This Council forbade the consecrating of wooden altars:

> "Altaria nisi lapidea chrismatis unctione
> non sacrentur." [82]

But wooden altars were still used for Mass in isolated cases for the next few centuries, for evidence of their existence in the light of contrary legislation can be found as late as the eleventh century in England,[83] Spain [84] and France.[85] These altars likewise had to be

[81] The Council of Paris (829), Lib. I, c. 47: ". . . in altaribus ab episcopis consecratis . . ."—*MGH,* Legum Sectio III, *Concilia,* Tom. II, pars 2, p. 641; the Council of Mainz (888), c. 9: ". . . tabula altaris consecrata . . ."—Mansi, XVIII A, 67. Cf. Gattico, *De Oratoriis Domesticis,* Pars II, c. I, n. 9.

[82] C. 26—*MGH,* Legum Sectio III, *Concilia,* Tom. I, p. 25; Burchardus, *Decretum,* Lib. III, c. 25—*MPL,* CXL, 677. Pope Benedict XIV (*De Missae Sacrificio,* Tom. I, c. 15) stated that some held Pope St. Sylvester I (314-335) to have been the first to order stone altars, but a solid basis for such a decree cannot be found. Similar legislation which required that the altars be of stone is found also in the Capitularies of Charlemagne (806 or later), n. 47, *Excerpta de canone,* c. 16—*MGH,* Legum Sectio II (in 4° H), *Capitularia,* Tom. I, p. 133, and in Hincmar (857), *Capitula,* III, c. 3: "Nemo presbyterorum in altario ab episcopo non consecrato ante consecrationem cantare praesumat . . . tabulam . . . de marmore vel nigra petra . . . nobis ad consecrandum afferat . . . in qua sacra mysteria secundum ritum ecclesiasticum agere valeat"—Mansi, XV, 492.

[83] The Council of Winchester (1070), c. 5—Mansi, XX, 460.

[84] The Council of Coyanza (1050), c. 3—Mansi, XIX, 786.

[85] Martène (*De Antiquis Ecclesiae Ritibus,* Lib. I, c. III, art. IV, n. 5) referred to a letter found in the archives of the monastery of Tours, written by Hardouin de Malliaco, dated 1298, declaring that the monks had the faculty of using wooden altars. Incidentally, after the persecutions metal altars made of silver or gold were also found, for example, the altar used by St. Ambrose in Milan before 385—*Dictionnaire d' Archéologie Chrétienne et de Litugie* (14 vols. in 27, Paris, 1907—), fig. 1130, t. I, pars II, col. 3171; Pope St. Sixtus III (432-440) had a silver one in St. Mary Major—*MGH, Gesta Pontificum Romanorum,* I, 97; Pulcheria (399-453), the sister of the Emperor Theodosius II (408-450), gave a gold altar to the church of the Holy Wisdom—(Sozomenus, *Hist. Eccles.,* Lib. IX, c. 1)—*MPG,* LXVII, 1596.

consecrated by the bishop, before it was permitted to say Mass on them. As regards the exact date when the Church first ordered that no Mass be said except on a consecrated stone, there is no certainty.[86]

But St. Ephraem of Syria, who died about 373, had already referred to the anointing of the altar in order that sacrifice might be offered on it.[87] The first definitely known legislation is that of the Council of Agde in 506.[88] From then on the consecration of altars became the universal practice.[89] Thus Pope Nicholas I (858-867), when speaking for the Roman practice in 860, stated that the altar for the Sacrifice was of natural and common stone converted into a sacred and a holy table by the help of God.[90]

Instead of a consecrated altar stone the Greeks used the *antimension,* a piece of decorated linen or silk, into which was sewn a tiny bag which contained the relics of the saints.[91] Just when this practice began is not definitely known. Balsamon (1140- ca. 1195) referred to it in his commentary on the Trullan Synod.[92]

As has been noted with reference to the early century persecutions, it was often the practice to celebrate Mass on the tomb of some martyr.[93] Hence, after the Edict of 313, the churches of Rome were

[86] Bona, *Rerum Liturgicarum Libri Duo,* Lib. I, c. XX, n. 1.

[87] *De Oleo,* Lib. I, c. 3—T. Lamy, *Hymni et Sermones St. Ephraem* (4 vols., Mechliniae, 1882-1902), II, 787. Cf. also St. Gregory of Nyssa, *Bapt. Christi, Oratio in Diem Luminum—MPG,* XLVI, 581.

[88] C. 14: "Altaria placuit non solum unctione Chrismatis, sed etiam sacerdotale benedictione sacrari."—Mansi, VIII, 327.

[89] The II Council of Braga (562), c. 19—Mansi, IX, 779; *De Gloria Confessorum* (ca. 538-594), c. 20—*MPL,* LXXI, 842; *Capitulare Primum Karoli Magni* (769 vel paulo post), c. 14—*MGH,* Legum Sectio II, *Capitularia* (4° H), Tom. I, p. 46; the Council of Mainz (888), c. 9—Mansi, XVIII A, 67; the Council of Coyanza (1050), c. 3—Mansi, XIX, 786; Ivo, *Panormia,* Lib. II, c. 17—*MPL,* CLXI, 1086.

[90] *Prima Epistola ad Res Orientales, Filio Michaeli,* n. 82—*MGH, Epistolae,* Tom. VI. (in 4 W), pars II, fasciculus I, Sectio IV, p. 438; Jaffé, n. 2682.

[91] Cf. Cabrol, "Antimension"—*Dictionnaire d'Archéologie Chrétienne et de Liturgie,* Tom. I, pars II, pp. 2319 ff.

[92] Gattico, *De Oratoriis Domesticis,* Pars II, c. II, n. 12.

[93] Cf. Schuster (*The Sacramentary,* I, 138): "The *Liber Pontificalis* attributes the custom of saying Mass on the tombs of martyrs to Pope Felix I (274), but in Asia Minor it would seem that the custom was very much older, so perhaps the Pope merely restricted such celebration to the tombs of those

built over the tombs of martyrs, and it became the custom to bury great men under or near the altar. Thus there evolved the practice of having the relics of martyrs in the altar stone on which Mass was said. But this practice never became universal, nor was it chrystalized as strict law during that early period. Thus the Roman Missal of 1478, in the instruction relative to the consecration of the altar, still noted the possibility of the non-insertion of the relics in the altar stone.[94]

The requirements that the altar for Mass be of stone, and that it be consecrated, brought with it the more widespread use of portable altars.[95] Mass could permissibly be celebrated on this type of altar while the priest was on a journey,[96] or also in the private houses of the sick, or even when he offered the Sacrifice out of private devotion.[97]

Some restrictions were placed on the practice of saying two Masses on the one altar on the same day. It was not lawful for the same priest to say two Masses in any one day on the same altar.[98]

who died a violent death for their faith." Cf. also Gattico, *De Oratoriis Domesticis*, Pars II, c. I, n. 10.

[94] Gattico, *De Oratoriis Domesticis*, Pars II, c. III, nn. 22, 23. Cf. the so-called IV Council of Carthage (398), c. 4, which ordered the destruction of all altars in which there were no relics. But it seems that this decree was aimed primarily at the eradication of false shrines in the rural districts—Mansi, III, 971; Burchardus, *Decretum*, Lib. III, c. 225—*MPL*, CXL, 722; Anselmus Lucensis, *Collectio*, Lib. V, tit. 14.

[95] Also called *"Altaria Viatica"*—Gattico, *De Oratoriis Domesticis*, Pars II, c. VI, n. 7 sqq.; c. VIII.

[96] The VIII Council of Paris (829), Lib. I, c. 47; Lib. III, c. 6—*MGH*, Legum Sectio III, *Concilia*, Tom. II, pars 2, pp. 641, 672; the Council of Mainz (888), c. 9—Mansi, XVIII A, 67; Burchardus, *Decretum*, Lib. III, c. 56 —*MPL*, CXL, 683; Ivo, *Decretum*, Lib. III, c. 59—*MPL*, CLXI, 210.

[97] Beda Venerabilis, *Historia Ecclesiae Anglicae*, Lib. V, c. 10—*MPL*, XCX, 244; Hincmar, *Capitula*, Lib. III, c. 3—*MPL*, CXXV, 794; Mansi, XV, 492.

[98] The Council of Auxerre (580), c. 10—Mansi, IX, 913; Burchardus, *Decretum*, Lib. III, c. 226—*MPL*, CXL, 722. This canon was not incorporated in Gratian, but Rufinus (*Summa Decretorum*, c. 47, D. I, *de cons.*—ed. Singer, p. 547, & note 'h') as late as 1159 reminded priests of this law which he had based on the "Breviarium Complutense super canones e Concilio Urbico sub Illario papae", although it cannot be found there (Mansi, VII, 959). Cf. Thomassinus, *Disciplina circa Beneficia*, Pars I, lib. II, c. 23, n. 17; Benedictus

In this way were developed the beginnings of the modern practices in regard to a consecrated stone altar, fixed or portable and containing relics, as the necessary place for the celebration of the Holy Sacrifice.

It is evident that, not only in the earlier period but also throughout the Middle Ages in the Western Church, liturgical legislation concerning matters that did not affect the validity of the substance of the rites remained within the power of the local bishops and of the provincial councils. It was such factors as widespread custom and general usage that set up the norm of a universal application.

XIV, *De Missae Sacrificio,* Tom. II, c. 40. Martène (*De Antiquis Ecclesiae Ritibus,* Lib. I, c. III, art. VI, n. 12) declared that this same law was found in the statutes of St. Boniface of Mainz, and in a council held at Bourges. But a divergency is found in the *Poenitentiale Theodori,* Lib. II, c. 2: "In unoquoque altari duas missas facere conceditur in uno die"—Haddan & Stubbs, *Councils and Ecclesiastical Documents,* III, 190, 210.

CHAPTER III

FROM GRATIAN (CA. 1140) TO THE COUNCIL OF TRENT (1545-1563)

THE Roman rite, which reached a certain degree of perfection under Pope Gregory the Great (590-604), was accepted everywhere in the Western Church (excluding some local differences, as in Milan and Toledo) by the time of Pope Gregory VII (1073-1085), and flowered to a full bloom between the eleventh and the sixteenth centuries. However, during this period of development in the Church law as a whole, much of the legislation concerning the Mass was not yet clearly defined by the authorities. Consequently there crept in abuses which were uprooted only through the decree of the Council of Trent, which paved the way for the really unified liturgical law on some of the more basic institutes. This unification was effected through the liturgical books which Pope Pius V (1566-1572) ordered to be published.[1]

ARTICLE 1. THE LAW IN GRATIAN

For the study of Gratian, who compiled the law as it existed in his time (ca. 1140), one can construct a general summary of the previous legislation and a brief synopsis of the current regulations governing the factors of time and place with reference to the celebration of Mass.

(*a*) *Time of Mass*

There was a daily offering of the Holy Sacrifice in commemoration of the Passion of Christ.[2] This daily Mass was to be regularly cele-

[1] Cf. Van Hove, *Commentarium Lovaniense in Codicem Iuris Canonici,* Vol. I, Tom. I, *Prolegomena* (2. ed., Mechliniae-Romae: H. Dessain, 1945), p. 194; Wernz, *Ius Decretalium* (6 vols., Romae, et Prati, 1898-1905), Tom. III, *Ius Administrationis Ecclesiae Catholicae,* pars II, n. 325.

[2] Cf. c. 71, D. II, *de cons.*: "Iteratur quotidie haec oblatio," as based on the exegesis offered by Paschasius Radbertus (785-860) in his work *De Corpore et Sanguine Domini* (831); and c. 13, D. III, *de cons.*, which borrows from the Epistle of Pope Innocent I (416), who in referring to Friday and Saturday wrote: ". . . Isto biduo Sacramenta penitus non celebrari" (cf. Jaffé,

brated in the early part of the day,[3] especially at nine o'clock in the morning.[4]

There were some exceptions to this general rule, such as the Mass on the night before Christmas Day,[5] the Mass on Holy Saturday night, or rather early in the night of Easter Sunday morning,[6] the Mass at three o'clock in the afternoon during Lent,[7] and the Mass celebrated at the vesperal hour after the ember fasts.[8] But it seems

n. 311). This could be interpreted to mean that no Mass was to be said on Friday and Saturday. The rubric of Gratian, however, implied that it referred to the fast to be observed on those two days, "Ob reverentiam sepulturae dominicae sabbato ieiunare debemus." Many (*Praelectiones de Missa,* n. 14), Gasparri (*De Sanctissima Eucharistia,* I, n. 87) and other authors interpreted this decree of Pope Innocent I as referring simply to the omission of Mass on the last two days of Holy Week.

[3] Cf. c. 51, D. I, *de cons.,* taken from an epistle of Pope Leo I (445); Jaffé, n. 406.

[4] Cf. c. 48, D. I, *de cons.*: ". . . missarum celebrationes ante horam diei tertiam minime sunt celebrandae . . .," as based on a pseudo-Isidorian letter attributed to Pope St. Telesphorus (125-136). Friedberg, in a footnote (n. 538) to this *caput,* pointed to *Caput Pseudo-Isidorianum,* n. 2, as contained in Hinschius, *Decretales Pseudo-Isidorianae,* p. 110.

[5] C. 48, D, I, *de cons.*: ". . . nocte sancta Nativitatis domini . . ."

[6] Dictum post c. 50, D. I, *de cons.*: ". . . in sabbato vero sancto circa noctis initium missarum solemnia sunt celebranda." This Mass followed the ordinations which began at dusk on Holy Saturday, thus causing the actual Mass to be late at night, or really making it the Mass of Easter. This time for ordinations was determined by Pope St. Leo, I (440-461), St. Gelasius I (492-496) and Pelagius II (578-590), as noted in cc. 4, 5, 7, D. 75, and c. 14, D. 63, and c. 12, D. 76.

[7] C. 50, D. I, *de cons.*: "Ante missarum solemnia, circa horam nonam decantata, nulli in Quadragesima comedere licet . . .," as based on a decree attributed to the Council of Chalon-sur-Saône (650) by Ivo and Gratian, to Pope St. Sylvester I by Burchard, but as actually found in the Capitularies of Theodulph of Orleans (797). Cf. Friedberg's note (n. 564) to the rubric of c. 50, D. I, *de cons.*

[8] *Dictum* post c. 50, D. I, de *cons.*: "In ieiuniis etiam quatuor temporum circa vespertinas horas . . . missarum solemnia sunt celebranda." Gratian here left the impression that Mass was celebrated earlier during Lent than on the ember days, whereas the opposite seems to have been the case from a consideration of the decree of Theodulph (797) and the Council of Mainz (813). According to Rufinus (1190) in his *Summa Decretorum* (on. c. 47, D. I, *de cons.*), the distinction was no longer made. Generally on all fast days

that on these exceptional days (i. e., the fast days) it was also lawful to say Mass in the earlier part of the day, for after speaking of the vesperal Mass on fast days Gratian concluded by saying:

> "Prima quoque parte diei Missarum solemnia
> non incongrue celebrantur." [9]

(*b*) *Place of Mass*

As regards the place for the celebration of Mass, the law which required a church that was consecrated by the bishop was an established institution.[10] Cases of necessity fell outside the demand made

Mass was to follow the public recitation of Nones. Many (*Praelectiones de Missa,* n. 19, [2]) and Gasparri (*De Sanctissima Eucharistia,* I, n. 98) declared that in Lent the Mass was celebrated *"sub vesperam,"* and on other fast days *"hora nona."* Pope Benedict XIV (*De Missae Sacrificio,* II, 386) pointed out the common teaching of the authors that according to the old discipline the Mass on the ember days was said after Nones (mid-afternoon), while during Lent it was celebrated at a later hour, namely, at dusk after vespers. Gonzalez-Tellez (+1673) reconciled the difficulty thus: "In Lent Mass was originally said in mid-afternoon after the Vesperal office; but in his day the conventual Mass was normally celebrated in the morning after the recitation of Nones, and during Lent Vespers were to be said before noon to allow for the celebration of Mass in the morning—*Commentaria Perpetua in Singulos Textus Quinque Librorum Decretalium Gregorii IX* (5 vols. in 4, Lugduni, 1715), Tom. III, lib. III Decretalium, tit. XLI, c. I, n. 12.

[9] *Dictum* post c. 50, D. I, *de cons.*

[10] C. I, D. I, de *cons.*: "De . . . missarum celebrationibus non alibi quam in sacratis Domino locis absque magna necessitate fieri debere, liquet omnibus, quibus sunt nota novi et veteris testimenti praecepta."; c. 2, D. I, *de cons.*: "Non in aliis quam in Domino sacratis ab episcopis, et non a chorepiscopis, missas celebrare debemus," with immediate reference to the decree of the Council of Laodicea (343-381), which prohibited the celebration of Mass in private houses; c. 11, D. I, *de cons.*: "Sacrificia non nisi . . . in locis Deo consecratis offerantur," as borrowed from a pseudo-Epistle of Pope Felix IV (526-530) (cf. Friedberg's note 129 to c. 11, D. I, *de cons.*, and note 2 on c. 1, D. I, *de cons.;* Jaffé, n. 878), which added: "In domibus tamen ab episcopis sive presbyteris oblationes celebrari nullatenus licet," as attributed to the Council of Tribur (895), but as actually taken from the Council of Mainz (888) (cf. Friedberg's note 144); c. 14, D. I., *de cons.*: "Sacrificare et missas celebrare non licet nisi in locis sacratis," as borrowed from an epistle which the pseudo-Isidorian Collectors attributed to Pope Clement (cf. Friedberg's note 153); c. 15, D. I, *de*

by this general law.[11] Incidentally this law explicitly excluded private oratories as suitable places for the celebration of Mass,[12] unless, as in other special cases, the consent of the bishop was first secured.[13]

The law which required that Mass be said in a consecrated church implied also that if the church lost its consecration it was no longer a fit place for the Divine Sacrifice until it was reconsecrated.[14] It was also unlawful to celebrate Mass in a church that had become

cons., makes added mention of a penalty (*abiiciatur*) for a priest who presumed to celebrate in places not made holy by the bishop. This canon is an apocryphal decree attributed to Pope St. Sylvester I (cf. Friedberg's note 166).

[11] C, 1, D. I, *de cons.*: ". . . absque magna necessitate . . .," c. 2, D. I, *de cons.*: ". . . si summa necessitate agere compulerit, non is domibus offerre prohibita sunt"; c. 30, D. I, *de cons.*: "sicubi . . . ecclesiae fuerint incensae et combustae, in capellis cum tabula consecrata missas interim celebrari permittimus . . . In itinere vero positis, si ecclesia defuerit, sub divo seu in tentoriis, item si tabula altaris consecrata ceteraque sacra mysteria ad id officium pertinentia ibi affuerint, missarum solemnia celebrari concedimus." This text is attributed to the Council of Tribur (895), but is actually derived from the Council of Mainz (888), c. 9. Cf. Friedberg, note 317.

[12] C. 33, D. I, *de cons.*, Rubrica: "In privatis oratoriis licet orare, sed non missas celebrare." This canon is attributed to a Council of Orleans (Friedberg, note 352). In reality it is a pseudo-Capitulary taken from the work of Benedict the Levite.

[13] C. 12 D. I, *de cons.*: ". . . vel ubi ipse [episcopus] permiserit, [missarum solemnia] celebranda esse censemus."; c. 14, D. I, *de cons.*: ". . . nisi in his in quibus episcopus iusserit, aut ab episcopo regulariter ordinato, . . . consecrata fuerint."; c. 34, D. I, *de cons.*, Rubrica: "In privatis oratoriis absque consensu episcopi nullus ministrare praesumat." This latter text, borrowed from canon 13 of the Trullan Synod (692), admittedly however does not directly refer to the celebration of Mass. Cf. c. 7, D. XLII: "In oratorio praeter orandi et psallendi cultum penitus nihil agatur . . .", a *Palea* taken from an epistle of St. Augustine. Further consideration of the bishop's authority over oratories is found in c. 10, C. 18, q. 2, and c. 7, D. I, *de cons.*

[14] Such loss of consecration occurred when the church was destroyed (cf. c. 24, D. I, *de cons.*, attributed to Pope St. Julius I (337-352), but in reality a letter of Pope Vigilius (537-552), as contained in Mansi, IX, 31), or the altar was removed (cf. c. 19, D. I, *de cons.*, attributed to Pope St. Hyginus (136-140), but uncertain in its origin, and found in the Excerpt of Egbert, who gives it under the name of Pope Vigilius according to Friedberg, note 209) or the crime of homicide or the shedding of human blood was perpetrated in the place (cf. c. 20, D. I, *de cons.*, and c. 3, D. LXVIII, both attributed to the I Council of Nicaea (325), but not found there, as Friedberg states in note 28),

violated by means of the burial of infidels therein.[15] If a church which was formerly in the hands of heretics, and which had been dedicated by them in some form contrary to the one used in the Roman rite, was taken over by Catholics, Mass was not permitted there until the church was reconsecrated validly.[16]

Finally, Gratian showed that Mass was permitted only on a consecrated [17] altar [18] of stone,[19] which contained relics of the saints.[20]

or acts of a carnal character were committed therein. Cf. cc. 19, 20, D. I, *de cons.*

[15] C. 27, D. I, *de cons.*, attributed to a Council of Orleans, but found in the Penitential of Theodore, n. 148 (cf. Friedberg, n. 283); c. 28, D. I, *de cons.*, also found in the same penitential (cf. Friedberg, n. 240). Both of these applied strictly to the burial of pagans and infidels in the church.

[16] C. 20, D. I, *de cons.;* c. 21, D. I, *de cons.*, a pseudo-Isidorian attribution to Pope John (cf. Friedberg, note 218); c. 22, D. I, *de cons.*, taken from the Dialogue of Pope Gregory. These canons refer to the reconsecration of the Arian churches, for they were not originally consecrated in the form of the Catholic Church. Thus if a church was only doubtfully consecrated, it too had to be consecrated before Mass was permitted in it. Cf. *Gloss* on c. 20—*Decretum Gratiani una cum Glossis, Gregorii XIII, Pont. Max. iussu editum* (2 vols., Romae, 1582), II, 2480, 2481; St. Thomas, *Summa Theologica,* III, q. 83, art. III, ad 3—Editio XXII diligenter emendata, (6 vols., Taurini-Romae: Marietti, 1939), V, 208.

[17] C. 30, D. I, *de cons.*: ". . . cum tabula consecrata missas iterum celebrare permittimus . . . si tabula altaris consecrata . . . ibi offerunt." Note also c. 22, D. I, *de cons.*, taken from the Council of Agde (506): "Altaria placuit non solum unctione chrismatis, sed etiam sacerdotali benedictione sacrari."

[18] C. 11, D. I, *de cons.*: ". . . sacrificia non nisi super altare . . . offerantur." Thus it seems likely that c. 30, D. I, *de cons.*, referred to what must have been a portable altar.

[19] C. 31, D. I, *de cons.*: "Chrismate non ungantur altaria, nisi fuerint lapidea." The text here was borrowed from canon 6 of the Council of Epaôn (517).

[20] C. 26, D. I, *de cons.*: "Evertantur altaria quae sine sanctorum reliquiis eriguntur . . .", based on the V Council of Carthage (401). The gloss on this canon indicates that the purpose of the law was to rebuke those who built altars in fields and villas, but failed to furnish them with the relics of the saints. Thus the bishop was ordered to destroy these false altars, or at least to tell the people to forego using them. C. 29, D. I, *de cons.*, forbade priests in carefree presumptuousness to say Mass on the tombs of the dead. The gloss understood this prohibition as invoking a necessary safeguard against the pagan belief, according to which the shades of the dead were considered as remaining in the vicinity of their tomb.

Article 2. Further Explanation and Development of the Gratian Canons

The *Glossa Ordinaria,* that is, the classic interpretation of Gratian's text as joined with that text by the decretists, in elaborating the notion of necessity as a cause excusing from the requirement of a consecrated church for Mass, listed as an example the celebration of Mass for the troops in the army. Yet it emphasized the fact that no cause excused from the requisite use of a consecrated altar stone.[21] Even if a private house had a special prayer-room, the celebration of Mass was not permitted there except in the greatest necessity and with the consent of the bishop.[22]

With regard to the hours of Mass, St. Thomas (1225-1274) [23] and the *Glossa Ordinaria* [24] declared that the "first part of the day" mentioned in Gratian indicated above all that Mass was to be said during the day, and not at night.[25]

St. Thomas identified the beginning of the day with the appear-

[21] Gloss on c. 1, and c. 11, D. I, *de cons.*

[22] Gloss on c. 11 and c. 23, D. I, *de cons.* It should be noted here that if the church had burned down, then Mass could be said in non-consecrated chapels until the church was restored, though otherwise such a manner for the celebration of Mass was not lawful without a special permission from the bishop—Gloss on c. 30, D. I, *de cons.* St. Thomas (1225-1274) stated that the factor of necessity allowed Mass to be said in non-consecrated or even in violated places with the consent of the bishop (*Summa Theologica,* III, q. 83, art. III, ad 2). But when he emphasized the necessity of a consecrated altar stone, he added that a church is never consecrated without an altar, but that an altar with its relics may be consecrated apart from a church. For this doctrine he relied on the text of c. 26, D. I, *de cons.*—*Summa Theologica,* Marietti edition, V, 208.

[23] *Summa Theologica,* III, q. 83, art. II, ad 4—Marietti edition, V, 206.

[24] On c. 48, D. I, *de cons.,* additio.

[25] Rufinus in his *Summa Decretorum,* c. 47 and c. 51, D. I, *de cons.,* claimed that the summary of Gratian, namely, "Etiam prima parte diei missas celebrare licet," did indeed correctly reflect the existing custom of the celebration of Mass during the day, but that in representing this custom as being based on the declaration of Pope St. Leo I (440-461) to Dioscurus, Patriarch of Alexandria (444-451), Gratian proved inaccurate, since the Pope's epistle dealt simply with an individual case when on the more solemn feasts not all the faithful could be accommodated in the church at once, and for that reason Mass was to be repeated as often as a new group arrived—Singer edition, p. 547.

ance of the aurora.[26] He listed three reasons for the daily celebration from nine o'clock in the morning until three in the afternoon,[27] adding as Rufinus (1190) had done,[28] that the regular time for the daily solemn Mass was at nine in the morning, for the Mass on certain special feasts at noon, and for the Mass on the fast days of Lent, on the ember days and on certain vigils, in mid-afternoon. On ordination days, that is, on the four Ember Saturdays and on Holy Saturday, the Mass, as really pertaining to the following day, began *"circa noctis tempus."* [29] Besides the temporal limitations attached to the celebration of Mass on these five Saturdays, the only day on which Mass could not be said was Good Friday.[30]

[26] *Summa Theologica,* III, q. 83, art. II, ad 4, referring to c. 51, D. I, *de cons.*: ". . . in die et non in nocte . . . ita tamen quod principium diei accipitur non a media nocte, nec etiam ab ortu solis, id est, quando substantia solis apparet super terram, sed quando incipit apparere aurora; tunc enim quodammodo dicitur sol ortus, in quantum claritas radiorum eius apparet"—Marietti edition, V, 206. This seems to be the first widespread explanation of the rule that the celebration of Mass could be begun only after the aurora, and so it seems probable that this custom became universal only by that time. Walafrid Strabo (*De Rebus Ecclesiasticis,* c. XXIII—*MPL,* CXIV, 951), when writing in 849, declared that Mass was not to be started before the aurora except on Christmas Day, but it is probable that he referred solely to the celebration of public solemn Masses.

[27] *Ibid.,* in corp. art.—Marietti edition, V, 205, 206. Cf. also Gulielmus Durantis (1237-1296), *Rationale Divinorum Officiorum* (ed. V. d'Avino, Neapoli: Apud Josephum Dura, Bibliopolam, 1859), Lib. IX, c. 1, n. 20.

[28] *Summa Decretorum,* c. 47, D. I, *de cons.*—Singer ed., p. 547.

[29] *Summa Theologica,* Pars III, p. 83, art. II, ad 3 and 4—Marietti edition, V, 205, 206. It may be noted that the beginning of a change in this matter can be indicated in the thirteenth century. Before this time the first Easter Mass was said to be celebrated *"in nocte,"* but St. Thomas added to this *"circa principium"* (IV *Sent.,* dist. XIII q. 1, art. II, ulterius quaest. I, solutio), implying that the Mass had been moved to an earlier hour on Saturday evening—*Commentaria in Quatuor Libros Sententiarum Petri Lombardi, emendata per Joannem Nicolai* (4 vols. in 2, Parisiis: Apud Societatem Bibliopolarum via Jacobae, 1659), IV, 208 (hereafter cited *In Quatuor Libros Sententiarum*). Durantis (1237-1296), in his treatment of the Holy Saturday service, did not clearly state when the Mass began. But he did indicate that the services had become proper to Holy Saturday itself, and were no longer of Easter Sunday, and that they began in most places about 4 P. M.—*Rationale Divinorum Officiorum,* Lib. VI, c. LXXVIII, nn. 2, 3.

[30] St. Thomas, *Summa Theologica,* Pars III, q. 83, art. II, ad 2: "In die

On Christmas Day the first Mass was said at midnight (*in nocte*), the second at dawn (*in aurora*), and the third in mid-morning (*clara luce seu circa tertiam horam*).[31] Rufinus had taught that private Mass could be celebrated at any hour of the day, either before or after nine o'clock, provided that by such a celebration of the Mass the people were not distracted away from the public solemnities of the day.[32]

Article 3. Legislation Between Gratian and the Council of Trent

Between the time of Gratian (ca. 1140) and the XXII Session of the Council of Trent (1562) there was comparatively little legislation that dealt explicitly with the factors of time and of place for the celebration of Mass. The general ruling which required that Mass be said in a consecrated church and on a consecrated altar stone was fairly clear, and its import seemed well established, as Gratian had intimated, and the time, particularly for the celebration of private Mass, was left to the dictates of local usage and custom, which differed somewhat in the various localities. However, there were a few legal developments which affected particularly the factor of place for the celebration of Mass.

After Alexander III (1159-1181) the removal of the altar was no longer a cause for the desecration of the church.[33] The notions

quo ipsa passio Domini recolitur . . . non celebratur consecratio huius sacramenti."

[31] St. Thomas, *Ibid.*, ad 4; Rufinus, *Summa Decretorum*, ad c. 47, D. I, *de cons.*—Singer edition, p. 547.

[32] St. Thomas (*ibid.*, ad 3) taught that Mass (solemn?) could be offered even before nine o'clock in a case of necessity. It may be noted that the first mention of any restriction concerning the latest time in the day at which the celebration of Mass was permitted occurs in the writings of Duns Scotus (ca. 1266-1308). He indicated (*In Quatuor Libros Sententiarum*, Lib. IV, dist. 13, q. 2, scholium unicum, pars *de hora*) that Mass was not to be said after the ninth hour of the day [i. e., three o'clock in the afternoon]—"Cavendum est ne ante auroram celebretur. Et potest celebrari usque ad nonam."—*Opera Omnia* (Editio nova, 26 vols., Parisiis, 1891-1895), XXIV, 199.

[33] C. 1, X, *de consecratione ecclesiae vel altaris*, III, 40; Jaffé, n. 14204.

of desecration and of violation became considerably clarified at that time. Thus a church lost its consecration only through destruction.[34] On the other hand, the effects of the consecration or of the blessing were only suspended in their operation if the church was violated.[35] If the violation occurred during the celebration of Mass, then the sacred function had to cease until the church, whether consecrated or blessed, was reconciled.[36]

The celebration of Mass was not allowed in a church which was placed under a local interdict. This ecclesiastical penalty entailed the prohibition of divine services and the abstention from the use of sacred things in a specified place or by designated persons. It was probably introduced around the sixth century as a modification of the general excommunication. The penalty of interdict as entailing the prohibition of the celebration of Mass already existed in the ninth century,[37] and the Council of Limoges in 1031 definitely declared that no divine services were permitted in a church upon which rested the ban of an interdict.[38]

However, it was only in the time of the Decretals that the use of interdict as a canonical penalty became widespread, and that its

[34] Decree of Pope Innocent III (1212)—c. 6, X, *de consecratione ecclesiae vel altaris,* III, 40; Potthast, *Regesta Pontificum Romanorum inde ab anno post Christum natum MCXCVIII ad annum MCCCIV* (2 vols. Berolini, 1874-1875), n. 4603 (hereafter cited Potthast).

[35] E. g., by the perpetration of homicide (c. 4, X, *de consecratione ecclesiae vel altaris,* III, 40 [Pope Innocent III 1198-1216]; Potthast, n. 3123); by the unjust and grave shedding of human blood (*loc. cit.*); by the illicit and voluntary effusion of the human seed (c. 10, *eiusdem tituli* [Pope Gregory IX (1227-1241)]; Potthast, n. 9203); or by the burial of infidels or of the *excommunicati vitandi* (c. 7, *eiusdem tituli* [Pope Innocent III] Potthast, n. 4722).

[36] Cf. cc. 4, 7, 9, 10, X, *de consecratione ecclesiae vel altaris,* III, 40; c. 18, *de consecratione ecclesiae vel altaris,* III, 21, in VI (Pope Boniface VIII [1295-1303]).

[37] Cf. for example, the interdict imposed in 861 by Hincmar, Bishop of Laon (858-879), as recorded in the epistle (n. III) of Hincmar, the Archbishop of Rheims (845-882)—Hardouin, *Acta Conciliorum et Epistolae Decretales ac Constitutiones Summorum Pontificum* (12 vols., Parisiis, 1714-1715), V, 1373 (hereafter cited Hardouin).

[38] Mansi, XIX, 541. For another example see the Council of Poitiers (1070), c. 6—Mansi, XX, 498.

nature became clearly differentiated from that of excommunication.[39] Legislation was enacted in the General Councils in regulation of its use and extent,[40] and its severity was somewhat modified in the later papal decretals.[41] Finally, under Pope Boniface VIII (1294-1303) the legislation regarding interdicts reached its full development, and it has remained substantially the same to the present day.[42]

In the thirteenth century priests began to apply to the Holy See for the privilege of a portable altar. Before that time Mass could be celebrated outside of a dedicated place only with the permission of the bishop. From the fact that bishops could permit this to be done, it was conceded that by law they had the privilege of a portable altar. Many examples of the use of this privilege by bishops in sickness or on journeys are recorded in history.[43]

Pope Boniface VIII (1298-1303) declared that the bishops could use this privilege even outside their own territories.[44] Honorius III (1216-1227) had granted this privilege to the Friars Minor and the

[39] E. Krehbiel shows that 57 general local interdicts were imposed under the Pontificate of Pope Innocent III between 1198 and 1216—*The Interdict, Its History and Its Operation* (Washington, D. C.: American Historical Association, 1909), p. 43, and Appendix.

[40] Cf. the III Lateran Council (1179), c. 9; the IV Lateran Council (1215), c. 57; the I Council of Lyons (1245), c. 7—Schroeder, *Disciplinary Decrees of the General Councils* (St. Louis, Mo.: Herder Book Co., 1937), pp. 222, 284, 322.

[41] Cf. the example of Gregory IX (1227-1241) who permitted the celebration of Mass once a week in an interdicted church with a view to renewing the Sacred Species in the tabernacle—c. 57, X, *de sententia excommunicationis*, V, 39. Cf. also c. 18, *de sententia excommunicationis, suspensionis et interdicti*, V, 11, in VI°; c. 8, *de privilegiis*, V, 7, in VI°.

[42] In churches under interdict Mass was permitted on certain days such as Christmas, Easter, Pentecost, and the Assumption of the Blessed Virgin Mary—C. 24, X, *de sententia excommunicationis, suspensionis et interdicti*, V, 11, in VI°.

[43] Cf. c. 12, D. I, *de cons.*; Gattico, *De Oratoriis Domesticis*, Pars II, c. VII, nn. 2, 3, 4.

[44] Cf. c. 12, *de privilegiis*, V, 7, in VI°: "Quoniam episcopi eorumque superiores se habent diversis ex causis a suis ecclesiis et diocesibus absentare frequenter . . . indulgemus eisdem, ut altare possint habere viaticum, et in eo celebrare ac facere celebrari, ubicunque absque interdicti transgressione illis permittitur celebrare vel audire divina."

Order of Preachers, and he at the same time reminded bishops and pastors that their own permission for its use was not required.[45]

Provincial Councils at the time reiterated the principle that to celebrate in private oratories was allowable only if permission was obtained from the local bishop.[46]

With reference to the factor of place for the celebration of Mass the legislation just prior to the time of the Council of Trent (1545-1563) had become universally uniform, definite and stabilized. It is with regard to the factor of time for the celebration of Mass that the law differed in accord with the divergent practice in the various countries. It is in this latter respect that a change in the legislation and its consolidation according to a universally uniform and stabilized pattern was still to follow.

[45] Cf. c. 30, X, *de privilegiis,* V, 33 (anno 1225); Potthast, n. 7467.

[46] Cf. the Council of Tours (or Angers, 1488), c. 6—Mansi, XXXII, 75; the Council of Sens (or Paris, 1528), c. 14—Mansi, XXXII, 1189; the Council of Mainz (1549), c. 95—Mansi, XXXII, 1435. Canon 15 of the Council of Sens (or Paris, 1528) reminded the bishops that they were not to consecrate portable altars until they had enquired about the need of them for present or future use—Mansi, XXXII, 1189.

CHAPTER IV

FROM THE COUNCIL OF TRENT (SESS. XXII, 1562) TO THE PRESENT CODE OF CANON LAW (1918).

THE twenty-second Session of the Council of Trent, the sixth under Pope Pius IV (1560-1565), was held on September 17, 1562. It legislated concerning the Holy Sacrifice of the Mass. After the doctrinal chapters and the dogmatic canons on this subject, there was issued the *Decree concerning the things to be observed and avoided in the celebration of Mass.* In this decree the assembled prelates declared in part:

> ". . . the holy council decrees that the local ordinaries shall be zealously concerned and be bound to prohibit and abolish all those things which either covetousness . . . or irreverence . . . or superstition . . . have introduced. And that many things may be summed up in a few . . . each in his own diocese shall . . . not suffer the holy sacrifice to be celebrated by any seculars and regulars whatsoever in private houses (*privatis in domibus*) or entirely outside the church or the oratories dedicated solely to divine worship and to be designated and visited by the same ordinaries . . . Finally, that no room be given to superstition, they shall by ordinance and prescribed penalties provide that priests do not celebrate at other than the proper hours (*aliis quam debitis horis*). All these things, therefore, which have been summarily enumerated, are in such wise set before all local ordinaries, that by the authority given them by this holy council, and also as delegates of the Apostolic See, they may prohibit, command, reform and establish not only the things aforesaid but also whatsoever else shall seem to them to be connected therewith; and they may by ecclesiastical censures and other penalties, which in their judgment they may impose, compel the faithful to observe them inviolately; any privileges, exemptions, appeals and customs to the contrary notwithstanding."[1]

As the Council itself indicated, this was a very summary statement of the law. The decree set down two basic principles with

[1] Conc. Trident., sess. XXII, *Decretum de observandis et evitandis in celebratione Missae*—Schroeder, *Canons and Decrees of the Council of Trent, Original Text with English Translation,* pp. 151-152; 423-424.

regard to the factors of time and place in the celebration of the Holy Sacrifice: first, Mass was prohibited outside of churches and oratories which were dedicated to divine worship; secondly, Mass was prohibited at other than the proper hours. Another important point was the abrogation of all privileges, exemptions, appeals and customs to the contrary. Finally, the Council indicated that a commission was to be established for the reform of the Roman Missal, in order that the celebration of Mass in the Roman rite might everywhere be made uniform.[2] This new reformed Missal, *Missale Romanum ex decreto S. S. Concilii Tridentini restitutum,* was finally published by Pope Pius V with the Bull *Quo primum* on July 14, 1570, in which the Pope commanded its use wherever the Roman rite was followed.[3]

[2] Cf. sess. XXV (Dec. 1563), *de ref.,* c. 21, Section concerning the Index of Books and the Catechism, Breviary and Missal: "The holy council in the second session . . . commissioned some Fathers to consider what ought to be done concerning various censures and books either suspected or pernicious and to report to this holy council. . . . it commands that whatever has been done by them be given over to the most holy Roman pontiff, that it may by his judgment and authority be completed and made public. The same it commands shall be done with regard to the catechism by the Fathers to whom it was assigned (sess. XXIV, Nov. 1563), and likewise with regard to the missal and breviary"—Schroeder, *op. cit.,* pp. 254-255. Peter Gonzales de Mendoza (1518-1574), writing on October 27, 1563, concerning the acts of the Council, stated that a commission was appointed for the editing of a new reformed Missal, but that the task could not be completed during the Council since it was a momentous undertaking and the work was commenced too late. Later, on November 10th of the same year, he wrote concerning the General Assembly which prepared the 24th Session, that in view of the manifold things yet to be considered the reform of the Missal was not to be undertaken by the Council itself—*Concilii Tridentini Diariorum, Actorum, Epistolarum, Tractatuum Nova Collectio* (ed. Societas Goerresiana, 13 vols. [incomplete], Friburgi Brisgoviae: B. Herder, 1901-), II, *Diariorum pars Secunda* (ed. S. Merkle, 1911), 706, 710.

[3] ". . . omnibus . . . in virtute sanctae obedientiae praecipientis, ut . . . Missam iuxta ritum, modum ac normam, quae per Missale hoc a Nobis nunc traditur decantent ac legant." Any rite which had been followed for over 200 years could however be tolerated. Thus Milan and Toledo retained their own rites, and the Dominicans, for example, retained certain ceremonies peculiar to their own Order—*Missale Romanum ex Decreto Sacrosancti Concilii Tridentini restitutum, S. Pii V Pontificis Maximi iussu editum, aliorum Ponti-*

With the publication of the reformed Missal the Roman liturgy (with a few minor exceptions) was standardized and became of legal force universally in the Western Church. Thus all control over even the accidentals of the liturgy was placed beyond the competence of the local bishop—a most important step towards unity in the precepts concerning the celebration of Mass. This unification was even more strongly established by Pope Sixtus V (1585-1590), who instituted the Congregation of Sacred Rites with full power to interpret all matters concerning the Sacred Rites, and to check any changes that might creep in.[4]

The Council of Trent and the new Roman Missal indicated the time and the place for the celebration of Mass much the same as it is done today. So with these two sources as a basis, the four general points under study will be considered in their development from the Council of Trent until the Code. These points, with reference to the time for the celebration of Mass, touch the day and the hour, and with reference to the factor of place, the church and the altar.

Article 1. The Days which Involved Limitations in the Celebration of Mass

The general Rubrics of the Missal begin with the statement: *"Missa quotidie dicitur secundum ordinem Officii."* Thus, according to the Latin rite, Mass could be said on any day except on Good Friday, which was entirely aliturgical, and only under certain restrictions could it be said on Holy Thursday and Holy Saturday.

ficum cura recognitum, a Pio X reformatum et Ssm̃i D. N. Benedicti XV auctoritate vulgatum (editio decima iuxta typicam, Turonibus, Typis Alfredi Mame et Filiorum [1926]), p. iii. The last time this Missal was reformed was when Pope Pius X issued the Constitution *Divino afflatu,* November 1, 1911, but his additions and variations did not affect the already established regulations regarding the factors of time and place in the celebration of Mass.

[4] Const. *Immensa aeterni,* 22 ian. 1588, Congregatio quinta, pro sacris ritibus et caeremoniis—*Bullarium Romanum,* a Leone I (440) ad Clementem XII (1740) (24 vols. cum appendice, Editio Taurinensis, 1857-1872), Tom. VIII, n. CXVII, p. 999 (hereafter cited *Bullarium Romanum*).

(a) *Holy Thursday*

The general rule for Holy Thursday was that a private or a low Mass was forbidden, and only one solemn Mass was permitted in all collegiate and parochial churches.[5] Suarez (1548-1617), writing in the beginning of the seventeenth century, held with others that, since there was no express law on the matter, and since no customary usage had acquired the force of law, a priest could celebrate privately on that day, provided that no scandal was given in his doing so.[6] This opinion however lost all probability through the subsequent decrees of the Holy See,[7] and of the Congregation of Sacred Rites.[8]

Yet private Masses were permitted on this day in exceptional cases. Thus in 1893 the Congregation of Sacred Rites granted this privilege to the Superior of the Third Order of St. Francis in order that Holy Communion might be distributed to the religious on that day, but it added that if the service was held in the church the doors were to be closed.[9] In places where the feast of the

[5] Benedictus XIV, *De Missae Sacrificio,* Tom. II, c. 22.

[6] *Commentarii et Disputationes in S. Thomam,* pars III, q. 83, disput. 80, sect. II, n. 6—*Opera Omnia,* XXI (editio nova a Carolo Berton, 28 vols., Parisiis, 1856-1878); he cited Soto (1494-1560), Navarrus (1492-1586) and Angelus Carleti (1495) as holding the same opinion. Schmalzgrueber (1663-1735) stated that in his day the more common opinion inclined to the view of Suarez, but he also mentioned that the Cardinal Vicar of Rome had prohibited private Masses on Holy Thursday in the diocese of Rome—*Ius Ecclesiasticum Universum* (5 vols. in 12, Romae, 1843-1845), Lib. III, tit. 41, c. 2, n. 45.

[7] Cf. *Institutiones Ecclesiasticae* Prosperi Lambertini, S.R.E. Cardinalis, Archiepiscopi Bononiensis, postea Benedicti XIV (Romae: Typis Sacrae Congregationis de Propaganda Fide, 1747), n. XXXVIII (Bulla Clementis XI, 15 mart. 1712)

[8] S. R. C., *Veneta,* 20 mart. 1762—*Decreta Authentica Sacrorum Rituum Congregationis* (6 vols., Romae, 1898-1927), n. 2465 (hereafter cited *Decr. Auth.*); S. R. C., *Urbis seu Minorum Observantiae S. Francisci,* 28 mart. 1775, ad V—*Decr. Auth.,* n. 2503.

[9] S. R. C., aug. 31, 1839: ". . . Superior celebret in privato oratorio ad ministrandam Religiosis communionem, et si desit oratorium, fiat in ecclesia ianuis clausis"—*Decr. Auth.,* n. 2799. The Dominicans received permission to continue the ancient custom of saying Mass in commemoration of the founding

Annunciation or of St. Joseph, when it coincided with Holy Thursday, was observed as a holy day of obligation, several private Masses were permitted on Holy Thursday before the regular Mass of the day, in order that the faithful could fulfill the precept of hearing Mass.[10]

As has already been mentioned, the one Mass celebrated in all cathedral, collegiate, and parochial churches was to be a solemn high Mass sung by the rector or pastor of the place.[11] However, when the celebration of a solemn high Mass was impossible in consequence of a lack of the necessary ministers, it was permitted to have an ordinary high Mass with three or four clerics assisting, according to the rubrics indicated in the *Memoriale Rituum,* edited in 1725 by order of Pope Benedict XIII, and extended to the use of the Universal Church in 1821.[12]

of the Rosary, which was said before dawn in the church of St. Dominic on that day—S. R. C., *Bononien.,* 14 mart. 1795—Pallottini, *Collectio Omnium Conclusionum et Resolutionum quae in causis propositis apud Sacram Congregationem Cardinalium S. Concilii Tridentini Interpretum Prodierunt ab eius Institutione anno MDLXIV ad annum MDCCCLX, distinctis titulis alphabetico ordine per materias digesta* (18 vols., Romae, 1868-1895), Tom. XIII, s. v. *Missa,* c. III, *Quoad Diem et Horam,* n. 50 (hereafter cited Pallottini).

10 S. R. C., *Decretum Generale,* 12 sept. 1716, approbata 27 sept.; ". . . in Annunciatione, . . . plures Missae privatae ante celebrationem Missae conventualis pro praecepti adimplemento"—*Decr. Auth.,* n. 2240; S. R. C., *Decretum Generale,* 13 sept. 1692 (for the feast of St. Joseph)—*Decr. Auth.,* n. 1883; S. R. C., *Viglevanen.,* 26 sept. 1868, not if it was not observed as a holy day of obligation—*Decr. Auth.,* n. 3179.

11 Cf. S. R. C., *Urbis et Orbis,* 10 dec. 1703, approbata 12 ian. 1704, concerning the argument between the local pastor and the chaplain of confraternities—*Decr. Auth.,* n. 2123.

12 S. R. C., *Resolutionis dubiorum,* 28 ian. 1821, ad I—*Decr. Auth.,* n. 2616; cf. *Ritual for Small Churches,* translation of the *Memoriale Rituum* issued by Pope Benedict XIII, and revised by authority of Benedict XIV, edited by Bartholomew Eustace (New York: Joseph Wagner, 1935). This ritual is not officially listed among the liturgical books of the Church, but its use has been canonized through frequent references to it in the responses of the Congregation. De Herdt (+1883) indicated that when this ritual calls for three or four clerics as serving at the Mass, the servers can be supplied from the ranks of the lay altar boys—*Sacrae Liturgiae Praxis iuxta Ritum Romanorum* (3 vols., ed. quarta revisa, Lovanii, 1863), Tom. III, pars V,

When the pastor could have neither a solemn high Mass according to the Missal, nor a high Mass with the required servers according to the *Memoriale Rituum,* the ordinary could permit him to say a low Mass early on Holy Thursday morning for the accommodation of the people.[13]

Outside the cathedral, collegiate, regular and parochial church (whether ruled independently by a pastor or subordinately by a vicar) even the one Mass on that day was not permitted, except when a special permission had been given, as indicated, or when the following four conditions were present. First, the church or oratory had to be entirely exempt from the jurisdiction of the local pastor;[14] secondly, the Blessed Sacrament had to be habitually reserved there;[15] thirdly, the Mass of the Presanctified had to be said on the next day[16] and finally it had to be a solemn Mass according to the ordinary rubrics.[17] Thus the chapels of seminaries, for example, could hold the Holy Week ceremonies under these conditions.

c. *De feria quinta in Coena Domini,* n. 44 (hereafter cited *Sacrae Liturgiae Praxis*).

[13] S. R. C., *Resolutionis dubiorum,* 28 iul. 1821, approbata 31 iul. 1821, ad I—*Decr. Auth.,* n. 2616.

[14] Pope Benedict XIV (*Institutiones Ecclesiasticae,* c. CV, n. 6) referred to the general decree, *Urbis et Orbis,* of 1703 (cf. *Decr. Auth.,* n. 2123). Cf. also De Herdt, *Sacrae Liturgiae Praxis,* Tom. I, pars V, c. *Ubi fit officium tridui sacri,* n. 34 (2).

[15] S. R. C., *Neopolitana,* 14 iun. 1659—*Decr. Auth.,* n. 1120.

[16] S. R. C., *Urbis seu Minorum Observantiae S. Francisci,* 28 mart. 1775, ad V—*Decr. Auth.,* 2503; *Responsio in Bellunen. et Teltren.,* 1 febr. 1895—*Decr. Auth.,* n. 3842; *Acta Sanctae Sedis* (41 vols., Romae, 1865-1908), XXVII (1894), 564 (hereafter cited *ASS*).

[17] S. R. C., *Mechlinien.,* 16 mart. 1876, approbata 23 mart. a Pio IX, declared that ordinarily the *Memoriale Rituum* was not to be used outside the parish churches; however, in special cases as for nuns in the enclosure, or when there was necessity or a great utility according to the judgment of the ordinary, it could be permitted—*Decr. Auth.,* n. 2390; S. C. Negotiis Ecclesiasticis Extraordinariis Praeposita, *Postulata patrum Concilii Plenarii Americae Latinae,* 1 ian. 1900, n. IV, in which the dioceses of Latin America received a ten-year indult from Pope Leo, XIII to use the *Memoriale Rituum* also in churches and oratories which were not parochial—*ASS,* XXXII (1899), 554; S. R. C., *Baltimoren.,* 1 sept. 1838, approbata sept. 7, a Gregorio XVI, permitted that the nuns have a low Mass celebrated in their oratory—*Decr. Auth.,* n. 4837.

(b) Good Friday

This was the only day of the year when no true Mass was said in the Roman rite.[18] However, in those and only in those churches where the ceremonies of Holy Thursday along with the procession and the reposition had been carried out, there was said on Good Friday the Mass of the Presanctified, which consisted in the consuming of the Host consecrated on the previous day.[19]

(c) Holy Saturday

In the fifth century Pope Innocent I placed this day on a par with Good Friday by declaring them both to be aliturgical. Hence, as shown in the previous section, no Mass was said on this day until after sunset, which Mass liturgically constituted the first Sacrifice of Easter morning. But gradually this evening service came to be more and more anticipated, so that finally it formed the Mass for Holy Saturday morning.[20]

The rule regarding the celebration of Mass on Holy Saturday was very similar to the rule that applied to Holy Thursday. One solemn high Mass was to be celebrated in all cathedral, conventual, collegiate, regular, and parochial churches (proper or vicarial), and other churches or oratories exempt from the jurisdiction of the local pastor. The ceremony was to be conducted according to the

[18] Benedictus XIV, *De Missae Sacrificio,* Tom. II, c. 21; cf. also Van de Burgt, *De Celebratione Missarum* (Ultrajecti, 1871), c. VII, pars II, n. 234.

[19] Benedictus XIV, *Institutiones Ecclesiasticae,* n. XXXVIII; Duchesne, *Christian Worship,* p. 249.

[20] Navarrus (1493-1586) already in his time stated that in view of the current customary usage it was lawful to say the Holy Saturday Mass even before noon, though it was perhaps difficult to see how that could be in harmony with the liturgical prayers for Holy Saturday. But he added that it was also licit to say this Mass at the third or fourth hour in the afternoon if all scandal was forestalled, for the custom of saying Mass before noon was introduced only in order that the faithful might not have to fast so long. The afternoon Mass on that day, he contended, fell within the "proper hours" which the decree of the Council of Trent called for—*Opera Omnia* (ed. novissima, 6 vols., Venetiis, 1618), disp. LXXX, sect. V, n. 6.

Caeremoniale Episcoporum and the Missal, or the *Memoriale Rituum*. Private and low Masses were not permitted.[21]

Suarez stated that according to a probable opinion current in his time (ca. 1600) one could say a private Mass on Holy Saturday if scandal was forestalled, and if the Mass was said after the solemn Mass had begun; but he did not counsel the use of this opinion.[22] Schmalzgrueber, about a century later, declared that this opinion had lost all probability after the decree of the Congregation of Sacred Rites on March 11, 1690.[23] Gasparri (1852-1934) [24] and Many (+1922) [25] advanced arguments to show that the prohibition of the celebration of private Masses on Holy Saturday was even more stringent than the similar prohibition with reference to Holy Thursday, for Holy Saturday was originally aliturgical, while on Holy Thursday the anniversary of the first Holy Sacrifice was celebrated.[26]

If the feast of the Annunciation fell on Holy Saturday, then this feast along with its accompanying precept to hear Mass was to be transferred after Low Sunday.[27]

[21] S. R. C., *Decretum Generale*, 11 febr. 1690, approbata 12 febr.—*Decr. Auth.*, n. 1822; S. R. C., *Senen.*, 26 apr. 1692—*Decr. Auth.*, n. 1873.

[22] *Opera Omnia*, XXI, disp. 80, *De Eucharistia*, Sect. II, n. 6.

[23] *Decretum—Decreta Authentica Sacrorum Rituum Congregationis*, collected by Aloysius Gardellini (5 vols., editio tertia, Romae, 1856-1888), n. 3204 (not included in the edition which was prepared under the authorization of Pope Leo XIII); Schmalzgrueber, *Ius Universum Ecclesiasticum*, Lib. III, tit. 41, c. 2, n. 44. Cf. also Benedictus XIV, *De Missae Sacrificio*, Tom. II, c. 22; St. Alphonsus, *Theologia Moralis* (ed. nova cura et studio Gaudé, 4 vols., Romae: Typis Polyglottis Vaticanis, 1905-1912), Lib. VI, n. 350.

[24] *De Sanctissima Eucharistia*, I, n. 87.

[25] *Praelectiones de Missa*, n. 16, (1-2).

[26] Cf. S. R. C., *Resolutionis dubiorum*, 28 iul. 1821, which revoked all personal indults for the celebration of private Mass on Holy Thursday, though there were retained certain local customs which permitted the celebration in certain places of one low Mass after the one solemn Mass of the day—*Decr. Auth.*, n. 2616; *Codicis Iuris Canonici Fontes cura Emi Petri* Card. Gasparri editi (9 vols., Romae [postea civitate Vaticana]: Typis Polyglottis Vaticanis, 1923-1939 (Vols. VII-IX, ed. cura et studio Emi Justiniani Serédi), n. 5842 (hereafter cited *Fontes*).

[27] S. R. C., *Decretum Generale*, 11 febr. 1690, approbata 12 febr.—*Decr. Auth.*, n. 1822; S. R. C., *Decretum Generale*, 23 apr. 1895, approbata 27 maii:

ARTICLE 2. THE HOUR OF MASS

The Council of Trent demanded that the ordinaries with the aid of legislation and even of penal measures were to see to it that their priests celebrated Mass only at the proper hours. This was the first universal legislation which dealt with the hour for the daily celebration of private Masses. In the time of St. Thomas it was customary not to begin Mass before dawn, but it was probably not until the sixteenth century that the hour of noon became generally recognized as marking the hour after which the celebration of Mass was not to take place.

Three years after the rather general decree of the Council of Trent the I Provincial Council of Milan (1565) decreed that Mass was not to be celebrated before dawn nor after mid-day, except for a reason permitted by law.[28] In 1566 Pope Pius V issued a general constitution which under penalty prohibited the celebration of Mass at the vesperal hour.[29]

Four years later the new Roman Missal was published. In it the general rubrics declared that "private Masses can be said at any hour from dawn (*aurora*) to mid-day (*ad meridiem*) after the recitation of Matins and Lauds;" and again, among the defects *in ministerio*, this Missal enumerated the celebration at an improper time, commonly any hour outside the period from dawn

"Ceterum, quotiescumque vel Feria VI in Parasceve vel Sabbato Sancto hoc Festum impediatur, toties Feria I post Dominicum in Albis . . . reponatur; in qua integra cum solemnitate et feriatione . . . celebrabitur"—*Decr. Auth.*, n. 3850; *ASS*, XXVII (1894), 57. De Herdt declared that if any other holyday fell on Holy Saturday the feast was to be transferred, but not the precept to hear Mass, so that all who could do so without too great inconvenience were bound to hear Mass on the actual feast day (*die a quo*)—*Sacrae Liturgiae Praxis*, Tom. I, pars IV, c. *De Translatione Festi*, n. 280. (Cf. S. R. C., *Barcinonen.*, 10 dec. 1733—*Decr. Auth.*, n. 2305). But, arguing from the 1895 decree, Gasparri contended that the decree at least implicitly transferred the same kind of precept that attached to any other holyday when it fell on Holy Saturday—*De Sanctissima Eucharistia*, I, n. 94.

[28] Pars II, c. 5—Mansi, XXIV A, 19.

[29] *Sanctissimus in Christo*, 29 mart. 1566, § 2—*Fontes*, n. 110. The penalty was that of perpetual suspension *a divinis*. This penalty was abrogated by Pope Pius IX, when on October 12, 1869, he issued the Constitution *Apostolicae Sedis*, which made no mention of the penalty. Cf. *Fontes*, n. 552.

until noon.[30] This was the first universal and definite law which determined the hours for the celebration of private Mass.[31] It was also the first universal law which limited the saying of private Mass to a period preceding the hour of noon.

(a) Dawn

By dawn or aurora is meant the dim glow or first radiation of light that by some time precedes sunrise. It is effected by the rays of the sun which, while the sun itself is still a certain distance below the horizon, begin to illuminate the horizon and the space above it. This illumination continues and increases in intensity as the sun gradually rises to the horizon until the actual ball of the sun itself appears, and then the dawn is terminated by sunrise.[32] In brief, dawn extends over the entire period of time intermediate between complete darkness and sunrise, that is, between night and day.[33] Due to the particular shape of the earth, its rotation on its axis, and its revolution around the sun on its oblique orbit, this period of dawn differs in different latitudes, and also at different seasons of the year. A detailed computation of the time which shows these variations will be furnished in the second part of this work.

In following the foregoing principle in regard to measuring the time of dawn independently of what the public clocks indicated,

[30] *Rubricae Generales Missalis,* c. XV, *De Hora celebrandi Missam;* tit. *De defectibus in Ministerio ipso occurrentibus,* n. 1.

[31] It may be noted that in the *General Rubrics* the law explicitly made mention only of private Masses when it set dawn and mid-day as the terms within which the celebration of Mass was to occur. In the section on the *Defects in the Ministry of the Mass* the Missal did not discriminate between public and private Masses by mentioning the latter and by leaving the former unmentioned. From this one can reasonably conclude that the law contemplated the public as well as the private Mass within its restrictive enactment.

[32] Cf. Many, *Praelectiones de Missa,* n. 20, (2, a); Gasparri, *De Sanctissima Eucharistia,* I, n. 102; Wernz, *Ius Decretalium,* III, n. 543.

[33] St. Alphonsus, *Theologia Moralis,* Lib. VI, n. 341. This period was also called *"crepusculum mane."* It corresponded to the period of dusk or twilight between sunset and night—Suarez, *Opera Omnia,* XXI, disp. 80, *De Eucharistia,* sectio IV, n. 4.

there arose in the Arctic regions a practical difficulty with reference to determining the time at which Mass could be started. Daybreak had no meaning in those districts, for there is no dawn in the Arctic in view of the extremely high latitude of the place. The Congregation of Sacred Rites replied to this difficulty by declaring that in those regions where there is no dawn the notion of aurora was to be taken in the moral sense. Thus dawn was to refer to the beginning of the civil and usual day, that is, to the time when according to the approved custom of the region men generally arise to begin their day's work.[34]

(b) Mid-day

Mid-day or high noon was the other limitative term set by the law for the celebration of Mass. This occurs when the sun passes directly over the local meridian. In relation to the hour indicated on one's clock or watch, dawn is a very relative thing and varies considerably in different latitudes and seasons. Noon however, is a comparatively stable point of time; it is the same for all latitudes, but differs at different longitudes. Because of the stability of noon and the changeableness of dawn, the period during which Mass could be said was subject to great variations in length.

The early writers found no difficulty with reference to the terminating point at noon. But as the use of the clock became

[34] S. R. C., *Missalis Romani,* 18 sept. and 2 nov. 1634—*Decr. Auth.,* n. 614; *Fontes,* n. 5354. Two sessions were held. In both the proposal to change the general rubric in the Missal for the sake of a better accommodation to conditions in the Arctic failed to win a majority support. Many (*Praelectiones de Missa,* n. 20) thought that a distinction was implicit in the response, so that its ruling was applicable only to the winter months when those regions have perpetual night. He contended that in the summer time, when the sun remains above the horizon even during the night, it was permissible to begin the celebration of Mass at the moment which corresponded to the middle of the night, which moment was to be determined as 12 hours after the time when the sun had passed directly over the local meridian. Wernz (*Ius Decretalium,* III, n. 543, note 170) and Gasparri (*De Sanctissima Eucharistia,* I, n. 106) seem not to have invoked any such distinction. Gasparri simply stated that aurora was to be understood as coinciding with that point of time at which it was usual for men to arise for their day's work.

more widespread, the true solar time was discarded for what was called mean solar time, that is, the average true time for the whole year. These two differ with a possible variation that involves an extreme difference of 30 minutes owing to the unequal motion of the earth in its revolution around the sun every year. Then, as commerce between cities became more widespread, it became necessary to set up a mean time for the whole region. Finally (1884) international time zones were agreed upon.

Quite naturally as a result of this development there were addressed to the Congregation of Sacred Rites many questions which sought to ascertain which of the different times, either local or legal, could be followed in the celebration of Mass and of other liturgical functions. As is the case with any other new juridical institute in the process of its development, the terms were not as yet clearly defined, and thus much confusion was occasioned for the interpretation of the various decrees which employed a divergent terminology.[35]

It was quite generally concluded that certainly mean sun time could be used, and also any legal time as shown on the public clocks, for a determination of noon in the celebration of Mass. Furthermore, most of the decisions were directed not specifically to the consideration of the precept regarding the celebration of Mass; yet all of the decisions ended with the same phrase which covered in general all ecclesiastical obligations. There was no common agreement among the authors concerning the use of the true sun time.[36]

[35] Cf., for example: *S. Poenit,* 18 iun. 1873—*Fontes,* n. 6430; S. R. C., *Clodien.,* 7 aug. 1875—Gardellini, *Decr. Auth.,* n. 5622; S. C. C., *Treviren.,* 22 iul. 1893—*Fontes,* n. 4287; S. C. S. Off., 9 aug. 1899, approbata a Papa Leone XIII, 11 aug.—*ASS,* XXXII (1899), 251-252; S. R. C., *Placentia in Hispania,* 12 maii 1905—*Decr. Auth.,* n. 4158; *Fontes,* n. 6338.

It should be noted here that the decision of August 7, 1875 as worded in the Gardellini edition of the decrees, reads: "Standum publicis horologiis," whereas in the authentic edition printed by the authorization of Pope Leo XIII it reads: "Posse stare publicis horologiis," in answer to the question whether by one's own choice one could follow mean or true time as one pleased —*Decr. Auth.,* n. 3365; *Fontes,* n. 6077.

[36] For example, Many (*Praelectiones de Missa,* n. 21) stated that it could not be used. On the other hand, Lehmkuhl (*Theologia Moralis* 4. ed., 2 vols., Friburgi Brisgoviae, 1887, II, 218) seemed to maintain that it could be used.

(c) Exceptions to the General Rule

The outstanding and universal exception to the general rule which called for the celebration of Mass after dawn was the first Mass on the night before Christmas Day.[37] According to the *General Rubrics* of the Missal [38] the first Mass for the feast of the Nativity of Our Lord was to be said after the middle of the night,[39] the second at dawn, the third in the morning. Private Masses however were generally excluded from the orbit of the privilege which warranted the celebration of midnight Mass.[40] But private Masses were permitted by special privilege,[41] and this privilege was finally extended in 1907 by Pope Pius X to all religious institutes, pious houses and clerical seminaries which had an oratory for which the faculty of reserving the Blessed Sacrament had been granted.[42]

Suarez had ventured the opinion that all three private Masses on Christmas Day could be read in succession after midnight,[43]

[37] Benedictus XIV, *De Missae Sacrificio,* Tom. II, c. 54.

[38] C. XV, n. 4.

[39] Any privileges to start before midnight were abrogated by the Bull of Pope Paul V, *Sanctissimus in Christo,* 29 mart. 1566—*Bullarium Romanum,* Tom. II, p. 433, n. VIII; cf. also S. R. C., *Societatis Iesu,* 11 maii 1878, ad XV —*Decr. Auth.,* n. 3448; *Fontes,* n. 6108; S. R. C., *Cuneen.,* 2 iun. 1883, ad X— *Decr. Auth.,* n. 3576; *Fontes,* n. 6148.

[40] This exclusion can be inferred from the reading of the rubric which seems to apply only to the solemn and conventual Masses, and it was confirmed by the decree of S. R. C., *Trium Missarum in Nocte Natalis Domini,* 7 dec. 1641—*Decr. Auth.,* n. 781; and S. R. C., *Aretina,* 18 sept. 1781—*Decr. Auth.,* n. 2520.

[41] For example, S. R. C., *Aquilein.,* 27 iul. 1720, for the Ursulines and their pupils—*Decr. Auth.,* n. 2267; S. R. C., *Urgellen.,* 7 aug. 1871, ad IX, for the nuns of the monastery of the Society of Mary—*Decr. Auth.,* n. 3254; *Fontes,* n. 6041; S. R. C., *Congregationis Clericorum Regularium Sancti Pauli,* 22 iul. 1848—*Decr. Auth.,* n. 2975; *Fontes,* n. 5959.

[42] S. C. S. Off., decr., 1st aug. 1907—*ASS,* XL (1907), 478-479; *Fontes,* n. 1284; further explained, 26 nov. 1908, as being a concession for three Masses, but as not granted to places where the doors were open to the faithful—*Acta Apostolicae Sedis, Commentarium Officiale* (Romae, 1909-), I (1909), 146 (hereafter cited *AAS*); *Fontes,* n. 1285.

[43] *Opera Omnia,* XXI, disput. 80, *De Eucharistia,* sectio IV, n. 5; cf.

but this opinion lost its probability through later decrees of the Congregation of Sacred Rites.[44]

Beyond this exception authors speculated on how far one could extend the dawn to mid-day period without involving a grave contravention against the law.[45] In 1724 Pope Benedict XIII permitted that Mass be commenced twenty minutes before the aurora and terminated twenty minutes after noon in Rome.[46] After this permission was extended to the Roman Province in 1725, the authors held that the practice which derived from it could be followed everywhere.[47]

also Schmalzgrueber, *Ius Ecclesiasticum Universum,* Lib. III, tit. 41, c. 2, n. 40, 46.

[44] S. R. C., *Bituntina.,* 14 nov. 1676—*Decr. Auth.,* n. 1548; *Aretina.,* 18 sept. 1871—*Decr. Auth.,* n. 2520. Pope Benedict XIV *(De Missae Sacrificio,* Tom. II, c. 166) listed also the decree of December 7, 1641 (*Decr. Auth.,* n. 781) as prohibiting it, and so likewise did St. Alphonsus (*Theologia Moralis,* Lib. III, n. 243). The Sacred Congregation of the Sacraments could however give an indult to permit this. Cf. *Ordo Servandus in S. Congregationibus, Tribunalibus, Officiis Romanae Curiae,* 29 sept. 1908, pars altera, c. VII, art. III, n. 10, e—*AAS,* I (1909), 87; *Fontes,* n. 6460. Such an indult, as noted, was included in the general privilege granted by Pope Pius X to religious and pious houses—*Fontes,* nn. 1284, 1285.

[45] Benedictus XIV, *Institutiones Ecclesiasticae,* n. XIII. The author here referred to a decree of Pope Clement XI (1700-1720) which definitely declared that one could not begin Mass before dawn or terminate it after noon. In his *De Missae Sacrificio* (Tom. II, c. 54) the same author referred to an epistle issued under the direction of Pope Clement XII (1730-1740), in which epistle there was condemned the abuse of celebrating several hours before dawn or after noon on certain solemnities.

[46] Benedictus XIV, *Institutiones Ecclesiasticae,* n. XIII.

[47] Cf. Benedictus XIV, *De Missae Sacrificio,* Tom. II, c. 54; *Institutiones Ecclesiasticae,* n. LXVIII; St. Alphonsus stated that many religious had the privilege of extending the time for the celebration of Mass over an even longer period. He also pointed with approval to several authors who held that Mass could be commenced at such a time that it was finished a little after the aurora, and that it could be started just a little before noon, for these two points of time were not to be taken mathematically but morally—*Theologia Moralis,* Lib. VI, nn. 341, 342. De Herdt noted that a grave violation was involved when Mass was said one hour earlier or later than within the legal limits—*Sacrae Liturgiae Praxis,* Pars I, tit. XV, n. 102 (IV). Cf. also Gasparri, *De Sanctissima Eucharistia,* I, n. 101; Many, *Praelectiones de Missa,* n. 20 (2b), and n. 23 (2, n. 1).

Among the exceptions to the general rule the authors [48] generally (with some variations) included the following:

(1) Any privilege granted by the Holy See after the Council of Trent; [49]

(2) the permission of the bishop, granted for a just cause and extended to a particular person or place; [50]

(3) the case of some special necessity, such as the need of a dying person to receive Holy Viaticum, the provision for a group of the faithful to enable them to fulfill the precept of hearing Mass, or the escape from threatened persecution;

(4) the existence of some reasonable custom, as when in certain sections of Germany Mass was said at a time earlier than the aurora in order that laborers might have the opportunity to hear Mass before going to work; and (5) the presence of a reasonable cause, such as, the need of setting out on a journey, of enhancing the solemnities on some unique festal occasion, or of making provision against some serious inconvenience or notable hardship.

A general rule in this matter was that the postponed celebrating of Mass after noon could be more readily permitted than an

[48] Schmalzgrueber, *Ius Ecclsiasticum Universum,* Lib. III, tit. 41, c. 2, n. 46; St. Alphonsus, *Theologia Moralis,* Lib. VI, nn. 343, 344; De Herdt, *Sacrae Liturgiae Praxis,* Tom. I, pars I, tit. XV, n. 102 (V); Gasparri, *De Sanctissima Eucharistia,* I, nn. 110-117; Many, *Praelectiones de Missa,* n. 23 (2-5).

[49] For example, the special faculties of the Jesuit missionaries to celebrate one hour before dawn and one hour after noon (Formula I, n. 23)—*Collectanea Sacrae Congregationis de Propaganda Fide* (2 vols., Romae: Typographia Polyglotta S. C. de Propaganda Fide, 1907), I, n. 660, note I (hereafter cited *Coll. S. C. de Prop. Fide*); S. C. de Propaganda Fide, instr. (ad Vic. Gen. Nankin.), 29 febr. 1836—*Fontes,* n. 4761. The author Many taught that cardinals, bishops and protonotaries also had this privilege—*Praelectiones de Missa,* n. 23, (2, n. 1); Gasparri held that in a cardinals chapel his chaplain enjoyed the same privilege—*De Sanctissima Eucharistia,* I, n. 112. Pope Benedict XIV pointed out that in the churches of Rome there existed the privilege of extending the time for the celebration of Mass by one hour at noon—*Institutiones Ecclesiasticae,* n. XIII.

[50] S. R. C., *Bonaeren.,* 7 iul. 1899, ad IV. In reply to the question whether a solemn Mass could be protracted until 2:00 P. M., the Sacred Congregation left the decision to the prudent judgment of the ordinary—*Decr. Auth.,* n. 4044; *Fontes,* n. 6301.

anticipated celebration before dawn, for, as St. Thomas explained, Mass was to be celebrated in the daytime.

Finally, for the perfect fulfillment of the rubrics the beginning of Mass was to coincide with the recitation of certain canonical hours, particularly when these were said in choir and conventual Mass was to follow.[51] But according to the more general practice, the rule which called for the recitation of certain canonical hours before Mass did not notably affect the actual time of the celebration of Mass. Instead of accommodating the celebration of Mass to the time set for the recitation of the canonical hours, it became the practice to determine the time of the recitation in relation to the time of Mass. This practice obtained particularly during Lent, when Mass was to be said after Nones. Had the law been applied in all its rigidity, the celebration of Mass would have to come at three o'clock in the afternoon.[52]

Probably the only practice which was followed generally was the practice in regard to the actual time for the celebration of the conventual or solemn Mass on Sundays and Feast Days. According to this practice the hour set for the celebration was nine o'clock in the morning after the recitation of Tierce.[53]

Article 3. The Remote Place for the Celebration of Mass

The Council of Trent required the bishops not to allow the Sacrifice of the Mass to be celebrated outside of churches or ora-

[51] *Rubricae Generales Missalis,* c. XV, nn. 1-5.

[52] On this particular point however, Navarrus (*Opera Omnia,* Tom. IV, *De Oratione et Canonicis Horis,* c. III, n. 44), who wrote shortly after the Council of Trent, still held that Mass could be celebrated in the afternoon on fast days. But Suarez (*Opera Omnia,* XXI, disp. 80, *De Eucharistia,* sectio IV, nn. 9-11), not so long after rejected that opinion as no longer tenable since the publication of the new Missal.

[53] Cf. *Caeremoniale Episcoporum Clementis VIII, Innocentii X, et Benedicti XIII iussu editum, Benedicti XIV et Leonis XIII auctoritate recognitum* (Mechliniae: H. Dessain, 1906), Lib. II, c. VIII, n. 5 (hereafter cited *Caeremoniale Episcoporum*). St. Alphonsus taught that to say private Mass without a cause before the recitation of Matins and Lauds implied a venial sin, but that to say the conventual Mass before the recitation of these canonical hours constituted a mortal sin—*Theologia Moralis,* Lib. VI, nn. 347, 348. Cf. also Benedictus XIV, *De Missae Sacrificio,* Tom. II, c. 102.

tories dedicated solely to divine worship. These churches or oratories were to be designated for that purpose by the bishops upon a previous canonical visitation of these places.[54] Furthermore the Missal enumerated as among the defects the celebration of Mass in a non-sacred place, or in a place not designated properly by the bishop.[55]

(a) The Church or Oratory

The celebration of Mass was permitted in dedicated churches [56] and in public oratories [57] which were blessed or consecrated and designated by the bishop. These public oratories were defined as oratories which were open to the common use of the faithful, inas-

[54] Conc. Trident., sess. XXII, *de observandis et evitandis in celebratione Missae;* Pope Benedict XIV reminded the bishops of their duty in this matter—Const. *Ad militantis,* 30 mart. 1742, n. 6—*Fontes,* n. 326.

[55] *Missale Romanum,* c. X, n. 1. Pallottini stated that one could not celebrate in churches and public oratories unless they were consecrated or blessed by the authority of the bishop, or at least visited and recognized by him as fitting places for the celebration of the Holy Sacrifice. Then he treated at considerable length of the restrictions the bishop could make in regard to Masses to be celebrated in public oratories. In general the conclusion was that some restrictions could be placed on the oratory before it was approved, but none could be added afterwards, unless the celebration of Mass in the oratory proved to interfere with the spiritual good of the faithful in the neighborhood—Pallottini, Tom. XIV, *Missa quoad locum,* c. VIII, nn. 1, 22; *ibid., Oratoria quoad Missas,* c. IV; cf. also Wernz, *Ius Decretalium,* III, n. 454.

[56] This dedication could be effected by means of a consecration or of a blessing. Cf. Schmalzgrueber, *Ius Ecclesiasticum Universum,* Lib. III, tit. 41, c. 2, n. 47; Gasparri, *De Sanctissima Eucharistia,* I, n. 149; Wernz, *Ius Decretalium,* III, nn. 436—437. The minister of consecration was a bishop (S. R. C., *Cameracen.,* 9 febr. 1608—*Decr. Auth.,* n. 246) or a priest empowered with an apostolic indult (S. R. C., *Massen.,* 7 oct. 1645—*Decr. Auth.,* n. 889); the minister of blessing was the bishop or a priest delegated by him (S. R. C., *Nolana,* 8 iul. 1904—*Decr. Auth.,* n. 4138). Cf. *Rituale Romanum, Pauli V Pontificis Maximi iussu editum, aliorumque Pontificum cura recognitum, atque auctoritate Ssmi D. N. Pii Papae XI ad Normam Codicis Iuris Canonici Accommodatum* (editio altera iuxta typicam, Ratisbonae: Typis Frederici Pustet, 1929), tit. VIII, cc. 27-28 (hereafter cited *Rituale Romanum*).

[57] S. C. C., *Florentina,* 2 dec. 1628; *Campansana,* 31 maii 1704—Pallottini, Tom. XIV, c. VIII, *Missa quoad locum,* n. 19.

much as their doors led to and gave free access from the public street.[58] But as regards private oratories there was some confusion due to the fact that there was no clear distinction between strictly private oratories and semi-public oratories until the decree of the Congregation of Sacred Rites in 1899.[59]

With this distinction as a basis, the celebration of Mass was permitted in certain other places besides public oratories. These places included episcopal residences,[60] seminaries, hospitals, orphanages, prison chapels, other pious places,[61] and the oratories of religious.[62]

(b) Exceptions to the General Requirements

The problem most controverted after the decree of the Council of Trent was the one which dealt with the extension of the bishop's

[58] Gattico, *De Oratoriis Domesticis,* Pars I, c. III, n. 2.

[59] S. R. C., *Decretum super oratoriis semipublicis,* 23 ian. 1899—*Decr. Auth.,* n. 4007. Wernz (*Ius Decretalium,* III, n. 544) summarized the legislation very well: the church or public oratory must be approved and blessed or consecrated; the semi-public oratory must be legitimately erected by the competent ordinary, and it could be blessed or even consecrated, but that was not required; private or domestic oratories could neither be consecrated nor solemnly blessed (Cf. S. R. C., *Decretum Generale,* 5 iun. 1899, ad VI: ". . . ea tantum formula benedicatur quae pro domo nova aut loco in eodem Rituale habetur"—*Decr. Auth.,* n. 4025), and the celebration of Mass was not permitted in them except by way of apostolic indult.

[60] Benedictus XIV, ep. encycl. *Magno cum,* 2 iun. 1751, § 2—*Fontes,* n. 413; Petra, *Commentaria ad Constitutiones Apostolicas seu Bullas Singulas Summorum Pontificum* (5 vols. in 2, Venetiis: Ex Typographia Balleoniana, 1729), Tom. IV, *De Constitutione II Urbani V, Sincere,* p. 150, n. 15 (hereafter cited Petra). Schmalzgrueber stated that among episcopal residences were included also the homes of patriarchs and cardinals—*Ius Ecclesiasticum Universum,* Lib. III, tit. 40, n. 8.

[61] Cf. S. C. C., *Calaritana,* 14 nov. 1648—*Fontes,* n. 2686; S. C. C., *Respons.,* 27 mart. 1847—*Thesaurus Resolutionum Sacrae Congregationis Concilii* (167 vols., Romae, 1718-1908), CVII, 227-233.

[62] Thus S. B. Smith (1845-1895), writing before the appearance of the 1899 decree, distinguished private oratories into episcopal, religious, pious and domestic, the last of which alone fell under the prohibition of the Council of Trent as a place for the celebration of Mass—*Compendium Iuris Canonici* (4. ed., New York: Benziger Brothers, 1890), Lib. III, pars II, c. I, art. III, n. 921.

faculty, namely, to what extent his former faculty to permit Mass outside of sacred places and on portable altars was restricted by the Council.[63]

The general conclusion was that the Council had removed from the bishops their general faculty to permit Mass to be said in domestic oratories of private houses, that is, the houses of laymen or of secular priests.[64] However, several exceptions were noted by the authors on this point:

(1) Bishops themselves and cardinals were permitted to say Mass anywhere in a decent place, even in private houses and on ships during a voyage at sea, as long as the necessary precautions for security in the celebration of Mass were duly taken.[65]

[63] Cf. Navarrus, *Opera Omnia*, Tom. I, *Manuale Confessariorum*, c. XXV, *De Peccatis Diversorum, De Peccatis Clericorum*, n. 81; Duranti, *De Ritibus Ecclesiae Catholicae Libri Tres* (Romae, 1591), Lib. II, c. VI, n. 3; Reiffenstuel, *Ius Canonicum Universum* (4 vols., Venetiis, 1735), Lib. III, tit. 41, n. 12; Schmalzgrueber, *Ius Ecclesiasticum Universum*, Lib. III. tit. 41, n. 11 (4); Petra, Tom. IV, p. 149, n. 12 sqq.; Benedictus XIV, *De Missae Sacrificio*, Tom. II, c. 42; ep. encycl., *Magno cum*, 2 iun. 1751, § 2—*Fontes*, n. 413; Gattico, *De Oratoriis Domesticis*, Pars I, c. XIII, n. 8 sqq., c. IX, nn. 6, 7; St. Alphonsus, *Theologia Moralis*, Lib. VI, nn. 357, 358; Ferraris, *Prompta Bibliotheca Canonica, Iuridica, Moralis, Theologica, necnon Ascetica, Polemica, Rubricista, Historica* (editio novissima, 8 vols. including Index, Romae: Ex Typographia Polyglotta S. C. de Prop. Fide, 1885-1892), Tom. V, "Missa, prouti est Sacrificium," art. IV, n. 10; Pallottini, Tom. XIV, *Oratoria*, c. II, n. 32; Lehmkuhl, *Theologia Moralis*, II, n. 223; Gasparri, *De Sanctissima Eucharistia*, I, nn. 209, 210; Many, *Praelectiones de Missa*, nn. 4-5; Wernz *Ius Decretalium*, III, n. 547.

[64] Benedictus XIV, ep. encycl. *Magno cum*, 2 iun. 1751, § 11—*Fontes*, n. 413; *De Missae Sacrificio*, Tom. II c. 42, where he referred to a decree of the Sacred Congregation of the Council in 1615 under Pope Paul V: "Celebrandi licentias in privatis oratoriis non nisi a Sede Apostolica esse concedendas . . ."; Pius VII, const. *Iamdiu*, 19 apr. 1816—*Fontes*, n. 478.

[65] Cf. Innocentius XIII, ep. *Apostolici ministerii*, 23 maii 1723, § 24—*Bullarium Romanum*, XXI, n. XXXIV; Benedictus XIII, ep. *In supremo militantibus*, 23 sept. 1724, § 20—*Bullarium Romanum*, XXII, n. XXXI. They, and practically all who after the Council of Trent treated the subject of the celebration of Mass outside of a church or an oratory, referred to the decree of Pope Clement XI, on December 15, 1703, which emphasized the strict interpretation of the restriction of the Council. Cf. Clemens XI, const. *Nonnulli*, 15 dec. 1703—*Fontes*, n. 264; Benedictus XIV, ep. encycl. *Magno*

(2) The bishop could permit the celebration of Mass in private houses if the permission was given in a particular case (*per modum actus*), and not for repeated use (*per modum habitus*), for at least a just cause.[66] Such a just cause was occasioned, for example, through the sickness of a priest or some important personage, or in view of the reception of Holy Viaticum which could be obtained in no other way.[67] Gasparri added that the bishop could temporarily permit the celebration of Mass in a church which was not blessed.[68]

(3) In special cases of necessity Mass could be celebrated outside of the regularly designated places, on a portable altar, but with the permission of the bishop if that was previously obtainable. Among these cases the authors enumerated the following: the case in which a church had been destroyed; the case in which a group was on a journey through a district where there were no churches; the case in which a church had become too small to accommodate large congregations; the case in which a priest worked in a mission field or in any place where there were no churches; the case in which a district had been ravaged by pestilence, by earthquake, in consequence of persecution, or by some other like calamity; the case in which there were army camps with no chapels,

cum, 2 iun. 1751, § 6—*Bullarii Romani Continuatio, 1740-1830* (14 vols., Prati, 1843-1867), Vol. III, n. XLVIII, p. 296; *Fontes,* n. 413.

66 The older authors required a grave cause or a great necessity, but this was somewhat modified after the decree of the Sacred Congregation of the Sacraments (*Romana et aliarum,* 23 dec. 1912, ad I), which declared in part: ". . . Ex iustis et rationabilibus causis, per modum actus, non tamen in cubiculo, sed in loco decenti, servatisque aliis de iure servandis et gratis omnino quocumque titulo"—*Fontes,* n. 2107. For a similar ruling about a half a century earlier cf. the II Plenary Council of Baltimore (1866), n. 362—*Concilii Plenarii Baltimorensis II, Acta et Decreta* (editio altera mendis expurgata, Baltimore: John Murphy, 1894), pp. 187, 188.

67 Benedictus XIV, ep. encycl. *Inter omnigenas,* 2 febr. 1744, § 22—*Fontes,* n. 339; S. C. de Prop. Fide, 14 dec. 1688—*Fontes,* n. 4480; decr., 30 apr. 1753, ad III—*Fontes,* n. 4517.

68 *De Sanctissima Eucharistia,* I, n. 210. It is to be noted that the permission given by the bishop did not have to be restricted for use exclusively on holy days of obligation. S. C. de Sacramentis, 22 mart. 1915, ad I—*Fontes,* n. 2110; *AAS,* VII (1915), 147.

or in which sailors had to be accommodated with the celebration of Mass on the seashore. Under ordinary circumstances these exceptions became applicable for use only on Sundays and on Feast Days, namely, in order that the faithful might fulfill the precept of hearing Mass.

(4) Mass could be celebrated in a private oratory, or on a portable altar, by way of an apostolic indult granted after the Council of Trent.[69] But such an indult did not at the same time allow the celebration of Mass on board ship, unless permission for celebration in this manner was explicitly included.[70]

(c) Place Where the Celebration of Mass Was Not Permitted

The law which prohibited the celebration of Mass in desecrated or violated churches remained about the same as it was in the earlier period.[71] But the Council of Trent pointed to an additional factor through which churches became desecrated, namely, the reduction of the edifice to secular or profane purposes.[72]

As formerly, Mass was not permitted in churches under general

[69] St. Alphonsus listed a number of days on which the use of such an indult was excluded, namely, the Feasts of Easter, of Pentecost, of Christmas, of the Ascension, of the Assumption, of Sts. Peter and Paul, and of All Saints—*Theologia Moralis,* Lib. VI, n. 359, nota 3.

[70] S. R. C., *Vicen.,* 4 mart. 1904, ad IV—*Fontes,* n. 6309.

[71] Concerning violated churches, cf. *Missale Romanum,* tit. *De defectibus,* c. X, *De defectibus in ministerio ipso occurrentibus,* n. 2. Concerning the reconciliation of violated churches, cf. S. R. C., *Cameracen.,* 9 febr. 1608—*Decr. Auth.,* n. 264; *Nolana,* 8 iul. 1904—*Decr. Auth.,* n. 4138; Schmalzgrueber, *Ius Ecclesiasticum Universum;* Lib. III, tit. 40, n. 65. Concerning desecration of the greater part of the walls, cf. S. R. C., *Ceasaraugustana,* 31 aug. 1872—*Decr. Auth.,* n. 3269; *Aretina,* 4 sept. 1875, ad II—*Decr. Auth.,* n. 3372; Wernz (1842-1914) stated that the common opinion held that this applied also to blessed churches—*Ius Decretalium,* III, n. 441.

[72] Sess. XXI, *de ref.,* c. 7—Schroeder, *Canons and Decrees of the Council of Trent,* p. 413.

or special interdict,[73] or in the churches of heretics or schismatics,[74] even if previously they had been dedicated for divine worship.[75]

Article 4. The Proximate Place of Mass

For the lawful celebration of the Holy Sacrifice, the altar is the most important of the four factors here considered, for as Pope Benedict XIV demonstrated, it has always been the constant and perpetual discipline of the Church to require that Mass be celebrated on the altar.[76]

(a) *Requirements in the Altar for Mass*

The *General Rubrics* of the Missal [77] declared that the altar on which Holy Mass was to be celebrated had to be of stone, consecrated by a bishop, or by an abbot who had the faculty from the Holy See, or at least had to have inserted in it a consecrated stone which was large enough to hold the host and the greater part of the base of the chalice. In the Missal among the defects [78] there is enumerated the celebration on a non-consecrated altar.

[73] Gasparri, in referring to the law in c. 24, *De sententia excommunicationis, suspensionis et interdicti,* V, 11, in VI, included the penalty called "*cessatio a divinis,*" which prohibited the ministry of the sacraments in a certain place—*De Sanctissima Eucharistia,* I, n. 241.

[74] S. C. de Prop. Fide, 21 maii 1627—*Coll. S. C. de Prop. Fide,* n. 34; *Fontes,* n. 4436; 13 febr. 1629—*Coll. S. C. de Prop. Fide,* n. 47; *Fontes,* n. 4442; Benedictus XIV, ep. *Iam inde,* 12 maii 1756, § 3—*Fontes,* n. 440; const. *Praeclaris,* 18 mart. 1746—*Fontes,* n. 366; ep. encycl. *Allatae nobis,* 26 iul. 1755, §§ 33, 35, 36—*Fontes,* n. 434. It should be noted that some exceptions were permitted by the Holy See in this matter. With reference to the promiscuous use of one and the same church for various kinds of religious services, cf. S. C. S. Off. (Vic. Ap. Malacen.), 5 iun. 1889—*Coll. S. C. de Prop.* Fide, n. 1707; *Fontes,* n. 1119; with regard to the celebration of Mass on a special altar in a schismatic church, cf. S. C. S. Off. (Archiep. Antibaren.), 1 dec. 1757—*Fontes,* n. 809.

[75] S. C. S. Off. (Archiep. Antibaren.), 1 dec. 1757—*Fontes,* n. 809.

[76] *De Missae Sacrificio,* Tom. I, c. 13.

[77] C. XX, *De Preparatione Altaris.*

[78] *De defectibus in ministerio occurrentibus,* c. X, n. 1.

Two types of altars then were indicated: the immovable or fixed altar, in which the entire stone tabletop together with its base was consecrated according to the ceremony given in the Pontifical,[79] and the movable altar, which consisted of a small piece of natural stone consecrated and inserted in or placed on the middle of the supporting altar or stand constructed of any reliable material.[80]

The altar always had to contain the relics of the saints, or at least a martyr,[81] which were placed in the cavity or sepulcher of the altar, and sealed or cemented with a piece of stone.[82]

Since Mass could not always be said in a church where a fixed altar was set up, many received from the Holy See the privilege of the use of a portable altar. This implied the faculty to celebrate in any decent place on a consecrated altar stone. Cardinals and bishops had this privilege by law,[83] but others also had received it

[79] *Pontificale Romanum, Summorum Pontificum iussu editum, a Benedicto XIV et Leone XIII, Pontificibus Maximis, recognitum et castigatum* (tres partes cum Appendice in 4 vols., Cincinnati: Pustet, 1908), Pars II, tit. *De Altaris Consecratione*. Cf. also Clemens VIII, const. *Ex quo,* 10 febr. 1596—*Fontes,* n. 180; S. R. C., *Cuneen.,* 7 aug. 1875, ad II—*Decr. Auth.,* n. 3364.

[80] An altar could be consecrated without any relation to the dedication of a church, but vice versa the same rule did not apply. Cf. S. R. C., *Molinen.,* 12 sept. 1857, ad XV—*Decr. Auth.,* n. 3059. In a strictly private oratory, which itself could not receive a solemn blessing, an immovable altar could not be lawfully consecrated—Schmalzgrueber, *Ius Ecclesiasticum Universum,* Lib. III, tit. 40, n. 31.

[81] S. R. C., *Rhedonen.,* 6 oct. 1837—*Fontes,* n. 5894; *Vivarien.,* 7 dec. 1844, ad II—*Fontes,* n. 5925; *Vilnen.,* 16 febr. 1906, ad III—*Decr. Auth.,* n. 4180. St. Alphonsus (*Theologia Moralis,* Lib. VI, n. 369, 3) questioned whether the relics were absolutely necessary for the valid consecration of an altar. In fact, the Holy Office (17 ian. 1900) permitted in certain places for a time the use of altars without relics—*Fontes,* n. 1235.

[82] S. R. C., *Sancti Hippolyti,* 31 aug. 1867, ad II—*Decr. Auth.,* n. 3162; S. R. C., *Dubiorum,* 4 aug. 1905, ad I—*Decr. Auth.,* n. 4165; *Pontificale Romanum,* Pars II, tit. *De Altaris Consecratione,* Rubrica: ". . . sepulcrum reliquiarum est in medio tabulae altaris, a parte superiori vel in stipite a parte anteriori, aut posteriori. Si vero sepulcrum est in medio summitatis stipitis supra autem sit ponenda ipsa tabula, sive mensa altaris . . .".

[83] S. R. C., decr., 19 maii 1896, approbata 8 iun. 1896—*Decr. Auth.,* n. 3903; Benedictus XIV, *De Missae Sacrificio,* Tom. I, cc. 45, 46.

from the Holy See after the Council of Trent.[84] This privilege, as has been pointed out above, could not be used on board ship unless that special faculty was expressly mentioned in the rescript.[85]

(b) Altars on Which the Celebration of Mass was not Permitted

(1) Mass was to be celebrated ordinarily in one's own rite, but in cases of necessity the altar of another Catholic Rite could be used; never however was a priest of the Roman Rite permitted to celebrate on a Greek antimension.[86]

(2) The celebration of Mass was prohibited on an altar under which, or even within a certain distance of which, was interred some corpse (except of the Blessed or the Saints).[87]

[84] Session XXII abrogated all previous privileges. The Jesuits and Mendicants on the missions, for example, received it from Pope Gregory XIII on October 1, 1579: ". . . non obstante Concilii Tridentini dispositione . . ."—*Bullarium Romanum,* Tom. VIII, n. CVI, p. 298.

[85] Cf. S. C. de Prop. Fide, decr., 1 mart. 1902: "Normae ad rite celebrandam Missam super Naves. (1) Videant nempe utrum mare sit adeo tranquillum, ut nullum adsit periculum effusionis Sacrarum Specierum e calice. (2) Curent ut alter sacerdos, si adfuerit, rite celebranti adsistat. (3) Si in navi non habeatur Capella propria vel altare fixum caveant . . . ne locus . . . indecens aut indecorum praeseferat . . . (sicut) in cellulis"—*AAS, XXXV* (1902), 48. Cf. S. R. C., *Vicen.,* 4 mart. 1904, ad IV—*Fontes,* n. 6309.

[86] Benedictus XIV, const. *Etsi pastoralis,* 26 maii 1742, § VI, nn. VI, VII, XIX—*Fontes,* n. 328; const. *Imposito Nobis,* 29 mart. 1751, §§ 1, 2, 4, 6, 7, 8 —*Fontes,* n. 410, these constitutions refer to the rareness with which permission was given to celebrate on an antimension. Cf. ep. encycl. *Allatae sunt,* 26 iul. 1755, §§ 33, 35, 36—*Fontes,* n. 434; S. C. S. Off., 7 iun. 1726—*Fontes,* n. 434; S. C. S. Off., 7 iun. 1726—*Coll. S. C. de Prop. Fide,* n. 306; *Fontes,* n. 786. The former discipline (cf. the Council of Auxerre [580], c. 10), which demanded that only one priest a day celebrate Mass on any one altar, at a later time applied only to the Greek Church. Cf. Benedictus XIV, *De Missae Sacrificio,* Tom. II, c. 40; ep. *In postremo,* 20 oct. 1756, § 9—*Fontes,* n. 442.

[87] *Rituale Romanum,* tit. VI, c. 1, *De exsequiis,* n. 9; S. R. C., *Decreta ad Missale pertinentia,* 13 feb. 1666, ad V: "In eo altari, sub quo vel sub cuius *predella* humata sunt corpora defunctorum, non debet celebrari Missa, donec alio transferantur"—*Fontes,* n. 5556; S. R. C., *De Queretaro,* 18 iul. 1902, ad V —*Fontes,* n. 6321; S. R. C., *Gallipolitana,* 19 iun 1908, ad I—*Fontes,* n. 6366; Petra, Tom. II, *Constitutio III Coelestini III* (1119), sect. I, n. 12, p. 108.

(3) Mass was not permitted on an altar that had lost its consecration. An altar lost its consecration: (a) when the *mensa* of a consecrated fixed altar was detached from its base;[88] (b) when the altar suffered a large break, the extent of which was to be judged either in relation to the altar as a whole, or with reference to the location of the break, as when a crack ran through the consecrated crosses;[89] and (c) when the relics were removed from the altar, or their seal was broken.[90]

(4) Mass was not allowed on an altar which was affected with a particular local interdict.[91]

(5) Mass was not to be said on an altar whereon the Blessed Sacrament was publicly exposed, except for some grave cause, or on a special feast or occasion (v.g., Corpus Christi or the Forty Hours' Devotion), or with an indult.[92]

[88] S. R. C., *Neapolitana,* 23 febr. 1884, ad VII—*Fontes,* n. 6156; *Brixinen.,* 7 iul. 1759—*Decr. Auth.,* n. 2450.

[89] S. R. C., *Carpen.,* 3 mart. 1821—*Fontes,* n. 5840; *Rhedonen.,* 6 oct. 1837—*Fontes,* n. 5894. The desecration of a church did not simultaneously involve the desecration of the altar, but when the church was polluted the fixed altar was also, and hence no Mass was permitted there until the church was reconciled—Schmalzgrueber, *Ius Ecclesiasticum Universum,* Lib. III, tit. 40, nn. 46, 47.

[90] S. R. C., *Vivarien.,* 7 dec. 1844, ad II—*Fontes,* n. 5925; S. R. C., *Sancti Flori,* 3 iul. 1846—*Fontes,* n. 5939; *Ord. Cisterciensis,* 25 sept. 1875, approbata 30 sept. 1875—*Decr. Auth.,* n. 3379.

[91] Wernz, *Ius Decretalium,* III, n. 544.

[92] S. R. C., *De Nicaragua,* 27 sept. 1864, ad II, III, IV—*Decr. Auth.,* n. 3124; S. R. C., *Societatis Iesu,* 11 maii 1878: "Non licere sine necessitate, vel gravi causa, vel in speciali indulto"—*Decr. Auth.,* n. 3448. Special provision was also made for Mass in the presence of the choir. Cf. *Gnesnen. et Posnanien.,* 20 dec. 1878, ad I: "Missam privatam in altari maiori, illo tempore quo in choro Horae Canonicae dicuntur, Decreta S. R. C. celebrari prohibent. Quaeritur autem: An sub denominatione Horarum Canonicarum etiam Officium Defunctorum in casu intelligatur? Affirmative"—*Decr. Auth.,* n. 3474. According to the *Caeremoniale* it was more fitting that the bishop should not pontificate at an altar where the Blessed Sacrament was reserved—Lib. I, c. XII, nn. 9, 16.

(6) Finally, only the Pope himself was permitted to celebrate Mass on the so-called papal altars, unless other persons received a special indult granting the privilege.[93]

[93] Benedictus XIV, ep. *Dilectus Filius,* 15 ian. 1745, § 1—*Fontes,* n. 352; allocut. *Postquam,* 30 sept. 1750, § 3—*Fontes,* n. 408; const. *Ad honorandum,* 27 mart. 1752, § 16—*Fontes,* n. 420; const. *Fidelis Dominus,* 25 mart. 1754, § 6 —*Fontes,* n. 427; ep. *In postremo,* 20 oct. 1756, § 9—*Fontes,* n. 442. These altars were called papal altars either because they were consecrated by the pope or because he said Mass upon them or because he directly granted this special distinction to them. For a list of the principal papal altars, cf. *infra,* Chapter IX, pp. 173-174.

Canonical Commentary

With the foregoing historical treatment of the evolution of the law in regard to the time and the place of the celebration of Mass as a background, it is the intention of the writer to give in a measure of detail the present legislation on this matter as contained in canons 820-823 of the Code of Canon Law.

CHAPTER V

DAYS ON WHICH MASS MAY BE SAID AND THE EXCEPTIONS

Can. 820. Missae sacrificium omnibus diebus celebrari potest, exceptis iis qui proprio sacerdotis ritu excluduntur.

THE Code on this question speaks in very general terms, and evades the issue of a discussion on the various rites of the Church. This canon does however recognize and respect the binding force of the liturgical laws of these rites. Two rites are distinguished in the Church, namely, the Latin and the Oriental. Since it is stated in the first canon of the Code that the laws of the Code regard only the Latin Church and do not bind the Oriental Church except in matters which of their very nature also affect the Oriental Church, the Latin rite alone is treated here. Furthermore the second canon of the Code states that generally the Code does not treat of the rites and ceremonies which the liturgical books of the Latin Church prescribe with regard to the celebration of Mass, the administration of the sacraments and sacramentals, and of other sacred functions. All the liturgical laws of the Latin Church retain their binding force, unless they are expressly corrected in the Code.[1]

The Holy Mass then may be said on all days, except on those excluded by the respective rite of the celebrant. In the Latin Church the general rubrics or the liturgical laws prescribe that no private Masses be celebrated on the last three days of Holy Week, namely, on Holy Thursday, Good Friday, and Holy Saturday.[2] The term

[1] Cann. 1, 2.

[2] Augustine, *A Commentary on the New Code of Canon Law* (8 vols., Vol. IV, 3. ed., St. Louis: Herder & Co., 1925), IV, 160 (hereafter cited *A Commentary*); Vermeersch-Creusen, *Epitome Iuris Canonici* (3 vols., Vol. I, 6. ed., Romae: Dessain, 1937; Vol. II, 6. ed., 1940; Vol. III, 5 ed., 1936), II, n. 98; Noldin-Schmitt, *Summa Theologiae Moralis* (3 vols., 21. ed., Vol. III, *De Sacramentis*, Oeniponte, 1932), III, n. 202 (hereafter cited *De Sacramentis*).

"rite" as used in canon 820 is taken in the wide sense to comprehend both the sacred actions of divine worship called ceremonies and the recitation of the prescribed prayers while these actions are being performed.[3]

Of the two rites in the Church, the Latin rite, which is the subject of discussion, is further subdivided into the Roman rite and the Ambrosian rite, the latter being of very much less importance than the former. In the Latin Church the Ambrosian rite forbids the celebration of Mass on all Fridays during Lent, and in this rite not even the Mass of the Presanctified can be said on Good Friday. Since the Ambrosian liturgy is not used universally in the Western Church, further detail would be of little practical value.[4] The Roman rite, which is universally used in the Latin Church, is the only one referred to throughout the following commentary, since, as already explained, the Code only refers to the Latin Church.

Article 1. Holy Thursday

The opinion of the older theologians that private Mass was not absolutely forbidden on Holy Thursday now lacks all probability, consequent on later decrees of the Holy See, and especially on the decree of the Congregation of Sacred Rites.[5] The present legislation definitely forbids a private Mass on this day. This prohibition does not mean that the celebration of the Holy Sacrifice is forbidden, but rather that it should be celebrated with the greatest possible solemnity. In its efforts to accomplish this purpose the Church in the liturgy and ceremonies of Holy Week has made the Mass the centre of each day's sacred functions, and safeguards its solemnity by stringent liturgical laws. Accordingly the celebration of the Mass is permitted on Holy Thursday in the following cases.[6]

[3] Beste, *Introductio in Codicem* (2. ed., Collegeville, Minn.: St. John's Abbey Press, 1944), p. 50.

[4] Cf. Coronata, *Tractatus Canonicus de Sacramentis* (3 vols., Romae: Marietti, 1943-1946), I, n. 231 (hereafter cited *De Sacramentis*); Gasparri, *De Sanctissima Eucharistia,* I, n. 69.

[5] Cf. *supra,* Chapter IV, p. 42.

[6] Regatillo, *Ius Sacramentarium* (2 vols., Santander: Sal Terrae, 1945-1946), I, n. 185; Cappello, *Tractatus Canonico-Moralis de Sacramentis* (3

(a) Only the conventual Mass with full liturgical rites is to be celebrated in the cathedral and collegiate churches according to the *Caeremoniale Episcoporum.*[7]

(b) In parish churches only one solemn Mass may be celebrated according to the Roman Missal. If this solemn Mass cannot be said because a deacon and subdeacon cannot be had, then a sung Mass (*Missa cantata*) is permitted in accordance with the *Memoriale Rituum* of Pope Benedict XIII.[8]

Finally, if not even a sung Mass can be celebrated, as may be the case in the more remote districts and in newly established parishes where organists and choirs cannot or only with difficulty can be had, then a low Mass may be read.[9] Heretofore in this case the permission of the bishop was required for a low Mass on this day, but according to some authors such permission is not demanded at present.[10]

With the permission of the bishop, however, a private Mass or low Mass can be celebrated before the solemn high Mass in parochial churches for the infirm and aged people who cannot be present at the solemn Mass, or even for the faithful who are physically able to attend but for whom morally it would be difficult or impossible owing to circumstances, for example, workers who cannot attend the solemn Mass because of their working hours. The fervent desire to hear Mass, and certainly the wish of some of the faithful to receive Holy Communion, are reasons sufficient to justify the celebration of low Mass in parish churches on Holy Thursday.[11]

Furthermore, the existence of a legitimate custom seems to dispense with the necessity of requiring the permission of the bishop. Since the Code does not deal with liturgical laws, such a custom need

vols. in 6, Vol. I, 4. ed., Romae: Marietti, 1945), I, n. 737 (hereafter cited *De Sacramentis*).

[7] Lib. II, c. 23.

[8] Gasparri, *De Sanctissima Eucharistia,* I, n. 71; Many, *Praelectiones de Missa,* n. 15.

[9] Regatillo, *Ius Sacramentarium,* I, n. 185.

[10] Cf. Cappello, *De Sacramentis,* I, n. 737; Regatillo, *Ius Sacramentarium,* I, n. 185, (2).

[11] Regatillo, *Ius Sacramentarium,* I, n. 185.

not be immemorial or of a century duration.[12] Hence custom may undoubtedly be invoked and may where it exists be acted upon until the matter is authoritatively settled.[13]

(c) In churches which are not strictly parochial, but in some way united with the parish church, such as vicarial, subsidiary or filial churches, the same principles hold true for these as for the parochial churches above. Hence either a solemn high Mass, a *Missa cantata* or a low Mass may be celebrated there.[14]

(d) In the churches of Regulars who are bound to choir and to conventual Mass, only the celebration of the conventual Mass is permitted on Holy Thursday. Regulars here must be interpreted according to canon 488, 2°, to mean members of a religious Order who profess solemn vows. Included in this category also are the churches of nuns (*moniales*) who profess solemn vows. The nuns here referred to, according to most of the authors, are only those who profess solemn vows, but Davis states that also those women religious are included whose vows are solemn according to their institute, but who in some places by order of the Holy See take simple vows.[15] This question has been definitely settled by means of a decree of the Sacred Congregation of Religious to the effect that these are truly equal to nuns who have actually taken solemn vows.[16] Hence they too enjoy the privilege of Regulars in regard to the conventual Mass on Holy Thursday.

If the solemn conventual Mass cannot be said in the church of Regulars, the superior can allow it to be celebrated in an oratory. If however there is no oratory, the superior may permit a private Mass in the parish church or any one of the diocesan churches most convenient to the house of the Regulars. This Mass must be celebrated privately and with the church doors closed.[17] The reason

[12] Vermeersch, *Theologiae Moralis Principia-Responsa-Consilia* (4 vols., 3. ed. Romae: Pont. Universitas Gregoriana, 1933-1937), III, n. 337.

[13] Davis, *Moral and Pastoral Theology* (3. ed., 4 vols., London: Sheed and Ward, 1938), III, 136, 137.

[14] S. R. C., *Goritien.*, 4 sept. 1875—*Decr. Auth.*, n. 3366.

[15] Davis, *op. cit.*, III, 136.

[16] S. C. de Religiosis, 23 iun. 1923—*AAS,* XV (1923), 357.

[17] S. R. C., *Tertii Ordinis S. Francisci,* 31 aug. 1839—*Decr. Auth.*, n. 2799.

required for the use of this privilege is that Holy Communion may be administered to the religious.

(d) In churches and oratories of other religious, of seminaries, hospitals, colleges and other such institutions, the following distinctions are made:

(1) In churches and oratories where the Blessed Sacrament is not reserved, the general rule holds that Mass cannot be celebrated on Holy Thursday.[18]

(2) Similarly neither a solemn Mass nor a *Missa cantata* can be celebrated in churches and oratories in which the sacred ceremonies of Holy Week, namely, the Mass and procession of the Blessed Sacrament to the altar of Repose (*processio ad Sepulcrum*) and the Mass of the Presanctified of the following day are not carried out. The exception made in favor of parish churches cannot be extended to other churches and oratories.[19]

(3) In oratories of Confraternities, provided that by legitimate custom the Blessed Sacrament is reserved there, a solemn Mass, a *Missa cantata* or a low Mass can be said. The reason given for the extension of the privilege in this case is that this Mass is not exclusively reserved to the pastor. Canon 462 enumerates the functions reserved to the pastor, and the celebration of the Holy Thursday Mass is not mentioned in the canon.[20] This negative and somewhat weak reason is strengthened by the fact that there will always be present the ardent desire of the priest to celebrate Mass and of the faithful to receive Holy Communion on this day.

(4) In churches and oratories of both men and women religious who profess only simple vows, also in those of seminaries, hospitals, colleges, and similar institutions, Mass can be celebrated unless there exists a particular prohibition or a peculiar disposition to the contrary. Two decrees of the Congregation of Sacred Rites granted

[18] S. R. C., *Neapolitana,* 14 iun. 1659—*Fontes,* n. 1120.

[19] S. R. C., *Urbis seu Minorum Observantiae S. Francisci,* 28 mart. 1775, ad V—*Decr. Auth.,* n. 2503; S. R. C., *Bellunen. et Feltren.,* 1 febr. 1895, ad I—*Decr. Auth.,* n. 3842.

[20] Cappello, *De Sacramentis,* I, n. 737.

permission for a low Mass on Holy Thursday even though the ceremonies of Holy Week were not performed in these churches.[21]

If Holy Thursday should coincide with a feast day of obligation, as for example the feast of St. Joseph or some particular feast day, the bishop should provide for the spiritual needs of the people of the places affected. He ought to see to it that a sufficient number of Masses be said before the parochial or conventual Mass for the purpose of enabling all the faithful of the locality to fulfil the obligation of hearing Mass.[22] Where the obligation to hear Mass on a certain feast has been suppressed, for example on the Feast of the Annunciation, the obligation to hear Mass also ceases and the reason for these Masses no longer exists; hence they cannot be said. The general rubrics which allow only the solemn Mass must then be followed.[23] Cappello ventures to say that where a feast is held in high esteem and celebrated with particular piety and devotion among the majority of the people, even though it is not a feast to which is attached the obligation to hear Mass, the bishop can permit several Masses to accommodate the faithful, who cannot otherwise attend the usual parochial or conventual Mass.[24]

(5) Cardinals and Bishops. The Code grants cardinals and bishops a special privilege with regard to Mass on Holy Thursday. By virtue of this privilege they can either themselves say Mass privately, or can permit another priest to celebrate one Mass in their presence. To cardinals this is given absolutely, but to bishops it is allowed only on condition that they are not already bound to celebrate in their cathedral. The term "bishops", as is evident from the canon in the Code, includes both residential and titular bishops.[25]

[21] S. R. C., *Mechlinien.*, 16 mart. 1876—*Decr. Auth.*, n. 3390; cf. *supra*, Chapter IV, p. 44; S. R. C., *Comen.*, 9 dec. 1899, ad II—*Decr. Auth.*, n. 4049.

[22] Cappello, *De Sacramentis,* I, n. 737 (8); S. R. C., *Decretum Generale,* 13 sept. 1692—*Decr. Auth.*, n. 1883; *Hispalen.*, 13 sept. 1692, ad I—*Decr. Auth.*, n. 1885; *Galliarum,* 10 ian. 1693, ad VI—*Decr. Auth.*, n. 1890; *Decretum Generale,* 27 sept. 1719—*Decr. Auth.*, n. 2240.

[23] S. R. C., *Viglevanen.*, 26 sept. 1868—*Decr. Auth.*, n. 3179; S. R. C., *Segusien.*, 18 aug. 1879, ad II—*Decr. Auth.*, n. 3503.

[24] *De Sacramentis,* I, n. 737, (8).

[25] Canons 349, § 1, 1°, and 239, § 4. Cf. Benedictus XIV, *Institutiones Ecclesiasticae,* XXXVIII, n. 4.

By special indult from the Holy See permission is sometimes granted for the celebration of Mass in private oratories on Holy Thursday, and also individual priests have been similarly permitted to say private Mass on this day. These privileges to private oratories and to individual priests for no other reason than private devotion show the attitude of the Holy See, and the general trend of readiness on the part of the Holy See to allow the celebration of Mass in reference to Holy Thursday.[26]

The question whether the bishop can grant permission for low Mass for the sick on Holy Thursday was doubted by some of the older authors.[27] The doubt was based on the fact that this faculty was given to bishops by a decree of the Congregation of Sacred Rites sent to the Carmelite Order in Poland. In this decree it was declared that a low Mass (*Missa lecta*) could be permitted "arbitrio episcopi."[28]

In the later editions of the *Decreta Authentica,* this section giving the faculty to the bishops was omitted from the decree of 1773, hence it was concluded that the bishops no longer had the faculty. Cappello and Cardinal Genari (1838-1914) held that merely because mention of this faculty was omitted in the new edition of the decrees of the Congregation, it did not follow that it was thereby revoked. They were of the opinion that the concession was peremptorily granted, and still continues until specifically revoked. This opinion of the modern authors who treat the question, seems to be the better one and more in line with the consideration of the general trend of the decrees concerning the Holy Thursday Mass. For example, it has already been mentioned that a low Mass can be said even without the permission of the bishop if there exists a legitimate custom. Even where no custom exists a low Mass can be said privately in religious houses for the purpose of administering Holy Communion to the sick who fervently desire to receive on Holy Thursday.[29]

[26] Regatillo, *Ius Sacramentarium,* I, n. 185, (9).

[27] Cf. Many, *Praelectiones de Missa,* n. 15.

[28] S. R. C., *Ordinis Carmelitarum Excalceatorum Prov. Poloniae,* 27 mart. 1773, ad IX—*Decr. Auth.,* n. 4212 in editione Gardellini anno 1825.

[29] S. R. C., *Tertii Ordinis S. Francisci,* 31 aug. 1839—*Decr. Auth.,* n. 2799.

Furthermore, authors of eminence state that the bishop can permit a low Mass to be said privately not only for the accommodation of the sick, but also for workers, students, etc., for a just cause. In exempt clerical religious houses the faculty of permitting a low Mass on this day belongs to the religious superior; in all other cases the local ordinary grants the privilege. These authors state the desired ideal that many more priests should receive the faculty to celebrate Mass on Holy Thursday, so that they may the better commemorate the institution of the august Sacrifice. The Holy See seems to honor this ideal by the ease with which it grants the faculty.[30]

Lastly, the question is disputed among the authors, namely, whether a priest who celebrates a prohibited Mass either solemnly or privately commits a grievous sin. The opinion of the best authority is that, provided there is no scandal, the sin is probably venial.[31] From the present study of the decrees of the Sacred Congregation and the opinions of the authors, it is evident that the Church, while it wishes to preserve the dignity and enhance the solemnity of the Holy Week services, also desires that both the clergy and the faithful be provided every opportunity of hearing Mass on Holy Thursday.

Article 2. Good Friday

The most contrary exception to the general law that Mass can be said on all days of the year is Good Friday. In the Roman rite this is a unique exception, since this is the only day of the year on which Mass can never be celebrated. St. Thomas gave the liturgical reason underlying the prohibition as follows:

> ". . . veniente veritate, cessat figura . . .; et
> ideo in die quo ipsa passio dominica recolitur
> prouti realiter gesta est, non celebratur
> consecratio huius sacramenti." [32]

[30] Cf. Cappello, *De Sacramentis*, I, n. 737, (11); Regatillo, *Ius Sacramentarium*, I, n. 185, (9); Coronata, *De Sacramentis*, I, n. 233.

[31] Cappello, *De Sacramentis*, I, n. 737, (10); Davis, *Moral and Pastoral Theology*, III, p. 137.

[32] *Summa Theologica*, III, q. 83, a. 2, ad 2.

On this day, however, the Mass of the Presanctified is said, which is not a full sacrificial offering of the Holy Sacrifice, as the essential part, namely the consecration, is omitted. It is but the consuming of the Sacred Host consecrated on the previous day. Nowhere then in the Latin Church is the Mass said on Good Friday, and this prohibition binds all Latin priests *sub gravi,* although by apostolic indult a relaxation of the law may be granted. Such a dispensation is very rarely given by the Holy See.[33]

It is commonly agreed that celebration is permitted on Good Friday to administer Holy Viaticum to the sick in danger of death. In practice this case will very seldom arise, as the Blessed Sacrament must be reserved for the sick on Holy Thursday, a provision which eliminates the possibility of having to say Mass for this purpose on the following day. If however in extraordinary circumstances such as times of war, pestilence, etc., there is grave necessity and Consecrated Hosts for the administration of Holy Viaticum are not available, the Mass of the passion may be celebrated, so that the dying may not be deprived of the spiritual benefits of Holy Communion in their last moments.[34]

If a particular feast day falls on Good Friday,[35] the office with the Mass is transferred, the obligations however are not transferred. Hence the obligation to abstain from servile work must be observed; on the other hand, the obligation to hear Mass ceases, since there is no obligation of assisting at the Mass of the Presanctified which, as mentioned heretofore, is not a true Mass. That the obligation to hear Mass ceases in this case has been definitely declared by the Congregation of Sacred Rites.[36]

[33] Cappello, *De Sacramentis,* I, n. 736.

[34] Coronata, *De Sacramentis,* I, n. 231; Cappello, *De Sacramentis,* I, n. 736; Regatillo, *Ius Sacramentarium,* I, n. 184; Many, *Praelectiones de Missa,* n. 14; Noldin-Schmitt, *De Sacramentis,* III, n. 203; Gasparri, *De Sanctissima Eucharistia,* I, nn. 84-86.

[35] A feast day of obligation for the universal Church cannot coincide with Good Friday, for in the present discipline (can. 1247, § 1) the feast of the Annunciation is no longer a feast day of obligation and the feast of St. Joseph which is celebrated on March 19th cannot coincide, since Easter Sunday cannot fall before March 22.

[36] S. R. C., *Monopolitana,* 20 mart. 1706—*Decr. Auth.,* n. 2164; S. R. C., *Barcinonen.,* 10 dec. 1773—*Decr. Auth.,* n. 2305.

Article 3. Holy Saturday

It has been seen that the celebration of Mass on Holy Thursday in general is permitted in all cathedral, collegiate, conventual and parochial churches, and also in other churches and oratories under the aforementioned conditions, which are not difficult to fulfil. Consequently the Holy Sacrifice is said generally in most churches on this day. On the other hand, on Good Friday, the only aliturgical day of the year, the law is strict in the extreme in that it does not allow Mass to be said, except in a case of extreme necessity to give Viaticum to the dying. On Holy Saturday, however, though of old it was an aliturgical day on which no Mass was said, the present legislation allows the celebration of Mass with many restrictions. Indeed, in some sense it can still be called aliturgical, in so far as the Mass said on this morning is the Mass which was celebrated after midnight of old, and which liturgically constitutes the first Mass of Easter morning.[37] Following the old disciplinary trend the present law, while it does not approach the severity of the restriction affecting Good Friday, does not extend the privilege of celebration as often or as easily as on Holy Thursday.

The general principle is that all private or low Masses are strictly forbidden in all churches and oratories either public or private on Holy Saturday. Mass can be offered on that day only in the following cases:

(1) In cathedral, collegiate and conventual churches only the solemn Mass can be celebrated on this day.

(2) In parish churches a solemn Mass can and ought to be said if there are sufficient ministers; if this cannot be done, then a *Missa cantata* can be celebrated by special indult according to the *Memoriale Rituum* of Pope Benedict XIII.

(3) In other churches and oratories solemn Mass or a *Missa cantata* can be said provided that the sacred functions of Holy Week are held there on the two previous days. If the Holy Week services are not held in the church, the celebration of Mass on Holy Saturday

[37] Cf. *supra*, Chapter IV, p. 45.

is not lawful except by apostolic indult, which however is occasionally given.[38]

(4) In parish churches having a baptismal font the blessing of the font must be performed on Holy Saturday prior to the Mass; in other churches and oratories this part of the function of Holy Saturday morning may legitimately be omitted, and the solemn Mass or the *Missa cantata* celebrated alone, even though the full Holy Week services were held according to the *Memoriale Rituum.*[39]

If at least a *Missa cantata* cannot be celebrated on account of a lack of ministers or for some other reason, it is not therefore lawful for the pastor to say a low Mass for the blessing of the Easter Fire, the Paschal candle and the baptismal font.[40] If however, there exists a contrary custom, which many authors maintain can be legitimately introduced, then it is contended that low Mass can lawfully be celebrated on Holy Saturday.[41]

As regards the admission of custom against liturgical law Pope Benedict XIV declared that it can be legitimately introduced under the required conditions, namely, that it is reasonable, and that it has run the full term of legal prescription.[42] While admitting that these customs can exist, the popes and the Congregation of Sacred Rites are strict in their attitude. Those only which are immemorial are favored with approval.[43]

It is also required as a condition that such customs be not openly repugnant to the rubrics. Though the Congregation of Sacred Rites permits and approves only those which are in conformity with the existing rubrics, still it tolerates customs which

[38] Cappello, *De Sacramentis,* I, n. 738, (3) ; Noldin-Schmitt, *De Sacramentis,* III, n. 204, b.

[39] S. R. C., *Comen.,* 9 dec. 1899, ad I—*Decr. Auth.,* n. 4049.

[40] S. R. C., *Resolutionis dubiorum,* 28—31 iul. 1828, ad I—*Decr. Auth.,* n. 2616.

[41] Gasparri, *De Sanctissima Eucharistia,* I, n. 95; Noldin-Schmitt, *De Sacramentis,* III, n. 204; Many, *Praelectiones de Missa,* n. 16; Coronata, *De Sacramentis,* I, n. 232.

[42] *De Synodo Diocesana* (13 books in 2 vols., Lovanii: E Typographia Academica, 1736), Lib. XII, c. 8, n. 8. Cf. also De Herdt, *Sacrae Liturgiae Praxis,* I, n. 10.

[43] Innocentius XIII, *Apostolici Ministerii,* 23 maii 1723—*Fontes,* n. 280.

are not fully in conformity with the liturgical law, but not openly repugnant to it.[44] It is manifest that the prohibition of the private or low Mass on Holy Saturday is a stringent one. Nevertheless, since the Church does admit of customs at variance with the rubrics, the authors hold that the practice of celebrating low Mass on this day is justifiable.[45]

Even where the custom permitting low Mass does not exist and the *Missa cantata* cannot be celebrated, there are some who support the opinion that low Mass can be said in parochial churches for the blessing of the font, if otherwise the blessing should be omitted.[46]

In view of the severity of the law forbidding low Mass on this day, and also after due consideration of the stringent principles of the papal and curial decrees in regard to the introduction of custom in this matter, it seems that this extension of the law assumes too much of a concession. In spite of this prohibition, however, it is true that the Code requires each parish church to have its own baptismal font,[47] and further reserves the blessing of the font on Holy Saturday to the pastor.[48] The argument based on this regulation

[44] Cf. S. R. C., *Hispalen.*, 23 maii 1603—*Decr. Auth.*, n. 128; S. R. C., *Nolana*, 23 maii 1603—*Decr. Auth.*, n. 129; S. R. C., *Comen.*, 13 mart. 1700—*Decr. Auth.*, n. 2051.

[45] Gasparri, writing of this custom even after the contrary responses of the Congregation, stated: "His non obstantibus, praxis est in pauperibus parochiis ut parochus Missam lectam celebret. Huic praxi favet Benedictus XIV (*Institutiones Ecclesiasticae*, XXXVIII, n. 11) . . . proinde putamus hanc praxim, ubi viget, servari posse, donec a S. Congregatione reprobetur. Immo in nonnullis locis permittitur, ob populi commoditatem, celebrare unam alteramque Missam privatam, praeter conventualem"—*De Sanctissima Eucharistia*, I, n. 95. Cf. also Noldin-Schmitt, *op. cit.*, III, n. 204; Coronata, *op. cit.*, I, n. 232; Many, *Praelectiones de Missa*, n. 16.

[46] Cappello, *De Sacramentis*, I, n. 738; Davis, *Moral and Pastoral Theology*, III, 139; Coronata, *De Sacramentis*, I, n. 232. Cappello goes so far as to say that the pastor in these circumstances not only can, but even ought, to celebrate a low Mass if otherwise the baptismal font would not be blessed—*op. cit.*, I, n. 738.

[47] Can. 774, § 1, reads: "Quaelibet paroecialis ecclesia, revocato ac reprobato quovis contrario statuto vel privilegio vel consuetudine, baptismalem habeat fontem, salvo legitimo iure cumulativo aliis ecclesiis iam quaesito." Cf. can. 1427, § 4.

[48] Can. 462, 7°.

does not seem convincing, however, and unless a custom existed or an apostolic indult was granted, it appears that the need for the blessing of the font does not justify a low Mass on Holy Saturday.

If a feast to which is attached the obligation of hearing Mass falls on Holy Saturday, the Office with the Mass is transferred to another day; the obligation however to hear Mass and to abstain from servile work still remain binding. Even though the faithful are bound to hear Mass on this day, it is not thereby lawful to celebrate low Mass to accommodate them. If those who are obliged to hear Mass cannot be present at the parochial or conventual Mass, then the obligation ceases for them.[49]

The bishop cannot on Holy Saturday say a private Mass as on Holy Thursday. He is bound to be in his cathedral on this morning; if however he does not celebrate Mass there, he is permitted to say the Ordination Mass in the chapel or in the oratory of his house. In this case he must begin with the prophecies, but by apostolic indult he can omit them, and begin in the usual manner, but without the *Introit*.[50]

It is true that the Holy See in the past has granted permission to celebrate low Mass on Holy Saturday, and also has allowed the omission of the *Prophecies* from the Holy Saturday Mass. At the present time such relaxations of the law are very reluctantly given. This practice and trend of the Holy See is evident from the replies of the Congregation of Sacred Rites, which revoked all personal indults, and manifested that local indults are very rarely granted.[51]

(5) The celebration of Mass on Holy Saturday for the sick, or for those who cannot attend the solemn Mass because of ill health, is not lawful. On Holy Thursday this is permitted, but the prohibition of private and low Masses on Holy Saturday is much more stringent and emphatic. The only exception made to this pro-

[49] Gasparri, *De Sanctissima Eucharistia,* I, n. 90; Cappello, *De Sacramentis,* I, n. 737.

[50] S. R. C., *Resolutionis dubiorum,* 28—31 iul. 1821, ad II—*Decr. Auth.,* n. 2616.

[51] S. R. C., *Resolutionis dubiorum,* 28—31 iul. 1821, ad II—*Decr. Auth.,* n. 2616; S. R. C., *Ordinis Carmelitarum Excalceatorum,* 22 iul. 1848, ad I, II—*Decr. Auth.,* n. 2970.

hibition is that Mass may be said to consecrate Holy Communion for the dying or those in danger of death from a cause which is truly grave and urgent.[52]

(6) The question is raised whether a legitimate custom of celebrating low Mass on Holy Saturday can be introduced. To furnish an adequate explanation to the problem the following distinctions must be made:

(a) In cathedral, collegiate, and conventual churches the question will not arise because of the absence of a cause for the introduction of the custom. First, these churches have a legitimate right to have a solemn Mass or a *Missa cantata* celebrated in them, and secondly the necessity for a low Mass will not arise since in these churches there will always be a sufficient number of ministers for at least a *Missa cantata.*

(b) As regards the introduction of the custom of saying a low Mass in parochial churches on Holy Saturday, some authors hold that such a custom is legitimate if the requisite conditions are present. These conditions are, first, that solemn Mass or *Missa cantata* cannot be said, and secondly that the baptismal font must be blessed.[53]

(c) As regards other churches or oratories it is commonly agreed that the custom of saying low Mass in them cannot be legitimately introduced. Such a custom for these non-parochial churches would be unreasonable. According to canon 462, 7°, the blessing of the font on Holy Saturday is enumerated among the functions reserved to the pastor, and again canon 774, § 1, gives each parochial church the right to have a baptismal font. Since these non-parochial churches and oratories generally have no baptismal font, the blessing of the font cannot be adduced as a reason for saying a low Mass on Holy Saturday. Therefore the custom of permitting a low Mass in non-parochial churches and oratories on Holy Saturday cannot be sustained as reasonable, and cannot be legitimately introduced.[54]

[52] Regatillo, *Ius Sacramentarium,* I, n. 186; Coronata, *De Sacramentis,* I, n. 232; Cappello, *De Sacramentis,* I, n. 738.

[53] Davis, *Moral and Pastoral Theology,* III, 139; Cappello, *De Sacramentis,* I, n. 738.

[54] Coronata, *De Sacramentis,* I, n. 232; Augustine, *A Commentary,* IV, 162; Cappello, *De Sacramentis,* I, n. 739.

To sum up the legislation regarding the celebration of Mass on Holy Saturday, in the Roman rite a solemn Mass, or if this is not possible a *Missa cantata* (according to the *Memoriale Rituum*) can be celebrated in all churches where the Blessed Sacrament is habitually reserved and where the sacred ceremonies of Holy Week are performed on the preceding days. Private or low Mass is strictly forbidden on Holy Saturday. According to the law the only exceptions to this prohibition are, first, a priest is permitted to say a low Mass to consecrate Holy Communion for the dying, and secondly, bishops are allowed to say Mass privately if they do not celebrate solemnly in the cathedral. Finally, authors add another exception by supporting the opinion that a low Mass may be said in parochial churches in order to perform the blessing of the font, if otherwise the blessing would be omitted.

CHAPTER VI

THE HOUR OF MASS

IN the foregoing chapter the days on which Mass can be said are indicated, and in particular the exceptional days which involve limitations on the general concession of the law have been treated in accordance with the liturgical laws, the decrees of the Congregation of Sacred Rites and canon 820 of the Code. It is found convenient here to adhere to the order preserved by the Code; consequently the present chapter treats of the hour at which Mass can be celebrated, as set forth in canon 821.

Canon 821, § 1. Missae celebrandae initium ne fiat citius quam una hora ante auroram vel serius quam una hora post meridiem.

The general rule for the hour of the day at which Mass can be said is contained in this paragraph, namely, that the celebration should not be commenced earlier than one hour before dawn, nor later than one hour after noon. As already noted,[1] the rubrics of the Roman Missal determined as a legitimate time for the celebration of Mass the period from dawn to mid-day; the Code, however, extends this period by two hours in permitting the celebration to begin one hour before dawn on the one hand, and one hour after noon on the other.

ARTICLE 1. FUNDAMENTAL PRINCIPLES IN RECKONING TIME

The full import of canon 821 cannot be adequately conveyed without a previous examination of canon 33, § 1, which states that in reckoning the hours of the day the common custom of the place is to be followed, but in the private celebration of Holy Mass, in the private recitation of the Divine Office, in the receiving of Holy Communion,

[1] Cf. *supra*, Chapter IV, p. 47.

and in the observance of the fast and abstinence, one may deviate from the common custom of the place to follow the local true time, or the local mean time, or the legal regional time, or the legal extraordinary time.[2] Canon 33, § 1, mentions, besides the usual time of the place, local time which can be either true or mean, and legal time which can be either regional or extraordinary.

The problem of reckoning time is abstract, relative, and for the most part conventional, but after much research and experimental use most of the civilized world has come to common grounds, at least in regard to the fundamental principles. In civil reckonings of time midnight is everywhere used as the beginning of the day for practical reasons. Astronomers, however, at least until a few years ago, were measuring the day from noon to noon. But in fact these days are the same.

The problem that must now be solved is the determination of noon and midnight. The two terms simply denote either the beginning or the middle of the day, but they themselves, even though regulated by the rotation of the earth on its axis, have no absolute value. They are relative quantities and the nature and length of the days which they measure depend on the starting point that one uses for the computation. If the starting point be a star or some fixed point in the heavens, one uses the sidereal time, but if the starting point be the sun, the system of computation is called solar time.[3] Since the sidereal time is no longer contemplated in Canon Law, the consideration of the solar time for practical purposes is sufficient here.[4]

True solar time depends on the actual motion of the earth around the sun. A true solar day is the interval of time that elapses

[2] Can. 33, § 1. In supputandis horis diei standum est communi loci usui; sed in privata Missae celebratione, in privata horarum canonicarum recitatione, in sacra communione recipienda et in ieiunii vel abstinentiae lege servanda, licet alia sit usualis loci supputatio, potest quis sequi loci tempus aut locale sive verum sive medium, aut legale sive regionale sive aliud extraordinarium.

[3] Dubé, *The General Principles for the Reckoning of Time in Canon Law*, The Catholic University of America Canon Law Studies, n. 144 (Washington, D. C.: The Catholic University of America Press, 1941), p. 43 (hereafter cited *The Reckoning of Time*).

[4] Cf. Dubé, *The Reckoning of Time*, p. 152.

between two successive transits of the sun over the same meridian. In this reckoning the duration of each day changes; the time involved varies throughout the year, and hence for practical purposes has many inconveniences, which render it inadequate in fulfilling the requirements of a civilized society.

In consequence of the shortcomings of true solar time men in civilized countries discarded it for the use of a modified form called mean solar time. This is nothing else but an average of all the true solar days of the year. This time is regular and can be kept by ordinary clocks and watches. It is often called civil time; its day always corresponds to twenty four of our watch or clock hours. Astronomers reckon this time from the motion of a fictitious sun which is imagined to move uniformly on the equator, and it differs from the true solar time. This difference is caused by the particular shape of the earth, its rotation on its axis, and the revolution around the sun on its oblique orbit.[5] These explanations of local time both true and mean agree with those given by practically all the canonists who define these terms.[6]

In canon 33, § 1, there is mention of another division of time called legal time. This is another generic expression and refers to the time that any duly constituted government prescribes for the fulfillment of at least one obligation, for example that of the railroads, or for that of telegraph offices.[7] The government referred to here is not restricted to the supreme legislative body of the country. It can be taken in the broad sense, which embraces federal, state, or municipal governments.[8]

There are three kinds of legal time. Two of these are mentioned

[5] Cf. Newcomb-Holden, *Astronomy* (3. ed., New York, 1887), p. 188; Dubé, *The Reckoning of Time*, p. 43.

[6] Maroto, *Institutiones Iuris Canonici ad Normam Novi Codicis* (2 vols., Vol. I, 3. ed., Romae: Apud Commentarium pro Religiosis, 1921), I, n. 258, 1, A, b (hereafter this work will be cited *Institutiones*); Cicognani, *Canon Law* (authorized English version by O'Hara and Brennan, Philadelphia: The Dolphin Press, 1934), pp. 666-669; Michiels, *Normae Generales Iuris Canonici* (2 vols., Lublin: Universitas Catholica, 1929), II, 127-129; Beste, *Introductio in Codicem*, p. 100.

[7] Michiels, *Normae Generales Iuris Canonici*, II, 139.

[8] Dubé, *The Reckoning of Time*, p. 145.

in the Code, namely, regional and extraordinary. The third is zone time and is new in Canon Law. It was considered in an answer given on November 10, 1925, by the Pontifical Commission established for the authentic interpretation of the Code, and recognized as a legal reckoning in Canon Law.[9]

Aware of the shortcomings of local time, men arrived at a medium of time reckoning called legal regional. If every place in the world had its own local time either true or mean, then each place would have a different time according to longitude. It is evident that such a diversity of times would be inconvenient and detrimental to practical, social and commercial life. Hence by a disposition of law or by decree of the public authority a certain mean meridian was selected from which time was measured for the region or the nation. In the larger nations a determinate time was computed for each zone, so that all the clocks in a specified zone followed the same time.

The equatorial circumference of the earth is divided into 360 degrees of longitude, and since the sun takes 24 hours to travel this distance, consequently the transition of the sun is 15 degrees every hour or four minutes for every degree of longitude. Greenwich, England, is the mean meridian, and every fifteenth degree removed from there constitutes the center meridian of a separate and distinct zone. This zone time, now recognized in Canon Law as legal, can be employed for the purposes mentioned in canon 33, § 1.[10]

Finally, legal time which is called extraordinary is specially constituted by public authority, on account of some unusual or accidental cause.[11] An example of this is daylight-saving time, which is one hour ahead of the legal regional time. Dubé gives what he regards as the best example of such reckoning, namely, the imposition of central European time on Belgium by the Germans in the first World War. Hence war-time in any country would be in the

[9] *AAS,* XVII (1925), 582; Bouscaren, *The Canon Law Digest* (2 vols., Milwaukee: Bruce, 1934-1943), I, 59.

[10] Cf. Beste, *Introductio in Codicem,* p. 100; Dubé, *The Reckonng of Time,* pp. 142-152. Both authors, especially the latter, give a detailed review of the problem of time.

[11] Michiels, *Normae Generales Iuris Canonici,* II, p. 131.

category of legal extraordinary time, if because of war the government imposed a special time.[12]

In reference to the reckoning of the hours of the day, however, a final remark should be made. It is commonly held today, just as it was before the Code, that the proper computation of the hours is the physical, and not the mathematical, reckoning. In other words, one need not worry about the precise and absolute time as indicated by the motion of the heavenly bodies. It suffices to use a good reliable clock or watch as one's guide. With regard to the clock the common opinion among canonists is that the hour ends with the first stroke of the clock.[13]

Article 2. Dawn

In order to determine accurately the starting point for the celebration of Mass, it is necessary here to settle as definitely as possible the duration of the period of dawn or daybreak. By dawn is meant the dim glow or first radiation of light that precedes sunrise. When the sun itself is still 18 degrees below the horizon its rays illuminate the horizon and the space above it. At 18 degrees below the horizon this brightness or illumination begins and can scarcely be discerned, but it continues and increases in intensity as the sun gradually rises, until the actual globe of the sun itself appears.[14] In brief, dawn extends over the entire period of time intermediate between complete darkness and sunrise, that is, between night and day.[15]

[12] Dubé, *The Reckoning of Time,* p. 145; Cappello, *Summa Iuris Canonici* (3 vols., Vol. I, II, 4. ed., Vol. III, 2. ed., Romae: Universitas Gregoriana, 1938-1945), I, n. 179, 2 (hereafter this will be cited as *Summa*).

[13] Dubé, *The Reckoning of Time,* p. 153; Cicognani, *Canon Law,* p. 684; Oesterle, *Praelectiones Iuris Canonici* (Vol. I, Romae: In Collegio S. Anselmi, 1931), I, 17.

[14] The author Many scientifically explains the actual beginning of dawn as follows: "Incipit aurora seu diluculum, quando sol jam *decimo octavo gradu* proximus est horizonti; sicut desinit crepusculum serotinum, quando sol jam recessit ab horizonte ultra decimum octavum gradum."—*Praelectiones de Missa,* n. 20, 2, a; Gasparri, *De Sanctissima Eucharistia,* I, n. 102; Wernz, *Ius Decretalium,* III, n. 543; Coronata, *De Sacramentis,* I, n. 234; Davis, *Moral and Pastoral Theology,* III, 139; Cappello, *De Sacramentis,* I, n. 741.

[15] St. Alphonsus, *Theologia Moralis,* Lib. III, n. 341. This period was

The accurate determination of any point of time belongs in the field of astronomy, and even the astronomers encounter innumerable perplexing factors and difficulties in fixing a uniform reckoning of time. Due also to the particular shape of the earth, its rotation on its axis, and its revolution round the sun on its oblique orbit, the period of dawn differs in the different latitudes, and also at different seasons of the year.[16]

Thus, in order to determine the precise moment of daybreak in a particular place on a certain day, first the exact latitude of the place must be known, and secondly the actual time of sunrise must be ascertained from the daily newspapers or local weather bureau. With these data the astronomical chart must be consulted. This chart scientifically compiled contains a list of the duration of the period of dawn on any day of the year, and for any latitude. Knowing the latitude and the hour of sunrise, one can determine the period of dawn for the given latitude on that particular day. If one subtracts the duration of the period of dawn from the time of sunrise, the result will be the initial moment of dawn or aurora.[17]

This is an easy and accurate reckoning of the beginning of dawn, but on most occasions the required data cannot be ascertained, especially the astronomic chart readings. However, most *Ordos* of the Divine Office and Mass calendars give a table indicating the hour

also called *"crepusculum mane."* It corresponds to the period of dusk or twilight between sunset and night—Suarez, *Opera Omnia,* Tom. XXI, disp. 80, sect. IX, n. 4.

[16] Cf. Gasparri, *De Sanctissima Eucharistia,* I, n. 103. There it may be noted for example that at 5 degrees latitude on January 1st the period of dawn is 1 hour and 16 minutes before sunrise, while on the same day at a latitude 60 degrees north the length of dawn is 3 hours and 42 minutes.

[17] For example, Washington, D. C. is 39 degrees latitude. On November 11th, the sun rises at 6:48 A. M. (Eastern Standard Time), and the astronomical chart gives the period of dawn as 1 hour and 32 minutes for this day and latitude.

Latitude	39
Sunrise	6:48 A. M.
Period of dawn	1:32
Moment of dawn	5:16 A. M.

Gasparri, *op. cit.,* I, n. 103.

of dawn. If a particular *Ordo* or Mass calendar does not contain this chart, the priest can use the moral or usual interpretation, namely the beginning of the civil day, when men arise for the day's work. It is understood in this case that sunrise is much later than the beginning of the civil day.[18]

At the end of this work there is given a chart showing the period of dawn for the different latitudes and different times throughout the year. Gasparri and Augustine also give a table from which the legitimate hour for the celebration of Mass may be ascertained.[19]

A point that should not be forgotten here is the fact that dawn depends completely on the hour of sunrise independently of the various computations in use on the public clocks. With reference to the foregoing principle in regard to measuring the time of dawn, there arose in the Arctic regions a practical difficulty in determining the time at which Mass could be started. Daybreak or dawn has no meaning in those regions, for there is none in the Arctic in view of the extremely high latitude of the place. The Congregation of Sacred Rites replied to this difficulty by declaring that in those regions where there is no dawn the nature of aurora is to be taken in the moral sense. Therefore dawn in those places refers to the beginning of the civil day, that is, according to the approved custom of the region, the time when men rise to begin their day's work.[20]

[18] Coronata, *De Sacramentis,* I, n. 234.

[19] Gasparri, *loc. cit.;* Augustine, *A Commentary,* IV, 163, appendix to canon 821.

[20] S. R. C., *Missalis Romani,* 18 sept., 2 nov. 1634—*Decr. Auth.*, n. 614; *Fontes,* n. 5354. Two sessions were held. In both, the proposal to change the general rubric of the Missal for the sake of a better accommodation to conditions in the Arctic regions failed to win a majority support. Many (*Praelectiones de Missa,* n. 22, (11), 20b) thought that a distinction was implicit in the response, so that its ruling was applicable only to the winter months when those regions have perpetual night. He contended that in the summer time, when the sun remains above the horizon even during the night, it is permissible to begin the celebration of mass at that moment which corresponds to the middle of the night. This moment is to be determined as 12 hours after the time when the sun has passed directly over the local meridian. Wernz (*Ius Decretalium,* III, n. 543, note 170) and Gasparri (*De Sanctissima Eucharistia,* I, n. 106) seem not to have invoked any such distinction. Gasparri simply stated that aurora is to be understood as coinciding with the time when men usually rise for their day's work.

Among modern authors who treat this problem there is common agreement that there is nothing in the law prohibiting the celebration of Mass at midnight in those regions where the sun never sets, or where it does not descend to a point more than 18 degrees below the horizon.[21] In the concession that is made to this opinion emphasis is to be placed on the fact that the celebrant must be careful to preclude the danger of anticipation, that is, of beginning Mass before midnight. Such an anticipation is never allowed, for the time which precedes midnight belongs to the preceding day.[22]

While admitting that it is lawful to begin at the exact moment of midnight, there are some who maintain that it is the mind of the Church that the Holy Sacrifice be postponed for a time afterwards. Some recommend that the celebration be deferred for a half an hour, while others advise as much as two hours.[23] Finally, in those regions where there is perpetual day or perpetual night, it is also permissible to follow the Roman hours for determining the beginning of dawn.[24]

Article 3. Noon

The other limitative term used in the law for the celebration of Mass is "meridies," mid-day or high noon. This occurs when the sun passes directly over the local meridian. In reckoning noon one may employ the various systems of time mentioned in canon 33 § 1.[25]

[21] Cappello, *De Sacramentis,* I, n. 741, d: Regatillo, *Ius Sacramentarium,* I, n. 188; Noldin-Schmitt, *De Sacramentis,* III, n. 205, b; Coronata, *De Sacramentis,* I, n. 234; Vermeersch-Creusen, *Epitome Iuris Canonici,* II, n. 96.

[22] Coronata, *loc. cit.*

[23] Regatillo; *loc. cit.,* Vermeersch-Creusen, *loc. cit.* These authors also recommend that the celebrant observe the fast for at least two hours before beginning the celebration of the Holy Sacrifice.

[24] S. R. C., *Missalis Romani,* 2 nov. 1634—*Decr. Auth.,* n. 614; *Fontes,* n. 5354; Regatillo, *Ius Sacramentarium,* I, n. 188; Coronata, *De Sacramentis,* I, n. 234; Vermeersch-Creusen, *Epitome Iuris Canonici,* II, n. 96. The latter gives the beginning of dawn in Rome on the following dates. Jan. 1st at 5:45 A. M.; March 8th at 4:45 A. M.; April 9th at 3:45 A. M.; May 10th at 2.35 A. M.; July 29th at 3:00 A. M.; September 6th at 4:00 A. M.; October 28th at 5:00 A. M.

[25] Cf. *supra,* Chapter VI, p 81.

In relation to the hour indicated on one's watch or clock, dawn is a very relative thing and varies considerably in the different latitudes and seasons. Noon, however, is a comparatively stable point of time; it is the same for all latitudes, but differs at different longitudes. In earlier times the determination of noon constituted little difficulty, but with the introduction of the use of the clock and the additional creation of the various time reckonings much confusion was occasioned in the interpretation of the decrees of the Congregations which employed a divergent terminology.[26]

The Code in canon 33 allows full freedom in following any one of the time reckonings mentioned therein, and hence recognizes all times as in use on the public clocks. In fixing the hour of noon one may permissibly follow local sun time, whether true or mean, or legal time, whether regional, zonal, or extraordinary.

Article 4. The Law Explained

Canon 821 states that the celebration of the Holy Sacrifice can be commenced one hour before dawn and one hour after noon. According to canon 33, § 1, freedom to follow any one of the various computations of time is granted. It is very important here to note that the freedom of time-reckoning as conceded in canon 33, § 1, refers only to the *private* celebration of Mass. The code uses the expression *"in privata Missae celebratione."*

The explanation of this phrase is approached in divergent ways by the authors. Some give the liturgical divisions of Masses, and accordingly hold that *private Mass* in the canon is to be understood liturgically as opposed to solemn Mass, either conventual or non-conventual.[27] Others understood the word "private" in the juridic sense to mean Mass which is not celebrated under the obligation of a choral office. In this sense the Midnight Mass on Christmas sung by the pastor with deacon and subdeacon would be a private Mass.[28]

[26] Cf. *supra,* Chapter IV, p. 49.

[27] Ojetti, *Commentarium in Codicem Iuris Canonici* (4 vols., Romae, 1927-1931), I, 199; Toso, *Ad Codicem Iuris Canonici Commentaria Minora* (5 vols., Romae: Marietti, 1920-1927), I, 103.

[28] Vermeersch, *Epitome Iuris Canonici,* II, n. 115; Wernz-Vidal, *Ius*

Beste seems to offer the most acceptable explanation. He maintains that the private celebration of Mass in the canon cannot mean a low Mass in the liturgical sense as opposed to a *Missa cantata,* but that it must be taken in the juridic sense as any Mass either low, *Missa cantata,* or solemn, the celebration of which is not connected by force of law with any ecclesiastical office. Hence, from the favor granted by canon 33, § 1, in regard to the hour of celebration, conventual, capitular, and parochial Masses are excluded.[29] In the celebration of these Masses the favor of canon 33, § 1, cannot be allowed; the usual time of the place must be followed.[30]

Usual time has a rather loose meaning. It simply refers to the time actually followed in the place, and generally corresponds to some one of the types of reckoning time as mentioned in canon 33, § 1. This computation offers little difficulty, since the celebrant of the conventual, capitular, or parochial Mass has to accommodate himself to the needs of the community, or of the faithful in the case of the parochial Mass, in fixing the hour of celebration. Hence, once for all a definite hour for beginning the Mass has been determined, it is obvious that there is no question of following the various reckonings offered for the private celebration of Mass. The time followed must be, according to the canon, the one in common use in the locality, as indicated in the ordinarily well regulated public clocks.[31]

Before the enactment of the present Code there was an opinion that Mass could be started twenty minutes before dawn and twenty minutes after noon. Since the promulgation of the Code it is commonly held that a similar extension of the present law is not legitimate and cannot be maintained.[32]

Canonicum ad Codicis normam exactum (7 vols., in 8, Romae: apud aedes Universitatis Gregorianae, 1923-1946), I, n. 248 (hereafter this will be cited *Ius Canonicum*).

29 *Introductio in Codicem,* p. 100. Cf. also Regatillo, *Ius Sacramentarium,* I, n. 188.

30 Can. 33 § 1. "In supputandis horis diei standum est communi loci usui; . . ."

31 Cappello, *Summa,* I, n. 179; Beste, *Introductio in Codicem,* p. 100; Dubé, *The Reckoning of Time,* p. 143.

32 Coronata, *De Sacramentis,* I, n. 234; Cappello, *op. cit.* I, n. 741.

It also appears, according to Augustine, that exempt and other religious who claim the privilege, granted after the Council of Trent, of celebrating an hour before dawn and an hour after noon, cannot since the promulgation of the Code extend this time to two hours. For the author asserts that the legislator by extending the time has not extended the starting point (dawn) for the privilege. Furthermore it seems that the extension granted by the Code should be enough for all reasonable demands. The permissible use of this privilege as granted after the Council of Trent appears at least doubtful, and it is in the ordinary power of bishops to compel even exempt religious to abide by the ruling of the Code for the hour of the celebration of Mass.[33] However, it is commonly held that religious can celebrate lawfully two hours before dawn and two hours after noon by reason of privileges acquired before the Code. Authors say that privileges of celebrating before or after the time defined by the law are not abrogated by the Code.[34]

Article 5. Exceptions

The common law allows a few exceptions to the general rule regarding the hour at which Mass can be said. The exception best known and of rather practical importance is the Christmas midnight Mass. After a statement of the general law the Code formulates the first exception with its limitations in canon 821, § 2.

Canon 821, § 2.—In Nocte Nativitatis Domini inchoari media nocte potest sola Missa conventualis vel paroecialis, non autem alia sine apostolico indulto.

The Code like the former law allows only one Mass at midnight on Christmas, and furthermore this privilege is permitted only in churches where the parochial and conventual Mass is said. In all

[33] *A Commentary,* IV, 163. Cf. also Benedictus XIV, *Institutiones Ecclesiasticae,* LXVIII, n. 11.

[34] Genicot-Salsmans, *Institutiones Theologiae Moralis* (13. ed., 2 vols., Bruxellis; L'Edition Universelle, S. A., 1936), II, n. 237; Prümmer, *Manuale Theologiae Moralis* (7. ed., 3 vols., Friburgi Brisgoviae: Herder & Co., 1931), III, n. 290; Coronata, *De Sacramentis,* I, n. 234.

other churches the Christmas midnight Mass cannot be celebrated. The Congregation of Sacred Rites, as well as the General Rubrics of the Missal, demand that care be taken that midnight Mass should never begin before midnight; not even is it permitted to anticipate the hour for the beginning of Mass by so much as to permit the consecration of the Mass to take place after midnight. With regard to this ruling there is no toleration of abuses.[85]

There is no strict obligation to commence at midnight. The law says that Mass can be commenced (*inchoari potest*) at that time, but it may be postponed for some time after midnight if there be any hindrance. The rubrics require of those who are bound to say the public office, such as the members of cathedral chapters, and of most of the regular institutes that they sing Matins before the Mass and Lauds after it. This order may not be changed on that day.[86]

Canon 821, § 3. In omnibus tamen religiosis seu piis domibus oratorium habentibus cum facultate Sanctissimam Eucharistiam habitualiter asservandi, nocte Nativitatis Domini, unus sacerdos tres rituales Missas vel, servatis servandis, unam tantum quae adstantibus omnibus ad praecepti quoque satisfactionem valeat, celebrare potest et sacram communionem petentibus ministrare.[87]

This exception to the general ruling is extended to religious houses, which are specified in the present law as the residences of any religious community. A religious community or *"religio"* is a society, approved by the legitimate ecclesiastical authority, whose

[85] S. R. C., *Cuneen.*, 2 iun. 1883, ad X—*Decr. Auth.*, n. 3576; S. R. C., *Societatis Iesu*, 11 maii 1878, ad XV—*Decr. Auth.*, n. 3448; *Rubricae Generales Missalis*, XV, n. 4; Vermeersch-Creusen, *Epitome Iuris Canonici*, II, n. 97.

[86] S. R. C., *Gerunden.*, 3 apr. 1830—*Fontes*, n. 5857.

[87] Can. 821, § 3. "In all religious and pious houses which possess an oratory with the faculty of habitually keeping the Holy Eucharist, one priest may say one or three Masses according to the rubrics Christmas night. Those who assist thereat comply with the obligation of hearing Mass, and Holy Communion may be administered to such as desire it."—Augustine, *A Commentary*, IV, 164.

members strive after evangelical perfection by living according to the special laws of the society itself and by taking public vows, either perpetual or temporary, to be renewed, if temporary, when the time of the vows expires.[38]

The privilege of celebrating three Masses consecutively at midnight on Christmas is also given by the Code to priests who celebrate the community Mass in pious houses. A pious house is defined as one in which the inmates, not necessarily under vow, are professedly engaged in pious or charitable works. In this category authors place orphanages, hospitals, seminaries, Catholic schools, episcopal residences and other like institutions.[39] A work of charity as contemplated in the canon comprises every species of good work, educational work, the corporal works of mercy, etc. But it is essential that such a house be superintended by ecclesiastical authority.[40]

A doubt may arise concerning hospitals, asylums for the aged, for the orphans, or for foundlings, when the work at these institutions is conducted by religious, but the administration is really superintended by the law or civil authority. In such circumstances if the religious who work in these institutions form a community of their own, and have their own oratory in which the Blessed Sacrament is habitually reserved, they are regarded as a religious house in the canonical sense, and the celebrant of the midnight Mass on Christmas can say three Masses consecutively. The same does not apply to State asylums and penitentiaries. Augustine stated that these are purely secular institutions, entirely managed by seculars, even though there be a temporary chapel where the Blessed Sacrament could hardly be kept. Therefore these chapels are not entitled to the favor in question.[41]

There are some, however, who hold that under the heading of "pious houses" one should also include prisons and penitentiaries.

38 Can. 488, 1°; Woywod, *A Practical Commentary on the Code of Canon Law* (2 vols., 9. ed. revised by Callistus Smith, New York: J. Wagner, 1945), I, 177 (hereafter cited *A Practical Commentary*).

39 Vermeersch-Creusen, *Epitome Iuris Canonici,* II, n. 97; Regatillo, *Ius Sacramentarium,* I, n. 189; Davis, *Moral and Pastoral Theology,* III, 141.

40 Devoti, *Institutionum Canonicarum Libri Quatuor* (3 vols., Romae 1785), I, 560.

41 *A Commentary,* IV, 166.

They contend that the office of the chaplain gives a sufficient character of piety to those places.[42] The office of the chaplain alone does not seem sufficient to constitute a pious house, however, if there is also attached to the prison or penitentiary an oratory or chapel endowed with the privilege of reserving the Blessed Sacrament habitually, there seems to be no reason why the term "pious house" should not apply.

The present law states furthermore that in a religious or pious house at midnight on Christmas one priest may say one or three Masses. Hence if there are present more than one priest in the given house, the others must wait until later in the morning. The three Masses must be said according to the rubrics, that is, as they follow each other in the Missal, and not all three according to the formulary of the Midnight Mass (*Missa in Nocte*). If a priest says only one Mass at midnight, as might happen in the case of an assistant at the cathedral who is also chaplain of a convent or a hospital, he is bound to observe what the law prescribes in regard to the time for the celebration of the other two Masses. In other words, he must say the other two Masses according to the rubrical time, that is, the second Mass is to be said at dawn, and the third in the morning *(de die)*.[43] Permission is given by the canons for one priest, and only one, to celebrate in these religious or pious houses one Mass or three Masses, but not two.[44]

All who assist at any of these three Masses fulfill the precept of hearing Mass on Christmas day, and the celebrating priest may administer Holy Communion to the faithful present. This concession of allowing three Masses at midnight on Christmas in religious and pious houses was formerly a special privilege of some communities.[45] The present law, however, extends the privilege to these houses notwithstanding decrees of the Holy Office in 1907

[42] Vermeersch-Creusen, *loc. cit.*, II, n. 97; Regatillo, *Ius Sacramentarium*, I, 189; Davis, *op. cit.*, III, 141.

[43] De Herdt, *Sacrae Liturgiae Praxis*, Tom. III, pars 5, n. 2. Cf. *supra*, Chapter IV, p. 51.

[44] Can. 821, § 3; Davis, *loc. cit.*

[45] *Supra*, Chapter IV, p. 51.

and 1908, which declared that the privilege was not extended to the chapel or oratory unless the doors were closed to the faithful.[46]

The decrees of the Holy Office of 1907 and 1908 required that the doors of the oratories of religious and pious houses be closed, but the present law has no such clause. Hence outsiders, for instance, friends and relatives, may be admitted and by assisting at the Mass they comply with the precept of hearing Mass on Christmas Day; if they so desire, they may also receive Holy Communion. This is plainly expressed in the words: *adstantibus omnibus,* all who assist.

But this favor cannot be extended to the churches of religious, whether exempt or not, for not only was the privilege directly denied to them by the decree of November 26, 1908, but the canon itself (can. 821, § 3) excludes such an extension, since it speaks only of religious and pious houses which have an oratory, and not of churches. The reason for the restriction obviously is to prevent a prejudice against parish churches. However the present law, as well as the decree of 1908, permits religious to have a midnight Mass for themselves even in their churches, but behind closed doors, at which the members may receive Holy Communion.[47]

On March 16, 1936, the Commission for the Authentic Interpretation of the present law stated in a reply that Holy Communion may be given at the midnight Mass on Christmas, whether the privilege to celebrate at that hour is granted either by law or by apostolic indult, but the local ordinary has the power in virtue of canon 869 to forbid the distribution of Holy Communion in particular cases and for just causes.[48]

Another exception regarding the hour for the celebration of Mass has been made in favor of Eucharistic Congresses if the Blessed Sacrament is exposed all night. In these cases, one Mass may be said at midnight, at which Holy Communion may be given to the faithful assisting. Priests who are present at adoration during the

[46] S. C. S. Off., decr., 1 aug. 1907—*ASS,* XL (1907), 478, 479; *Fontes,* n. 1284; this decree was further explained on November 26, 1908, as being a concession for all three Masses but not to places where the doors were open to the faithful—*AAS,* I (1909), 146; *Fontes,* n. 1285.

[47] Can. 821; Augustine, *A Commentary,* IV, 167; Vermeersch, "Ex audientia Sanctissimi,"—*Periodica,* IV (1913), 312.

[48] *AAS,* XXVIII (1936), 178.

night have the privilege of saying Mass after the midnight Mass, or at 1:00 A. M., and may recite the Office of the Blessed Sacrament instead of the Office of the day.[49] Furthermore, the Sacred Congregation of the Sacraments extended this privilege by giving permission to begin Mass at 12:30 A. M. In addition to the time of Eucharistic Congresses this faculty was further extended to the occasion of a triduum of devotion in honor of the Blessed Sacrament, to the time of a mission, or any other extraordinary occasion of prayer.[50]

Article 6. Excusing Causes

The present law concerning the hour at which Mass may be celebrated binds *sub gravi* when grave matter is involved. As to what constitutes grave matter there is some divergence of opinion. However, most of the authors are in agreement in regard to the basic principle, namely, that without a just cause a priest who says Mass a *notable* time before or after the time prescribed by the law is guilty of grievous sin unless particular circumstances excuse him. The notable time is regarded by most as the space of one hour. Hence to commence the celebration of Mass two hours before dawn or after noon is grievously sinful in the absence of an excusing cause.[51]

If there is no scandal and no inconvenience caused to the faithful, Cappello contends that to celebrate *privately* before or after the prescribed time very probably does not exceed a venial sin. He furthermore asserts that any just and reasonable cause excuses from the obligation of celebrating within the time specified by law. Such a cause, according to the same author, need not necessarily be a

[49] Pius, XI, litt. ap., 7 Mar. 1924—*AAS*, XVI (1924), 154.

[50] S. C. de Sacramentis, decr. *Romana et Aliarum*, 22 apr. 1924—*AAS*, XVII (1925), 100. In the apostolic letter of March 7, 1924, the condition that the Blessed Sacrament be exposed all night was required, but the later decree of April 22, 1924, only required three hours of prayer throughout the night.

[51] Noldin-Schmitt, *De Sacramentis*, III, n. 206; Cappello, *De Sacramentis*, I, n. 744; Vermeersch-Creusen, *Epitome Iuris Canonici*, II, n. 97; Coronata, *De Sacramentis*, I, n. 234; St. Alphonsus, *Theologia Moralis*, Lib. VI, n. 346.

public one; even a merely private cause either on the part of the celebrant or on the part of any one of the faithful suffices.[52]

The restrictive legislation which forbids the celebration of Mass earlier than an hour before dawn is more stringent than that which forbids a postponement to a time later than an hour after noon. Hence a more grave cause is required for the anticipation than for the postponement after 1:00 P. M. Authors commonly assert that the bishop in a particular case can dispense from the law in regard to the time set by it for the celebration of Mass.[53] There are some who say that the superiors of regulars have the same faculty in particular cases.[54] In the absence of an indult, a privilege or a dispensation, an excusing cause is necessary to justify the celebration of Mass outside the time limits specified by the law.

Among the causes excusing from the general ruling authors with some variations generally include the following.[55]

(a) In cases of special necessity such as the consecration of Holy Viaticum for the dying, the provision for a group of the faithful to enable them to fulfill the precept of hearing Mass, or the escape from threatened persecution, it is regarded as lawful to say Mass at any hour of the day or night, even at midnight.

(b) The existence of a reasonable custom justifies the celebrant in beginning Mass one hour before the time specified by the law. The example usually given is the custom of laborers and their families desiring to hear Mass even on week days.[56]

[52] *De Sacramentis,* I, n. 744.

[53] S. R. C., *Bonaeren.,* 7 iul. 1899—*Fontes,* n. 6301; Noldin-Schmitt, *op. cit.,* III, n. 206; St. Alphonsus, *op. cit.,* Lib. VI, n. 344; Lehmkuhl, *Theologia Moralis,* II, n. 117; Ballerini-Palmieri, *Opus Theologicum Morale* (7 vols., Prati: Giachetti, 1889-1893), IV, n. 1051.

[54] Noldin-Schmitt, *op. cit.,* III, n. 206; St. Alphonsus, *op. cit.,* Lib. VI, n. 344.

[55] Vermeersch-Creusen, *Epitome Iuris Canonici,* II, n. 96; Noldin-Schmitt, *op. cit.,* III, n. 206; St. Alphonsus, *op. cit.,* Lib. VI, n. 343, 344; De Herdt, *Sacrae Liturgiae Praxis,* Tom. I. pars I, tit. XIV, n. 102; *Gasparri, De Sanctissima Eucharistia,* I, nn. 110-117; Many, *Praelectiones de Missa,* n. 23 (2-5); Cappello, *De Sacramentis,* I, n. 744; Coronata, *De Sacramentis,* I, n. 234; Davis, *Moral and Pastoral Theology,* III, 142.

[56] Noldin-Schmitt do not even require the existence of such a custom.

(c) If a solemn Mass by reason of the solemnity is protracted beyond the mid-day limitation, and there is a custom of saying a low Mass afterwards in order that a large number of the faithful may fulfill the obligation to hear Mass, then it is lawful to begin the low Mass after the prescribed time.

(d) If a priest on a Sunday or Holy Day of obligation by reason of a journey is impeded from saying Mass at the proper hours, the necessity of making the journey is sufficient cause to allow him to begin the celebration even more than one hour before or after the limits set by law.

(e) Provided that the extension of the time for the celebration of Mass exists in a well ordered relation to the proportionate gravity of the cause, authors hold that the celebrant is excused. Such considerations as the necessity of enhancing the solemnities on some special festal occasion, or of avoiding serious inconvenience or notable hardship, are accepted as causes which reasonably warrant an exceptional arrangement for the hour at which Mass may be celebrated. The funerals of kings, of princes or of persons of eminence equivalent to these; the occasion of missions, of special sermons, or of public supplication; the conferring of Holy Orders or the celebration of nuptial Mass—all these are mentioned as some of the more common excusing causes.[57]

Article 7. The Determination of the Schedule of Masses in Churches

"In sacred edifices which have been legitimately dedicated, all ecclesiastical functions may be performed which do not prejudice the rights of parochial churches and the rights acquired by privilege or by legitimate custom. The Ordinary may for a just cause fix the hours for the sacred functions—not however in the case of the churches of exempt regulars except as provided by Canon 609." [58]

They simply say that a priest is justified in anticipating the specified time in order to accommodate workers and their families—*De Sacramentis,* III, n. 206.

[57] Noldin-Schmitt, "In funere magni principis, occasione contionis, publicae supplicationis, collationis ordinum, matrimonii, etc., licet in his adiunctis Missam serius quam integra hora post meridiem celebrare"—*De Sacramentis,* III, n. 206.

[58] Can. 1171, as translated by Woywod, *A Practical Commentary,* II, 12.

Canon 609 gives the ordinary the right to judge whether the services in the churches of the regulars interfere with the people's attendance at the explanation of the Gospel and the catechetical instruction in the parish church if the regular church does not also serve as a parish. If the bishop judges that the services at the monastery or convent church so interfere, he may forbid the regulars to have public services in their church during these hours. The religious superiors also are obliged to see to it that such services in their churches are not conducted contrary to the legislation of canon 609.

According to canon 1171 the ordinary has the power to prohibit Masses at certain hours in non-parochial churches if there is a just cause. The question is, does he have the power to determine the hours at which Mass can be said in the churches of exempt religious? Canon 609 was taken from the letter of Pope Benedict XIV, in which he asked for zeal on the part of pastors in the discharge of their duty of preaching the Gospel and of giving catechetical instruction to the faithful.[59]

The pope showed the danger to the faith of the people in rural districts who attended non-parochial churches to satisfy the precept of hearing Mass, and thereby cannot be present to hear the word of God or attend catechetical instruction. The encyclical letter provided remedies for this danger by laying down the rule that the bishop can either forbid Mass in these churches until the pastor finishes his Mass and the instructions in the parish church, or oblige the priests who celebrate Mass in non-parochial churches, even under heavy penalties, to preach the Gospel and to give religious instruction to the people.

In the non-parochial churches in cities, and especially in those of Regulars, very frequently solemn feasts are celebrated, and many parishioners attend, thus missing the opportunity of hearing the regular sermons and catechetical instruction in the parish church. Against this difficulty the encyclical letter stated that no general norms could be given. However, the ordinary was required by the letter to see to it that in the best possible way according to his prudent judgment provision was made for the religious instruction

[59] Benedictus XIV, ep. encycl. *Etsi minime*, 7 feb. 1742, § 15—*Fontes*, n. 324.

of the faithful, without detracting from the observance by the solemnities of the regulars.

Some authors state that the spirit of the law in canon 609 is that the parochial functions, especially preaching and the catechetical instruction, cannot be hindered by the functions of the regulars. On the other hand, they argue, the religious have the right to admit the faithful to their Masses, sermons, and religious instructions. Even though this admission may result in the increase of the congregations present at the services in the church of the Regulars, and in a considerable decrease in the attendance at the parochial church, this disadvantage to the parochial church is compensated, they contend, by the greater spiritual benefits to the faithful.

The principal benefits are, they insist, a general increase in devotion, added attendance at the sacred functions of the church, and greater numbers hearing the preaching of the Gospel. Whether the faithful derive these benefits from attendance at the parochial church or the regular church services is of secondary importance; the actual attendance at the sermons and religious instructions is the primary purpose of canon 609.[60]

Vermeersch-Creusen explain that the power invested in the ordinary by canon 609 does not extend as far as suppressing the ministrations of regulars or forcing them to abstain from the performance of their sacred functions; the law only allows him to pass judgment as to when and what services hinder the preaching of the Divine Word and the religious instruction of the faithful of the diocese. If warned by the ordinary, the religious superior is bound in virtue of the same canon to see to it that the sacred functions in his church do not interfere with the preaching and religious instruction in the parochial church. If the superior refuses to co-operate with the bishop, the matter is to be referred to the Holy See.

This manner of procedure is indicated in the encyclical of Pope Benedict XIV.[61] Canonists, in following the principle of canon 6,

[60] Vermeersch-Creusen, *Epitome Iuris Canonici,* II, n. 710; Regatillo, *Ius Sacramentarium,* I, n. 191.

[61] *Etsi minime,* 7 feb. 1742, § 15—*Fontes,* n. 324.

2°, after the publication of the Code,[62] strictly adhere to the norms of the papal encyclical, namely, that the bishop cannot prohibit the celebration of Mass in religious churches at hours coinciding with those in the parochial churches, provided that the explanation of the Gospel and of Christian doctrine is also given in the church of the religious.[63] Hence the determination of the particular hours at which Mass may be said on Sundays and feast days of obligation is summed up as follows:

(1) The Ordinary of the place for a just cause can fix the hours of Mass in all secular and non-exempt religious churches; as regards exempt religious, however, he has no power to determine the Mass schedule in their churches (Can. 1171).

(2) The pastor cannot legitimately prohibit Mass or other sacred functions in the churches of religious either on Sundays or on feast days of obligation. Neither can he demand that the functions take place at a specific time, either before, after, or simultaneously with the parochial functions.

(3) The power of the local ordinary to determine the Mass schedule extends only to the churches of non-exempt religious. The exempt religious, however, are not absolutely exempt, for the common law states that the superiors must so arrange the hours of Masses and of other Divine Services in their churches that the faithful may not be directly deprived of the opportunity of attending the sermons and religious instructions in the parochial church. The ordinary himself cannot subject the exempt religious to any prohibition, but once he has warned the superior that the schedule of the hours of services in the religious church hinders the preaching and religious instruction in the parochial church, he must look to the superior to remedy the harm. If the superior refuses to co-

[62] Can. 6, 2°.—Canones qui ius vetus ex integro referunt ex veteris iuris auctoritate, atque ideo ex receptis apud probatos auctores interpretationibus, sunt aestimandi.

[63] Schaefer, *Compendium de Religiosis ad normam Codicis Iuris Canonici* (2. ed., Münster i. W.: Ex Officina Libraria Aschendorff, 1931), p. 365; Regatillo, *op. cit.*, I, n. 191; Coronata, *Institutiones Iuris Canonici* (5 vols., Vols. I-II, 2. ed., 1939; Vol. III, 2. ed., 1941; Vol. IV, 2. ed., 1945; Vol. V, 1936, Taurini-Romae: Marietti, 1936-1945), I, n. 615.

operate, the ordinary can have recourse to the Holy See, which in each particular case solves the problem.[64]

In order to act justly in prohibiting the Divine Offices at certain hours in non-parochial churches, the ordinary of the place should be guided by the principle of the greater good of souls.[65] Hence, even though the congregation attending the parochial church may be considerably diminished, the prohibition of the ordinary does not seem to be opportune if the faithful can attend another non-parochial church more conveniently, and there also hear a sermon and have religious instruction.

(4) In larger towns and especially in cities such prohibitions of the ordinary are not expedient, for it is desirable that the faithful have every possible facility of hearing Mass in crowded urban districts; otherwise many tepid Catholics would neither hear Mass, nor the sermon, nor the religious instruction, as is well known from experience. However, ordinaries who use their power to prohibit Masses in non-parochial churches at certain hours usually do not include churches in cities and large towns. In rural districts where the non-parochial churches are far removed from the parochial, and the same difficulty arises, the mind of the legislator in canon 609, § 3, seems to be in accordance with the encyclical of Pope Benedict XIV, who provided the remedy that the priests celebrating in the non-parochial churches should give sermons and religious instruction to the faithful present.[66] The present law in canon 1334 binds superiors even of exempt religious to accede to the wishes of the ordinary of the place in the matter of preaching and religious instruction.[67]

Furthermore, the Code states that it is to be desired that in all churches and public oratories where people assist at Holy Mass on

[64] Can. 609, § 3; Regatillo, *Ius Sacramentarium,* I, n. 191.

[65] Can. 1162, § 3; 542. § 2; 2162.

[66] *Etsi minime,* 7 febr. 1742—*Fontes,* n. 324.

[67] Can. 1334—"Si, Ordinarii loci iudicio, religiosorum auxilium ad catecheticam populi institutionem sit necessarium, Superiores religiosi, etiam exempti, ab eodem Ordinario requisiti, tenentur per se vel per suos subditos religiosos, sine tamen regularis disciplinae detrimento, illam populo tradere, praesertim in propriis ecclesiis."

Sundays and on Holydays of obligation, a short explanation of the Holy Gospel or of some point of Christian doctrine be given to the people. If the local ordinary has given orders concerning this matter, they must be obeyed, not only by the secular clergy but also by religious both non-exempt and exempt, even in their own churches.[68]

(5) If there be a divergence of opinion in this matter between parish priests and religious, the opinions of both parties are to be referred to the ordinary, who is to solve the problem according to his prudent judgment. In cases of this nature special care ought to be taken to forestall all emergence of scandal among the faithful.[69]

[68] Can. 1345; Woywod, *A Practical Commentary*, II, 105.

[69] Can. 1345; Regatillo, *Ius Sacramentarium*, I, n. 191.

CHAPTER VII

THE REMOTE PLACE FOR THE CELEBRATION OF MASS

Canon 822, § 1.—Missa celebranda est super altare consecratum et in ecclesia vel oratorio consecrato aut benedicto ad normam iuris, salvo praescripto can. 1196.

THE legislation on the place for the celebration of Mass is briefly summarized in this canon of the Code. The canon makes mention of two types of place, namely, the church and the altar. For a clearer exposition of the section on the place of Mass, two main divisions are made under the headings: the *remote* place for the celebration of Mass, which is the church or oratory, and the *proximate* place, which is the altar. The present chapter is confined to a treatment of the remote place.

ARTICLE 1. THE CHURCH

The definition of the term "church" as given in the Code is that it is "a sacred edifice dedicated to divine worship, especially with a view to enabling all the faithful to practice public worship." [1] This definition of the term is given mainly for the purpose of distinguishing it from other sacred places used for divine worship. Other chapels, oratories and houses of prayer are either not open to all Catholics (but only to certain communities, confraternities, etc.), or, if they are open to all, they are not officially instituted for the public offering of divine worship, but rather for private devotion.[2] The primary note in the definition is that the church is erected specifically for the use and benefit of all the faithful, and

[1] Can. 1161. "Ecclesiae nomine intelligitur aedes sacra divino cultui dedicata eum potissimum in finem ut omnibus Christifidelibus usui sit ad divinum cultum publice exercendum." Translation by Woywod, *A Practical Commentary,* II, 5.

[2] Woywod, *loc. cit.*

hence is open to all. This is the specific difference between a church and an oratory, which, though it is destined for divine worship, does not have as its principal object the serving of the faithful at large.

No church can be erected legitimately without the explicit written consent of the local ordinary. The vicar general cannot give this consent without a special mandate, nor shall the ordinary give it unless he prudently foresees that the necessary means for the building and the maintenance of the new church, for the support of the necessary ministers, and for the defraying of other costs of divine worship, will not be wanting.

In order that the new church may not, without proportionate spiritual benefit to the faithful, injure the interests of churches already established, the local ordinary, before giving his consent for the building of a new church, should hear the rectors of the neighboring churches which may be concerned, with due attention also to the law of canon 1676.[3] "Religious organizations also, though they have obtained consent from the local Ordinary for the erection of a new house in the diocese or in a city, must obtain permission from the local Ordinary before they can build a church or public oratory in a certain and definite place." [4]

Furthermore, local ordinaries besides giving consent for the erection of new churches "should take care to have the churches built or restored according to approved Christian traditions of ecclesiastical architecture, and in conformity with the laws of sacred art, consulting for the purpose, if necessary, experts in ecclesiastical architecture. In a church there must be no door or window opening into a house of lay persons. The space below the floor or above the ceiling of the church, if there be any, shall not be used for purely profane purposes." [5]

[3] Can. 1676 gives to parties who think themselves injured through the erection of a new church, or through other new ecclesiastical undertakings, the right to object, and from the moment the process is instituted as a result of the objection, operations must come to a standstill until a decision has been reached by the ecclesiastical court.

[4] Can. 1162, § 4, translated by Woywod, *A Practical Commentary,* II, 5.

[5] Can. 1164, translated by Woywod, *op. cit.,* II, 6.

The ordinaries are commanded in canon 1164 to see that the churches are built in such a style and design as to be in harmony with ecclesiastical architecture and as serving to elevate the minds of those who use the church for divine worship. The highest human art and the best material, in so far as financial circumstances make it possible, should be made available for the house of God. Ordinaries in virtue of canon 1164 have the right and duty to study carefully and inspect the plans of the architect before acceptance.[6]

The Congregation of Sacred Rites has made decisions which determine the profane purposes forbidden by the ruling of canon 1164 with reference to the basement and the space above the ceiling of the church. To use the basement as a wine cellar, or to store there oil or other purely profane commodities is unlawful, even though the actual cellar is outside the body of the church. The storing of altar wine cannot be regarded as a profane commodity, as it is destined for use in divine worship.[7]

Also condemned is the practice of using the basement for theatrical entertainments or "movies," even though they are legitimate recreation, well conducted for the purpose of entertaining the youth in the parish. On no account are dances, parties, games, meetings, and other such noisy gatherings of a purely secular nature allowed in the basement or in the rooms above the ceiling of the church.[8] In like manner it is not lawful to convert the space above the church into cubicles or dormitories, or to use it as living quarters, even though destined for the use of clerics or religious.[9]

Authors do not include under the phrase *"ad usum mere profanum"* the use of the space above or below the church to store things which pertain to divine worship, or to serve as a parish library, or as a library for a religious house. Likewise the use of such a space for sodality meetings, for religious conferences, or for a parish school, provided that the scope is religious in purpose, can-

[6] Beste, *Introductio in Codicem*, p. 557; Woywod, *A Practical Commentary*, II, 7.

[7] S. R. C., *Mechlinien.*, 31 aug. 1867, ad V—*Fontes*, n. 6016; Beste, *Introductio in Codicem*, p. 558.

[8] S. R. C., *Taurinen.*, 4 maii 1882, ad II—*Fontes*, n. 6135.

[9] S. R. C., *Caiacen.*, 11 maii 1641—*Fontes*, n. 5401.

not be designated as a profane use. The end for which the space below or above the church is to be used will be the deciding factor for the local ordinary in judging whether or not the church building is being or will be employed *"ad usum mere profanum,"* and hence whether he can legitimately consecrate or bless such a building.[10] It is beyond the scope of this dissertation to discuss all the canonical requirements for the consecration and blessing of churches. These matters have been fully explained in a work by Ziolkowski.[11]

Article 2. The Oratory

Canon 822 states the general rule that the place for the celebration of the Holy Sacrifice of the Mass is a consecrated altar in a church or oratory, which must be consecrated or blessed in the manner prescribed by law. In the preceding article the nature of the term "church," and the requirements demanded by the common law for its erection have been explained. In the present law, besides the church, the oratory is also specified as the proper place for the celebration of Mass.

> **Canon 1188, § 1.—Oratorium est locus divino cultui destinatus, non tamen eo potissimum fine ut universo fidelium populo usui sit ad religionem publice colendam.**

This definition of the oratory given in the Code is general enough to include the three kinds of oratories (public, semi-public, and private), and at the same time is sufficiently specific to differentiate it from all other places, whether sacred or profane. The

[10] Ayrinhac, *Administrative Legislation in the New Code of Canon Law* (New York: Longmans, Green & Co., 1930), n. 11; Woywod, *A Practical Commentary,* II, 7; Beste, *Introductio in Codicem,* p. 558; Ziolkowski, *The Consecration and Blessing of Churches,* The Catholic University of America Canon Law Studies, n. 187 (Washington, D. C.: The Catholic University of America Press, 1943), p. 54.

[11] Cf. *The Consecration and Blessing of Churches,* p. 48.

definition consists of two parts. The first part points to an oratory as a place destined for divine worship, and thus there is specified the positive element that differentiates it from a profane place.[12] The second part of the definition points to what is the principal difference between a church and an oratory, namely, that the oratory is not destined *primarily* to the enabling of all the faithful to offer public worship.[13] The threefold division of oratories is given in canon 1188, § 2.[14]

(a) Public Oratory

A public oratory, therefore, is an oratory erected principally for the convenience of a certain group or corporation or even of private individuals, but in such a manner that all the faithful have the right, legitimately recognized, to frequent it at least at the time of divine services.[15] It is in this right of the faithful that a public oratory is distinguished from a semi-public oratory, for the fact that they are subject to different laws is consequent to rather than constitutive of their essential difference. If an oratory is open to the faithful merely by the gratuitous indulgence of its proprietor, it is not a public oratory; for in order to be public the faithful must have a strict right to frequent it, and its proprietor must be

12 Vermeersch-Creusen, *Epitome Iuris Canonici,* II, n. 497; Feldhaus, *Oratories,* The Catholic University of America Canon Law Studies, n. 42 (Washington, D. C.: The Catholic University of America, 1927), p. 64.

13 Ferreres, *Institutiones Canonicae* (ed. altera, 2 vols., Barcinone, 1920), II, n. 94; Coronata, *Institutiones Iuris Canonici,* II, n. 764; Cocchi, *Commentarium in Codicem Iuris Canonici* (8 vols. in 5, Vol. V, 4. ed., 1938, Vol. VII, 3. ed., 1940, Augustae Taurinorum: Marietti), V, n. 28 (hereafter cited *Commentarium*).

14 Canon 1188, § 2.—Est vero oratorium:

1°. *Publicum,* si praecipue erectum sit in commodum alicuius collegii aut etiam privatorum, ita tamen ut omnibus fidelibus, tempore saltem divinorum officiorum, ius sit, legitime comprobatum, illud adeundi;

2°. *Semi-publicum,* si in commodum alicuius communitatis vel coetus fidelium eo convenientium erectum sit, neque liberum cuique sit illud adire;

3°. *Privatum* seu *domesticum,* si in privatis aedibus in commodum alicuius tantum familiae vel personae privatae erectum sit.

15 Feldhaus, *Oratories,* p. 70.

bound by the corresponding obligation of not interfering with the free exercise of this right, and hence of affording an unimpeded admission to the faithful at least at the time of divine services. Both the right and the correlative obligation are perpetual.[16]

(b) Semi-public Oratory

The second type of oratory is the semi-public oratory, which is erected for the convenience of a certain community or group of the faithful who assemble there, but to which the other members of the faithful have not the right of free access. The element stressed in the definition given in the Code is the fact that the community or group in behalf of which the oratory was erected has the exclusive right to its use. Other persons have no right to frequent it; if they are admitted, it is a mere favor and can be withdrawn at will.[17]

A semi-public oratory may be erected for the convenience of either a community or a group of the faithful—*"communitatis vel coetus fidelium."* The term "community" here designates the persons resident in or pertaining to an institution, and therefore implies the existence of a moral person either ecclesiastical or civil.[18] The phrase "group of the faithful" designates simply a number of physical persons without reference to the existence of a moral person.[19]

The community for which the semi-public oratory is erected need not necessarily be a religious community, for the Code in legislating for semi-public oratories in canon 1192, § 4, includes the oratories erected in educational institutions, hospitals, prisons, barracks of soldiers, etc. The Congregation of Sacred Rites on October 18, 1901, stated in a particular reply that the term "group of the faithful" can be understood as any number of the faithful who frequent the forementioned oratory for the purpose of hearing Mass

[16] Many, *Praelectiones de Locis Sacris* (Parisiis, 1904), n. 73; Feldhaus, *Oratories,* p. 71.

[17] Feldhaus, *Oratories,* p. 73.

[18] Vermeersch-Creusen, *Epitome Iuris Canonici,* II, n. 498.

[19] Vermeersch-Creusen, *op. cit.,* II, n. 498.

even to fulfill the precept, provided that they have the assent of the proprietor of the place and the requisite consent of the ordinary.[20]

A semi-public oratory must be erected for the convenience of a community or group of the faithful, as the Code indicates. However, authors maintain that the oratory is also semi-public even if it was originally built for the convenience of a private family, or a private individual, but subsequently through the permission of the local ordinary was destined for the use of a certain community or group of the faithful.[21]

(c) Private Oratory

A private oratory is erected for the benefit or convenience of some family or of a private individual. Since this type of oratory is usually erected in a private home and destined exclusively for private use, it is also called a domestic oratory, though the term "domestic oratory" is less extensive than the term "private oratory." The faithful in general do not enjoy the right of frequenting a private oratory. This is evident from the Code and also from the fact that this right is denied the faithful even in regard to semi-public oratories. The term "family" as used in the definition of a private oratory must be taken in its usual and natural meaning; hence, corporations or moral persons whose physical members are sometimes referred to as a family are not included in the term. However, all the inhabitants of a house living under the authority of the same head of the family are included under the term.[22]

There is also another type of oratory which the Code regards as private and mentions in canon 1190. "Small chapels erected in a cemetery by private individuals or families over their burial place have the nature of private oratories." [23] The Code considers them

[20] Cf. Vermeersch-Creusen, *Epitome Iuris Canonici,* II, n. 498; Cocchi, *Commentarium,* V, n. 29. Both authors cite the decree of 1901, which is not found in any authentic collection.

[21] Coronata, *Institutiones Iuris Canonici,* II, n. 766; Vermeersch-Creusen, *Epitome Iuris Canonici,* II, n. 498; Feldhaus, *Oratories,* p. 74.

[22] Cf. Augustine, *A Commentary* (3. ed., St. Louis: B. Herder & Co., 1931), VI, 68; Feldhaus, *Oratories,* p. 75.

[23] Can. 1190, translated by Woywod, *A Practical Commentary,* II, 23.

private since they are erected by private persons for their own private use. Cemetery chapels of this kind, though numerous in Europe, are extremely rare in this country. The chapels erected in our cemeteries are not private but public chapels; they are erected and intended not for a singly private person or family, but for all the faithful of the locality in which the cemetery is situated, as well as for any other of the faithful who may wish to visit it.[24]

The oratories of cardinals and bishops, either residential or titular, although they are private oratories, nevertheless enjoy all the privileges of semi-public oratories.[25] The reason the Code devotes a special canon to them is not only to safeguard the privileges which they have long enjoyed, but also to obviate all doubt as to their status.[26]

Private oratories, therefore, may be subdivided into three classes: (1) oratories erected in private houses for the convenience of the family or of private individuals; (2) private oratories erected in cemeteries; (3) private oratories of cardinals and bishops.

Article 3. Dedication of Churches

The present law is very clear about the necessity and the obligation of dedicating new churches. The Code in canon 822, § 1, demands that churches and oratories be dedicated either by consecration, or at least by blessing; otherwise the Mass may not be celebrated there. Dedication is a sacred rite instituted by the Church. In virtue of it a profane place is rendered sacred and is perpetually destined for divine worship by a lawful minister.[27] The dedicatory rite may be performed in one of two ways: (1) by consecration; (2) by blessing.

[24] Vermeersch-Creusen, *Epitome Iuris Canonici*, II, n. 499; Brehm, *Synopsis Additionum et Variationum in Editione Typica Missalis Romani* (Ratisbonae, 1920), p. 201 (hereafter cited *Synopsis*).

[25] Can. 1189.

[26] Cf. Benedictus XIV, ep. encycl. *Magno cum*, 2 iul. 1751, § 2—*Fontes*, n. 413; Feldhaus, *Oratories*, p. 76.

[27] Cf. can. 1154; can. 1191; Wernz, *Ius Decretalium*, III, n. 436; Muratori, *Liturgia Romana Vetus*, II, 467-489.

It may be observed here that one should employ the words "consecration" or "blessing" in order to be more specific in describing the act of dedication. To say that a church was "dedicated" simply means that it was set aside for divine worship. Without further explanation the statement lacks full information whether the church was consecrated or blessed. If the rite is solemnly administered, it is called a consecration or a solemn dedication, otherwise it is known as a simple dedication or as a blessing. The Pontifical contains the rite of consecration,[28] and the Ritual, that of the blessing.[29] Though these rites differ as sacramentals, their canonical effects are identical; both render a hitherto profane place sacred with all the consequences that this implies. In the dedication of places to divine worship the prescriptions of the approved liturgical books must be observed.[30]

The present law enacts that new churches or oratories destined for public worship must be dedicated or set aside for that purpose only, either by the ceremony of solemn dedication called consecration, or by a simple dedication or blessing. Mass cannot be celebrated nor can other acts of public worship be held in a new church building before it is first dedicated to divine worship by solemn consecration or at least by simple blessing.[31]

If it can prudently be foreseen that the church will eventually be converted to profane purposes, the ordinary shall not give his consent for building the same, or, if it has already been built, shall neither consecrate nor bless it.

"Cathedral churches should be dedicated by solemn consecration and also, in so far as possible, collegiate, conventual, and parochial churches. A church built of wood, or iron or other metal, may be

[28] *Pontificale Romanum*, pars II, *De Ecclesiae Dedicatione seu Consecratione.*

[29] *Rituale Romanum,* tit. VIII, c. 27, *Ritus Benedicendi Novam Ecclesiam seu Oratorium Publicum.*

[30] Can. 2; can. 1154.

[31] Can. 1165, § 1.—"Divina officia celebrari in nova ecclesia nequeunt, antequam eadem vel solemni consecratione vel saltem benedictione divino cultui fuerit dedicata."

blessed, but it cannot be consecrated."[32] The Congregation of Sacred Rites replied to the bishop of San Salvador that a church built of wood, no matter how ornate in the interior and beautiful on the outside, cannot be consecrated.[33] The same Congregation later, in 1909, replied that cement churches could be consecrated, provided that the places for the twelve anointed crosses on the walls and the supports of columns of the main door, were of stone.[34]

The minister of the valid consecration of a church or oratory is any bishop, even a heretic or a schismatic, provided the substantial form of the *Pontificale Romanum* is used. This consists essentially in the anointing of the twelve crosses on the walls by a bishop following the prescribed form at least in substance.[35] Similarly any priest with a special privilege granted either by the Holy See or by the common law can validly consecrate, but only within the limits prescribed by the privilege or the concession.[36] Cardinals, abbots and prelates *nullius,* vicars and prefects apostolic by virtue of the common law enjoy this privilege.[37] Though the Code in canon 1155 gives the right to the local ordinary, it is commonly held that cardinals can validly consecrate churches and oratories throughout the world, even without the consent of the local ordinary.[38] According to the common law the right to consecrate a church or oratory, even though it belongs to regulars, pertains to the ordinary of the place where the building is situated, provided the ordinary has the episcopal character. The vicar general, even though he is a bishop, cannot without a special mandate consecrate new churches or oratories in the diocese.[39]

[32] Can. 1165, §§ 3-4, translated by Woywod, *A Practical Commentary,* II, 7-8.

[33] S. R. C., *Sancti Salvatoris in America,* 11 apr. 1902—*Decr. Auth.* n. 4094.

[34] S. R. C., *Portus Principis,* 12 nov. 1909—*Decr. Auth.*, n. 4240.

[35] Can. 1148; Augustine, *A Commentary,* VI, 5.

[36] Can. 1147.

[37] Cf. can. 1155, § 1; 239, § 1, 20°; 323, § 2; 294, § 2.

[38] Coronata, *De Sacramentis,* II, n. 238; Bliley, *Altars according to the Code of Canon Law,* The Catholic University of America Canon Law Studies, n. 38 (Washington, D. C.: The Catholic University of America, 1927), p. 70 (hereafter cited *Altars*); Feldhaus, *Oratories,* p. 86.

[39] Can. 1155.

"The right to bless the churches or oratories of both seculars and non-exempt religious belongs to the Ordinary of the place in which these are situated; if the place belongs to an exempt clerical religious body, the major superior has the right to bless it. Both the Ordinary of the territory and the major superior of the religious community may delegate a priest for the blessing of such places. Notwithstanding any privilege to the contrary, nobody can consecrate or bless a place without the consent of the ordinary." [40] Any priest, however, can validly perform the blessing of sacred places, but without the necessary permission his action would be illicit.[41] On the occasion of the solemn dedication or the consecration of a church the consecrating bishop and also those who ask for the consecration are bound to fast on the previous day. This fast before the consecration of a church follows the rules of the common law on fasting, that is, it does not include abstinence.[42] "Even though the present law permits the consecration of an altar separately from the church, it nevertheless requires that at least the main altar should also be consecrated in one and the same ceremony, or, if the main altar is already consecrated, another altar should be consecrated." [43]

Article 4. Dedication of Oratories

Oratories must be either consecrated or blessed in order to be constituted as a legitimate place for the celebration of Mass.[44] Since not all oratories are governed by the same laws in regard to consecration and blessing, it is necessary here to distinguish and clarify the characteristics of the different types of oratories.

In a few words the Code applies to public oratories all the laws that govern churches: *"Oratoria publica eodem iure quo*

[40] Can. 1156 and Can. 1157, as translated by Woywod, *A Practical Commentary,* II, 2.

[41] Can. 1147, § 3.

[42] Can. 1166, § 2; Pontifical Commission for the Interpretation of the Code, 20 iul. 1929—*AAS*, XXI (1929), Coronata, *Institutiones Iuris Canonici,* II, n. 737.

[43] Can. 1165, § 5, translated by Woywod, *A Practical Commentary,* II, 8.

[44] Can. 822, § 1.

ecclesiae reguntur."[45] Hence, what has been said above as regards the consecration and the blessing of churches applies also to public oratories. There is, therefore, a strict obligation which calls for the consecration or the blessing of these oratories. On the other hand, private oratories can neither be consecrated nor blessed in the manner of churches. They can, however, be blessed according to a specially prescribed form contained in the *Roman Ritual.*[46]

Although a public oratory must be consecrated or blessed, the same obligation is not to be extended to a semi-public oratory. Though a private oratory cannot be consecrated or blessed in the manner of churches, either of these sacred rites may be applied to a semi-public oratory, there is neither an obligation nor a prohibition to consecrate or bless a semi-public oratory. If it is not dedicated by consecration or blessing, a semi-public oratory may be blessed with the ordinary "*Benedictio Loci vel Domus.*"[47] Concerning the celebration of Mass in a place which is not consecrated or blessed more will be said later.

Article 5. Loss of Consecration and Blessing of Churches

The celebration of the Holy Sacrifice is permitted in churches and oratories only as long as their sacred character has not been lost by desecration or defiled by violation. Churches and oratories are endowed with a sacred character when they are dedicated to divine worship by the liturgical rite of consecration or blessing. Concerning this matter it is necessary at the outset to clarify the terms used in the Code. The term "*execratio*" is usually translated by "desecration," and the expressions "*pollutio*" and "*violatio*" convey the idea of a violation.[48]

The desecration of a church may be defined as the removal of the sacred character which was given to the church through its

[45] Can. 1191, § 1.

[46] *Rituale Romanum,* Appendix: *Benedictio Oratorii Privati seu Domestici,* n. 16.

[47] *Rituale Romanum,* tit. VIII, c. 6.

[48] Gulczynski, *The Desecration and Violation of Churches,* The Catholic University of America Canon Law Studies, n. 159 (Washington, D. C.: The Catholic University of America Press, 1942), p. vii.

consecration or blessing.[49] In other words, the desecration of a church is the loss of its consecration or blessing.[50] The Code mentions three ways in which a church may lose its consecration or blessing, namely: (a) by the total destruction of the church; (b) by the collapse of the major part of the walls; (c) by the conversion of the church to profane purposes by the authority of the local ordinary in accordance with the prescriptions of canon 1187.[51]

In the Code it is of importance to note that reference to the desecration of churches the term "desecration" is used indiscriminately in reference to both consecrated and blessed churches. This must be concluded both from the statement that is made in canon 1170, which specifically mentions both consecrated and blessed churches as governed by the same rule regarding the possibility of their desecration. The Code in listing the three causes which effect the desecration of a church indicates with the use of the word *"nisi"* that this is an exhaustive list. Hence, the desecration of a church cannot be brought about by any other cause except by the three enumerated in the law.[52]

(*a*) *Total Destruction*

The Code thus provides that a church becomes desecrated when it is totally destroyed. Hence, when the edifice is rebuilt it needs to be consecrated or blessed again before Mass can lawfully be celebrated there, since this reconstruction connotes the destruction of the old and the erection of a new building.[53]

In connection with the desecration of a church caused by total destruction, the question may be asked: What exactly is meant by a total destruction? The ordinary and obvious meaning is the

[49] Wernz-Vidal, *Ius Canonicum* (7 vols. in 8, Romae: apud Aedes Universitatis Gregorianae, 1923-1946), IV, n. 365.

[50] Many, *Praelectiones de Locis Sacris* (Parisiis, 1904), n. 25.

[51] Can. 1170. Consecrationem vel benedictionem ecclesia non amittit, nisi tota destructa fuerit, vel maior parietum pars corruerit, vel in usus profanos ab Ordinario loci redacta sit, ad normam can. 1187.

[52] Cf. Gulczynski, *The Desecration and Violation of Churches,* p. 50.

[53] Can. 1165, § 1; cf. also Wernz, *Ius Decretalium,* III, n. 441; Coronata, *De Locis et Temporibus Sacris* (Taurinorum Augustae: Marietti, 1922), n. 26.

complete leveling or demolition of the entire structure, so that no part remains standing. The Congregation of Sacred Rites issued a decree which declared that a newly constructed church had to be consecrated even though it was built upon the site of an old church which had previously fallen completely to ruins.[54]

Contemplated also is the case in which a church may become destroyed to such an extent that only one wall, or a small portion of the walls, remains standing, as may happen, for example, in consequence of an earthquake, or as a result of bombing in time of war. The destruction caused by these factors may weaken and shake the remaining walls to such an extent that they cannot be used in the reconstruction of the church, and hence the state of the building is equivalent to a total destruction. The term "total destruction," therefore, may be understood as including the demolition or collapse of the church, even though parts of the walls remain standing, once it is manifest that these walls cannot be used in the reconstruction of the building because of their unsafe condition.[55]

(*b*) *Destruction of the Major Part of the Walls*

According to canon 1170, the second cause effecting the desecration of a church is the destruction of the major part of the walls. The quantity and not the relative position or importance of the walls is considered here. The desecration is determined by the amount of the area of the destroyed walls, and not by the importance of the part destroyed.[56] The principle for determining the desecration is that the destruction of the slightest amount over and above half of the total area of the walls of the church will cause the loss of the consecration or blessing. The Congregation of Sacred Rites on several occasions in its responses declared that a church did not have to be reconsecrated when the destroyed part of the walls was comparatively less than the part which remained standing.[57]

[54] S. R. C., *Caesaraugustana*, 31 aug. 1872, ad I—*Fontes*, n. 6045; *Decr. Auth.*, n. 3269.

[55] Gulczynski, *The Desecration and Violation of Churches*, p. 50; Augustine, *A Commentary*, VI, 32.

[56] Coronata, *Institutiones Iuris Canonici*, II, n. 741.

[57] S. R. C., *Marianopolitana*, 20 febr. 1874—*Decr. Auth.*, n. 3326; S. R. C.,

It is further to be noted that, if one is to consider a church as desecrated, the destruction of the major part of the walls must be in evidence at one and the same time. It is the common opinion of the authors that a church does not lose the consecration or blessing when small portions of the walls are destroyed at different times but are immediately rebuilt, even though this is done with the intention of rebuilding the entire church, provided that at no one time the destroyed part was greater than the part remaining.[58]

(c) *Reduction of a Church to Profane Uses*

Canon 1170 states explicitly that a church loses its consecration or blessing when it is converted to profane uses by the authority of the ordinary. The Holy See is opposed to such reduction of churches to secular uses, as is evident from the prescriptions of canon 1165, § 2, whereby the local ordinary is forbidden to give his consent to the erection of a church, or if it is already built, to its consecration or blessing, when it can be prudently foreseen that in the course of time it will be used for profane purposes.

Occasionally it may happen that unforeseen circumstances will necessitate the reduction of a church to profane uses. The local ordinary in accordance with the norms of canon 1187 effects this reduction. When an unauthorized agent subjects a church to profane usage it does not lose its consecration or blessing, and consequently does not have to be dedicated again to divine worship; at most such unlawful usage might cause a church to become violated.[59]

Though the present law does not prescribe any rite to be used in the reduction of a church to profane use or secular status, it is

Barcinonen., 16 ian. 1886, ad I—*Decr. Auth.*, n. 3651; S. R. C., *Marianopolitana*, 11 mart. 1871—*Decr. Auth.*, n. 3240.

[58] Coronata, *De Locis et Temporibus Sacris*, n. 26; Gasparri, *De Sanctissima Eucharistia*, I, n. 181; Many, *Praelectiones de Locis Sacris*, n. 27; Schmalzgrueber, *Ius Ecclesiasticum Universum*, Lib. III, tit. 40, n. 28; cf. Gulczynski, *The Desecration and Violation of Churches*, p. 54.

[59] Coronata, *Institutiones Iuris Canonici*, II, n. 741; Ayrinhac, *Administrative Legislation*, p. 20; Augustine, *A Commentary*, VI, 33; Beste, *Introductio in Codicem*, p. 563.

only fitting that some liturgical rite should be used on such an occasion. There is suggested a ceremony based on that prescribed by IV Provincial Council of Milan (1576).[60]

Any church desecrated in any of the foregoing ways must be consecrated or blessed again. Only then is it constituted as a legitimate place for the celebration of the Holy Sacrifice.

Article 6. Violation of Churches

Even though the celebration of Mass is forbidden in violated churches as well as in desecrated churches, still the violation of churches differs radically from their desecration. By desecration a church loses its consecration or blessing, whereas by violation a church retains its consecration and blessing, but the effects of the consecration or blessing are suspended. According to law this suspension is caused by certain specified acts committed in the church. Suspension of the effects of consecration or blessing renders the church an unlawful place for the celebration of the divine services until the suspension is removed by means of the sacred rite of reconciliation.[61]

The violation of a church is brought about by the specific acts and conditions enumerated in canon 1172, § 1;

> Ecclesia violatur infra recensitis tantum actibus, dummodo certi sint, notorii, et in ipsa ecclesia positi:
> 1° Delicto homicidii;
> 2° Iniuriosa et gravi sanguinis effusione;
> 3° Impiis et sordidis usibus, quibus ecclesia addicta fuerit;
> 4° Sepultura infidelis vel excommunicati post sententiam declaratoriam vel condemnatoriam.

The canon here quoted clearly indicates that there are only four factors which can bring about the violation of a church. The wording of the first part of the canon is such that it excludes the possibility of the church becoming violated in any other way than by the commission of any one of the four acts specifically enumer-

60 Cf. Gulczynski, *The Desecration and Violation of Churches*, p. 60.
61 Gulczynski, *op. cit.*, p. 65; cf. can. 1173, § 1.

ated in the law. These four acts constitute an exhaustive list of the causes which can effect the violation of a church.[62]

If an act is to constitute a cause for the violation of a church the law postulates that the act be: (1) certain, that is, not involved in any reasonable doubt regarding its actual commission; (2) notorious, either in law or in fact; and (3) perpetrated within the church itself. The present law states that a church is violated if an act of homicide has been perpetrated therein; if an unjust and serious shedding of blood had taken place, if the church has been subjected to impious or sordid uses, and finally if an infidel or an excommunicate after the intervention of a condemnatory or of a declaratory sentence has received burial in the church. In addition to the commission of any one of these four acts the three aforementioned conditions must be present in each case, otherwise the violation and its consequences do not follow.[63]

Before the rite of reconciliation has been performed in a violated church, it is not lawful to celebrate the divine services, to administer the sacraments, or to bury the dead. When the violation happens during the divine services, these must cease immediately with the following exception. The general rubrics of the *Missal* prescribes that, if during the celebration of Mass the violation occurs before the Canon, the Mass must be discontinued at once; but if the violation occurs after the Canon of the Mass has already been begun, the Mass shall not be discontinued.[64] In consequence, however, of the present law this prescription of the rubric must be corrected. The present ruling is that, if a violation of the church occurs before the Canon of the Mass, or after the Communion, the Mass must be discontinued immediately; if it occurs between the Canon, i.e., beginning with the words "Te igitur . . .", and the Communion,

[62] Beste, *Introductio in Codicem,* p. 564.

[63] For a full explanation of the factors effecting the violation of a church and the three conditions required in the canon to make the act violative, one may consult the work of Gulczynski, *The Desecration and Violation of Churches,* pp. 69 ff.

[64] *Missale Romanum,* tit. *De defectibus in celebratione missarum occurentibus,* c. X, *de defectibus in ministerio ipso occurrentibus,* n. 2: "Si, sacerdote celebrante, violetur ecclesia ante Canonem, dimittatur Missa; si post canonem, non dimittatur."

the Mass is to be continued as far as the Communion, i.e., until the prayer "Corpus tuum . . ." inclusively.[65]

Before the Holy Sacrifice can be celebrated lawfully therein, a violated church must be restored to its pristine condition by means of the sacred rite of "reconciliation."[66] The reconciliation must take place as soon as possible according to the rites prescribed in the *Roman Pontifical* and in the *Roman Ritual.*[67] It has been officially declared that the need of saying of Mass in a violated church, even in a case of serious necessity, does not cancel the obligation of performing the rite of reconciliation.[68]

The obligation of reconciling a violated church is a grave one, and therefore the blemish effected by the violation must be effaced as soon as possible. This obligation exists only when the violation is certain;[69] if the violation is doubtful, a provisional (*ad cautelam*) reconciliation may take place, but there is no obligation to make it.[70] Since the liturgical rites of reconciliation of a consecrated and of a blessed church are explained in detail in books specifically dealing with this matter, it is unnecessary to treat the matter further here.[71]

It is appropriate, however, at this point to make a few observations in reference to oratories. The Code does not provide any specific legislation concerning the violation of oratories, but canon 1191, § 1, applies to public oratories all the laws that govern churches. The consecration of a public oratory is not prescribed in law, but is permitted. If it is not consecrated, a public oratory must at least be blessed, otherwise divine services cannot be celebrated therein.[72] By their consecration or blessing, therefore, public ora-

[65] Can. 1173, § 2; cf. also Gulczynski, *The Desecration and Violation of Churches,* p. 91.

[66] Can. 1173, § 1; Coronata, *De Locis et Temporibus Sacris,* n. 30; Cocchi, *Commentarium,* V, n. 19.

[67] Can. 1174, § 1.

[68] S. R. C., *Oppiden.,* 19 aug. 1634, ad II—*Decr. Auth.,* n. 611; *Coll. S. C. de Prop. Fide,* n. 78.

[69] Can. 1172, § 1.

[70] Can. 1174, § 2; Gulczynski, *The Desecration and Violation of Churches,* p. 93.

[71] Cf., for example, Gulczynski, *The Desecration and Violation of Churches,* p. 95.

[72] Can. 1165, § 3; can. 1191, § 1; can. 1165, § 1.

tories are constituted sacred places, and as such they are subject to violation in the same manner as consecrated or blessed churches.[73]

The possibility of semi-public oratories being subject to violation depends upon whether or not they are consecrated or blessed after the manner of churches. It is not required by law that such oratories be consecrated or blessed in a solemn manner; they may be blessed with the so-called *benedictio loci* or the *benedictio domus novae*. Such a blessing, however, is merely invocative, and does not constitute a semi-public oratory a sacred place; hence, such an oratory is not subject to violation.[74]

Private oratories, that is, domestic oratories and cemetery chapels, likewise are not subject to violation, since they are not sacred places in the canonical sense.[75]

Article 7. The Celebration of Mass in Oratories

Canon 822, § 1, prescribes that Mass be said in a church or oratory which must be consecrated or blessed. Canon 1191 states that public oratories are governed by the same laws as churches. Hence, what has been said of churches with regard to their erection, dedication, desecration, and violation in the preceding articles applies also to public oratories.

In semi-public oratories, in accordance with canon 1193, the present law allows the celebration of Mass on all days, unless the ordinary in granting permission for the erection of the oratory placed limitations on its use, for example, by forbidding the celebration of Mass there on certain solemn feasts.[76] To be effective, these limitations as affecting the celebration of Mass in a semi-public oratory must be introduced by the ordinary when he grants his permission for the erection of the semi-public oratory. The Holy See has in many decisions declared that after the oratory has been

[73] Coronata, *De Locis et Temporibus Sacris*, n. 28, (4).

[74] Vermeersch-Creusen, *Epitome Iuris Canonici*, II, n. 489.

[75] Can. 1196; Augustine, *A Commentary*, VI, 83; Coronata, *De Locis et Temporibus Sacris*, n. 28.

[76] Cappello, *De Sacramentis*, I, n. 708; Feldhaus, *Oratories*, p. 122.

erected it is unlawful for ordinaries to place these restrictions.[77] These limitations, as generally imposed, have reference to conflict with parochial rights, to the functions of Holy Week, and to the reservation, exposition and benediction of the Blessed Sacrament. With regard to the celebration of Mass in semi-public oratories there are usually no restrictions imposed by ordinaries for this is generally the primary purpose of their erection.[78]

The celebration of Mass in private oratories falls outside the scope of canon 822, § 1, since this canon requires for the celebration of Mass an oratory which must be either blessed or consecrated, and in virtue of canon 1196, § 1, private oratories cannot be either blessed or consecrated. The Code, however, in canons 1194-1195 clearly and specifically states the regulations with regard to the celebration of Mass in private oratories.

Canon 1194.—In privatis coemeteriorum aediculis, de quibus in can. 1190, Ordinarius loci permittere habitualiter potest etiam plurium Missarum celebrationem; in aliis oratoriis domesticis, nonnisi unius Missae, per modum actus, in casu aliquo extraordinario, iusta et rationabili de causa; Ordinarius autem has permissiones ne elargiatur, nisi ad normam can. 1192, § 2.

In private cemetery chapels the local ordinary can permit habitually the celebration of even several Masses daily,[79] and furthermore those who assist at Mass there fulfill their obligation to hear the preceptive Mass.[80] These chapels must be so constructed that the altar is removed by a distance of at least one yard from the nearest

[77] S. C. C., *Vercellen.*, 3 aug. 1675—*Fontes*, n. 2838; S. C. C., *Nitrien.*, 12 febr. 1735—*Fontes*, n. 3442; S. C. C., *Comaclen.*, 17 iun. 1769—*Fontes*, n. 3764; S. C. C., *Lunen.*, 4 apr. 1772—*Fontes*, n. 3782; S. C. C., *Savonen.*, 28 iul., 9 sept. 1724—*Fontes*, nn. 3281, 3285.

[78] Feldhaus, *Oratories*, p. 122; cf. also S. R. C., *Secovien.*, 10 nov. 1906—*Decr. Auth.*, n. 4192.

[79] Feldhaus, *Oratories*, p. 119.

[80] Can. 1249.

tomb; otherwise it is unlawful to celebrate Mass there.[81] This distance is computed by measurement from the tomb to the table of a consecrated altar, or to the table on which a portable altar is placed.[82]

The local ordinary is empowered to grant habitual or permanent permission for the celebration of several daily Masses in private cemetery chapels. In all other (non-cemetery) private oratories the local ordinary may permit not several but only one Mass to be said. Furthermore, this permission can legitimately be granted only under the following conditions: (1) He can only give permission for each individual case (*per modum actus*), not habitually or perpetually; (2) there must be in the prudent judgment of the ordinary a just and reasonable cause for the concession; and (3) canon 1194 requires that the local ordinary shall give his permission only on some extraordinary occasion. By the insertion of this phrase the Code restricts the power of the local ordinary to a great extent. The mere fact that there is a just and reasonable cause for granting the permission does not warrant its concession unless the ordinary judges that the case in question is also an extraordinary, exceptional or urgent one. Times of war, pestilence, etc., are given as examples of an extraordinary occasion.[83]

Although it is left to the judgment of the ordinary of the place to decide when the aforementioned conditions are verified, the wording of the canon is so emphatic that the power is to be used sparingly. If, however, he judges that the circumstances justify it, he can give permission for the celebration of one Mass. As the canon seems to imply, the term "one Mass" signifies not just one single Mass, but rather one daily Mass. He can permit the celebration of daily Mass as long as the circumstances that warrant its concession continue.[84]

[81] Can. 1202, § 2.

[82] S. R. C., 25 oct. 1933—Bouscaren, *The Canon Law Digest*, II, 348; Coronata, *De Sacramentis*, I, n. 245.

[83] Coronata, *Institutiones Iuris Canonici*, II, n. 770; Feldhaus, *Oratories*, p. 120.

[84] Cappello states that the ordinary can concede permission for as long as eight or ten days, and can renew it as often as the reason for its concession still continues. But if it is foreseen that the cause will continue for a very long or indefinite period of time, the ordinary should refer the case to the

That the power of the ordinary as stated in canon 1194 is not limited to the granting of permission for the celebration of one single Mass is defended by almost all commentators of the Code.[85] Thus an examination of the restrictions enacted in canon 1194 reveals that the power of the ordinary to allow the celebration of Mass in private oratories is very limited. These limitations are tantamount to a reservation of this power to the Holy See, for only in the exceptional cases noted in canon 1194 is he permitted to use his power. Though it is always lawful for any member of the faithful to seek and obtain permission for the erection of a domestic oratory destined for divine worship, still the permission to celebrate Mass daily or even frequently is obtained only by means of an apostolic indult.[86]

The general law governing the celebration of Mass in domestic oratories granted by apostolic indult is stated in canon 1195:

> § 1. "In oratoriis domesticis ex indulto Apostolicae Sedis, nisi aliud in eodem indulto expresse caveatur, celebrari potest, postquam Ordinarius oratorium visitaverit et probaverit ad normam can. 1192, § 2, unica Missa, eaque lecta, singulis diebus, exceptis festis solemnioribus; sed aliae functiones ecclesiasticae ibidem ne fiant.
>
> § 2. Ordinarius vero, dummodo iusta adsint et rationabiles causae, diversae ab eis ob quas indultum concessum fuit, etiam sollemnioribus festis permittere potest per modum actus Missae celebrationem." [87]

Holy See, though meanwhile he may permit one daily Mass—*De Sacramentis*, I, n. 790; cf. also Cocchi, *Commentarium*, V, n. 32; Feldhaus, *Oratories*, p. 121.

[85] For a full explanation consult Feldhaus, *Oratories*, p. 122.

[86] Vermeersch-Creusen, *Epitome Iuris Canonici*, II, n. 502.

[87] Can. 1195: "Unless the contrary is expressly stipulated in the indult Mass may be celebrated in private oratories which have been erected by indult of the Holy See, after the Ordinary has visited and approved the place as specified in canon 1192. One low Mass may then be said each day, except on the more solemn feasts of the Church, and other ecclesiastical functions shall not be held in the oratory. For good reasons other than those for which the indult was granted, the Ordinary may allow Mass even on the more solemn feasts *per modum actus*—which means, not habitually, but by way of an exception

Thus the more general regulations usually given in an apostolic indult which allows the celebration of Mass in private oratories are summarized in this canon. It is explicitly stated in the canon that, if the indult contains other provisions than those set up by the general law, the particular prescriptions of the indult, and not the general rulings of canon 1195, are to be observed.

The indult which permits the celebration of Mass in private oratories is commonly called the indult of a private oratory, and according to the present law is granted by the Holy See through the Sacred Congregation of the Sacraments.[88] The petition for the indult is to be sent through the ordinary of the place where the oratory is situated. He is to testify to the causes for the petition and to add his recommendations. The usually given causes are old age, infirmity, and distance from the church.[89]

The Holy See does not concede this special privilege unless it has moral certainty of the need and merits of the petitioner. The rescript granting the indult is in most cases sent to the ordinary, who in virtue of canon 1195, § 1, must inspect and approve the oratory as a fitting place for the offering of the Holy Sacrifice.[90] The general law in canon 1195 states that only one low Mass may be celebrated daily except on the more solemn feasts in a private oratory enjoying an apostolic indult. The Mass, therefore, must be a low Mass (*Missa lecta*). Hence, even though the indult does not contain the word *"lecta"* in its usual wording, this omission does not justify the celebration of High Mass.[91] However, if the indult explicitly permitted the celebration of High Mass or even Solemn Mass, these

in particular cases." Translated by Woywod, *A Practical Commentary,* II, p. 24,

88 Cf. can. 249, § 2; Pius X, const. *Sapienti consilio,* 29 iun. 1908, ad I—*Fontes,* n. 682; *AAS,* I (1909), 86.

89 Coronata, *De Locis et Temporibus Sacris,* n. 88; Regatillo, *Ius Sacramentarium,* I, n. 212; Gasparri, *De Sanctissima Eucharistia,* I, n. 235.

90 Feldhaus, *Oratories,* p. 124.

91 The author Many writes: "Missa *cantata* celebrari nequit in his oratoriis; quum enim missa sollemnis sit res valde gravis, ex eo quod indultum de ea sileat, concludi debet, praesertim sic rem interpretante consuetudine eam non concedi."—*Praelectiones de Locis Sacris,* n. 94, 6, a.

exceptional privileges can be used by virtue of the clause in canon 1195 which allows for other provisions of a particular nature.

The Code restricts the privilege by allowing only one Mass each day in domestic oratories. Though one Mass daily generally satisfies the needs of the petitioner, occasion may arise when the celebration of more than one daily Mass is required. The following are cases when a plurality of Masses is lawful:

(a) If Mass is offered in a private oratory by a cardinal in virtue of the privilege granted to him by canon 239, § 1, 14°, his Mass does not exclude the celebration of the daily Mass allowed by the indult;

(b) if the apostolic indult expressly allows it;

(c) in cases of grave necessity, for example, when a second Mass is required for the consecration of Holy Viaticum for the dying,[92] and (d) if the indult permits Mass on the feast of Christmas, not only one but three Masses may be celebrated, even if the indult does not explicitly mention this additional privilege. None of these three Masses may be celebrated on Christmas night contrary to the ruling of canon 821, unless the indult also grants this right. The Congregation of the Council in granting an indult to a sick priest conceded this further privilege.[93]

Pope Benedict XIV in treating of indults granted to infirm priests also permitted the privilege of three Masses on Christmas day.[94] Furthermore, the authors extend the same interpretation to all private oratories possessing the privilege of the celebration of Mass on Christmas Day, irrespective of the reason in virtue of which the privilege was granted.[95] They contend that if one Mass can be

[92] S. R. C., *Florentina,* 27 aug. 1836—*Decr. Auth.*, n. 2754; cf. Feldhaus, *Oratories,* p. 125.

[93] S. C. C., 20 ian. 1725. This reply is quoted in the work of Pope Benedict XIV, *De Sacrificio Missae,* Lib. III, c. 4 n. 7.

[94] Ep. encycl. *Magno cum,* 2 iun. 1751, § 18—*Fontes,* n. 413.

[95] Ferreres writes: "Si quacumque ex causa concederetur sacrum fieri in die Natalis Domini, tunc licet illa die tres Missas ibi celebrare"—*Compendium Theologiae Moralis* (13. ed., Barcinone: E. Subirana, 1925), 1, n. 438. Cf. also Gasparri, *De Sanctissima Eucharistia,* I, n. 235; Many, *Praelectiones de Locis Sacris,* n. 88; Coronata, *De Locis et Temporibus Sacris,* n. 87; Cappello, *De Sacramentis,* I, n. 609; Prümmer, *Manuale Theologiae Moralis* (7. ed., 3 vols., Friburgi Brisgoviae: Herder, 1931), III, n. 284.

said on the feast of Christmas in a private oratory by reason of an indult, it is legitimate to say three Masses in line with the interpretation of the Congregation of the Council (1725) and the decree of Pope Benedict XIV in regard to the indult for infirm priests. However, the indult of a private oratory usually does not permit Mass on Christmas Day, and hence the matter is of little practical importance.

A question of much more practical import is the celebration in a private oratory of three Masses on All Souls' Day. The same authors apply the liberal interpretation to All Souls' Day, and hold that in virtue of any indult which allows Mass in a private oratory three Masses can be said therein on the feast of All Souls. As yet there has been no official declaration on the matter from the Holy See. Hence, it seems safe to follow the authors who teach that it is lawful to say three Masses on this day in view of the statement which is contained in canon 806, § 1.

The feast days on which Mass is not permitted in private oratories are specifically mentioned in some indults, though in many cases the rescript through which the indult is granted contains only a general clause that excepts the more solemn feasts. As regards these more solemn feasts the Congregation of Sacred Rites in a reply declared that the more solemn feasts on which Mass is forbidden in all private oratories are those which are specified in the *Caeremoniale Episcoporum,* and are at the same time feasts to which is attached the obligation to hear Mass.[96] Thus according to this decision the feasts which exclude Mass in a private oratory must be not only listed in the *Caeremoniale Episcoporum* but also feasts on which the faithful are obliged to hear Mass.

The following days according to canon 1247, § 1, are the feasts on which the faithful are bound to hear Mass: Christmas, Circumcision, Epiphany, Ascension, Corpus Christi, Immaculate Conception, Assumption, the Feast of St. Joseph, the Feast of Sts. Peter and Paul, and the Feast of All Saints. Easter and Pentecost are understood as also included, though they are not mentioned in the canon

[96] *Caeremoniale Episcoporum,* "Illi per se sunt sollemniores, in casu, qui describuntur in Caeremoniali Episcoporum, L. II, c. XXXIV, § 2, et de praecepto servantur."

since they coincide with Sundays. Of these twelve feasts, only Circumcision and Corpus Christi are not mentioned in the *Caeremoniale Episcoporum;* hence the remaining ten feasts exclude the celebration of Mass in private oratories unless the contrary is stated in the indult. The last three days of Holy Week must also be excepted, since private Masses on those days are forbidden in all oratories.[97]

In the United States, in virtue of an indult obtained by the Fathers of the III Plenary Council of Baltimore (1884) the Feasts of the Epiphany, of Corpus Christi, of St. Joseph, and of Sts. Peter and Paul are not feasts to which the obligation to hear Mass is attached.[98] This indult still remains in force in view of canon 1247, § 3. Hence in the private oratories of this country, unless the contrary is indicated in the indult, Mass may be celebrated on all days of the year except the following ten: Christmas, the three last days of Holy Week, Easter, Ascension, Pentecost, Assumption, Immaculate Conception and the Feast of All Saints.

But even with reference to these more solemn feasts, canon 1195, § 2, also provides that the ordinary may permit the celebration of Mass under the condition that there exist just and reasonable causes other than those in virtue of which the indult was granted, and that such a permission be given not habitually, but only for each particular and individual case. The Code demands that these causes be different from those that induced the concession of the indult, as otherwise the ordinary would act directly against the will of the Holy See which forbade the celebration of Mass on these days despite the reasons given in the petition for the indult. These limitations on the power of the ordinary are based on a reply of the Sacred Congregation of the Sacraments, March 22, 1915, which contains these limitations.[99]

The Holy See in the indults granting privileges of private oratories to priests usually specifies those feasts on which the celebration of Mass is prohibited in the oratory, and generally the days specified are less numerous than the aforementioned ten. Usually indults

[97] Cf. *supra,* Chapter V, pp. 66ff.

[98] *Acta et Decreta Concilii Plenarii Baltimorensis Tertii A. D. MDCCCXXXIV,* (Baltimorae: John Murphy, 1886), n. III, p. 57.

[99] *AAS,* VII (1915), 147.

granted to sick or aged priests exclude only the last three days of Holy Week. In indults granted to the laity for their convenience in attending Mass all the more solemn feasts are usually excluded. The reason for excepting these feasts is contained in canon 467, § 2, which obliges the faithful to attend Mass in their own parish church frequently when this can be conveniently done.

There is another notable difference between the oratories of priests and those of the laity. In the oratories of priests the right of celebrating Mass is limited to the priest in whose favor the indult was granted, whereas in the oratories of the laity any priest with the ordinary faculty of saying Mass in the diocese can say the one Mass in the oratory.[100]

[100] Feldhaus, *Oratories*, p. 129.

CHAPTER VIII

THE PROXIMATE PLACE FOR THE CELEBRATION OF MASS

Article 1. The Altar

The general law concerning the place for the celebration of Mass demands that it be said in a consecrated or blessed church or oratory. Furthermore it requires that it be said in a particular place in the church or oratory, namely, on the altar.[1] The altar in the strict liturgical sense consists of a flat stone table, rectangular or square, fixed or movable, and consecrated for the offering of the Holy Sacrifice of the Mass. In the usual acceptation of the word, adopted in the rubrics themselves, the name altar is given both to the table that rests on the foundation, and also the support of the table.

According to the liturgical acceptation and with reference to the use and location of the altar in the church or oratory, the following distinctions are made in regard to altars upon which Mass may be celebrated.

In accordance with the manner of construction and its relation to the possibility of consecration in the strict liturgical sense, an altar is either fixed (*altare fixum seu immobile*) or portable (*altare portatile seu mobile, ara portatilis, petra sacra*). "A fixed or immovable altar is a permanent structure of stone, consisting of the upper table (*mensa*), upon which the Holy Sacrifice is offered, and the supports or base (*stipes*), all of which are consecrated together as a whole." [2]

A portable or movable altar consists of a solid piece of natural stone, generally of small size, which alone is consecrated; or the

[1] Can. 822, § 1.

[2] Can. 1197, § 1, 1°, as translated by Woywod, *A Practical Commentary*, II, 25.

same stone with its support, which, however, is not consecrated with the table as one whole.[3]

Midway between fixed and portable altars is another type of altar, quite prevalent in churches which may be called quasi-fixed, or in the words of the Congregation of Sacred Rites *ad modum fixi.*[4] This altar is a permanent structure of wood, cement, or any other suitable or becoming material or composition, in which a consecrated altar stone is inserted. In the liturgical and canonical sense these structures enjoy the character only of portable altars. They have, however, the advantage that they can be made privileged altars,[5] and also can receive the title of a saint, which portable altars in themselves cannot possess.[6]

The fixed altar is the altar in the truest sense of the word, and is the normal altar for the church, so that in every consecrated church there must be at least one fixed altar.[7] The portable altar supplies the place of the fixed altar in the church, when for a variety of reasons a fixed altar cannot be built. The present law sanctions the use of portable altars, and has regulations governing the construction and use of such altars.[8] By reason of excellence and location altars may be divided into: privileged, papal, high or side altars.[9]

Article 2. The Fixed Altar

A fixed or immovable altar is a permanent structure of stone, consisting of the table and the support consecrated together as one whole. The name fixed or immovable is given to it, not only because it is a permanent and immovable structure, but also because the

[3] Can. 1197, § 1, 2°. Cf. Woywod, *op. cit.*, II, 25.

[4] S. R. C., *Sancti Hippolyti,* 31 aug. 1867, ad I—*Decr. Auth.,* n. 3162; *Fontes,* n. 6018.

[5] S. R. C., *Sancti Hippolyti,* 31 aug. 1867, ad I—*Fontes,* n. 6018.

[6] Can. 1201, § 1, 2°.

[7] Can. 1197, § 2; "In ecclesia consecrata saltem unum altare, praesertim maius, debet esse immobile."

[8] Cf. can. 1197, § 2; can. 1198; can. 1199, § 1; can. 1201.

[9] Bliley, *Altars,* p. 14.

table is so firmly united to the support that one cannot be separated from the other without the resulting desecration of the altar.

The table of the fixed altar superimposed on the support must be a single entire natural stone and one not easily broken.[10] The Congregation of Sacred Rites requires natural stone of a certain degree of hardness and durability, as, for example, granite, marble, sandstone, or travertine,[11] but has refused the use of soft or brittle natural stone such as pumice stone or gypsum, in the construction of fixed altars.[12] The table of the altar must be one single slab of stone, so that a table composed of two or more pieces of stone cemented or put together in any other way cannot be validly consecrated.[13]

The support or base is that part of a fixed altar which props or holds the table of the altar. Though the Code of Canon Law does not make any particular demands as regards shape, size, or architecture, it specifically requires that the material of the support be of natural stone with the same qualities as the stone required for the table. It is not required that the base be one solid piece of stone; it may consist of at least four columns of stone.[14] At least that part of the support must be of stone where at the four corners the table of the altar comes in contact with the support, in order that the prescribed four unctions of the stone of the supports can be properly performed in the consecration of the altar; the remaining space between the columns may be empty, or may be built in with bricks or any other solid material.[15]

[10] Can. 1198, § 1.

[11] S. R. C., *Lamacen,* 29 apr. 1887—*Decr. Auth.,* n. 3674; *Fontes,* n. 6182; cf. also S. C. S. Off., 14 maii 1681—*Coll. S. C. de Prop. Fide,* I, n. 224; *Fontes,* n. 756.

[12] S. R. C., *Americae,* 13 iun. 1899—*Fontes,* n. 6297; *Decr. Auth.,* n. 4032.

[13] Coronata, *Institutiones Iuris Canonici,* II, n. 775; Bliley, *Altars,* p. 53; Many, *Praelectiones de Locis Sacris,* n. 114, 2; Gasparri, *De Sanctissima Eucharistia,* I, n. 294.

[14] Can. 1198, § 2: "stipes autem sit lapideus vel saltem latera seu columellae quibus mensa sustentatur sint ex lapide."

[15] S. R. C., *Pampilonen.,* 24 maii 1901—*Fontes,* n. 6313; cf. Augustine, *A Commentary,* VI, 88; Coronata, *De Locis et Temporibus Sacris,* n. 102; Bliley, *Altars,* pp. 56 ff.

The joining of the table of the altar to the support is an essential element in the construction of the fixed altar. The table and the support must have approximately the same length and width. The table, therefore, must cover the whole structure of the support over which it is placed, and must be united to it by means of cement or some other similar material. Furthermore, this conjunction of the table and support must be effected in a manner that fulfills the prescription of the *Roman Pontifical,* according to which the consecrator annoints these joinings with Sacred Chrism.[16]

Article 3. The Sepulcher for the Relics

A further canonical requirement in the construction of all altars is the sepulcher or cavity for the relics.

> **Canon 1198, § 4. "Tum in altari immobili tum in petra sacra sit, ad normam legum liturgicarum, sepulcrum continens reliquias Sanctorum, lapide clausum."** [17]

The sepulcher or cavity for the relics is a small square or oblong opening made in the table or the solid support of the altar, in which are placed the relics of the saints, as prescribed in the Roman Pontifical.[18] The size of the sepulcher for the relics varies in accordance with the size of the reliquary. This opening for the relics must be hewn in the natural stone of the altar. The usual location of the sepulcher is in the upper part of the table at its center and towards the front edge.[19]

[16] *Pontificale Romanum*: "coniunctiones mensae seu tabulae altaris, et tituli sive stipitis, in quatuor angulis, quasi illa coniunges. . . ."—Tit. *De ecclesiae dedicatione seu consecratione,* tit. *De altaris consecratione quae fit sine ecclesiae dedicatione;* cf. can. 1198, § 2.

[17] Can. 1198, § 4. "In an immovable altar as well as in an altar stone, there must be, according to the rubrical prescriptions, a sepulcher containing relics of the saints and closed with a stone."—Augustine, *A Commentary,* VI, 89.

[18] *Pontificale Romanum,* tit. *De ecclesiae dedicatione seu consecratione*: tit. *De altaris consecratione quae fit sine ecclesiae dedicatione.*

[19] Cf. Bliley, *Altars,* pp. 67 ff.

The cover or lid which closes the cavity that contains the relics must be a single natural stone.[20] It need not necessarily be the same kind of stone as that which is used in the rest of the altar,[21] although good taste and unity of design would demand that it be the same. If a metal cover instead of stone is used to seal the relics, although its use is unlawful, it seems that the consecration of such an altar is not invalid for that reason.[22] If the cover for the relics is of cement, or if cement alone is used for the sealing of the sepulcher, the subsequent consecration of the altar is invalid, as is evident from a declaration of the Congregation of Sacred Rites.[23]

The stone seal for the sepulcher must be fastened with the use of cement or some other similar material, and not simply with any material whatsoever. The material must have the binding force of cement, or something approaching this quality.[24]

Article 4. The Consecration of a Fixed Altar

(a) The Necessity of Consecration

Canon 1199, § 1. "Ut Missae sacrificium super illud celebrari possit, altare debet esse, secundum liturgicas leges, consecratum; idest vel totum, si agatur de immobili, vel ara tantum portatilis, si de mobili." [25]

It is unlawful to celebrate Mass on an altar that has not been consecrated. In addition to the regulation of the Code, the general rubrics of the *Missal* also demand that the altar on which Mass may be celebrated must be consecrated.[26] It has already been shown

20 Can. 1198, § 4.

21 S. R. C., *Sancti Joannis in America,* 15 dec. 1882, ad I—*Fontes,* n. 6144.

22 S. R. C., *Lauden.,* 23 iun. 1892—*Fontes,* n. 6216; Gasparri, *De Sanctissima Eucharistia,* I, n. 299; Coronata, *De Locis et Temporibus Sacris,* n. 103.

23 S. R. C., *Arichaten.,* 28 iul. 1883—*Fontes,* n. 6152.

24 Bliley, *Altars,* p. 70.

25 "In order that the Sacrifice of the Mass may be celebrated upon an altar, it must be consecrated according to the liturgical laws; that is to say, if the altar is fixed, the whole must be consecrated, if it is portable, the altar table."—Augustine, *A Commentary,* VI, 92. Cf. can. 822, § 1.

26 *Missale Romanum,* c. XX: "Altare, in quo sacrosanctum Missae Sacrificium celebrandum est, debet esse lapideum, et ab episcopo, sive abbate facultatem a Sede Apostolica habente, consecratum."

that this has been the law and the practice of the Church since the earliest centuries.[27] The Holy See very rarely allows the celebration of Mass without a consecrated altar,[28] and all authors are agreed that an altar must be consecrated before Mass can lawfully be said on it.[29] The obligation to have the altar consecrated is a most grave one, so much so that to celebrate Mass without a consecrated altar, whether fixed or portable, even in a case of urgent necessity, is objectively a grave sin.[30]

An altar must be considered as consecrated if it has been customary to say Mass upon it from time immemorial, even though there is no proof of consecration either of the church or of the altar.[31] If the consecration of an altar cannot be proved either through the fact of the celebration of Mass on it from time immemorial or in a legal manner, that is, by authentic document, or by witnesses, then such an altar must be consecrated before Mass can be licitly celebrated upon it.[32] If legal proof of the consecration of the altar is available, the repetition of consecration is not allowed; but if there is a doubt, the consecration must be performed provisionally (*ad cautelam*).[33]

(*b*) *The Relics for the Fixed Altar*

It is prescribed in the consecration of all altars, fixed and portable, that the relics of saints be placed in the sepulcher or cavity

[27] Cf. *supra*, Chapter II, p. 23.

[28] Cf. *Coll. S. C. de Prop. Fide*, n. 828.

[29] Coronata, *De Sacramentis*, I, n. 236; Cappello, *De Sacramentis*, I, n. 714; Gasparri, *De Sanctissima Eucharistia*, I, n. 311; Many, *Praelectiones de Locis Sacris*, n. 117; Wernz, *Ius Decretalium*, III, n. 464.

[30] Coronata, *De Sacramentis*, I, n. 236; Gasparri, *De Sanctissima Eucharistia*, I, n. 311; Suarez, *De Missae Sacrificio*, disp. 81, sect. V, n. 6—*Opera Omnia*, XXI, 808.

[31] S. R. C., *Mechlinien.*, 31 aug. 1867, ad VI—*Fontes*, n. 6016; Gasparri, *op. cit.*, I, n. 311; Many, *Praelectiones de Locis Sacris*, n. 124; Coronata, *De Locis et Temporibus Sacris*, n. 105.

[32] S. R. C., *Lauden.*, 23 iun. 1892, ad VI—*Fontes*, n. 6216; cf. can. 1159, § 2; can. 1158; can. 1159, § 1.

[33] Can. 1159, § 2.

prepared for them.[34] The present law does not, however, give any particulars about the depositing of the relics in the altar, but refers to the laws of the liturgy, which retain their force except when a change or correction is expressly made by the Code.[35]

The necessity of placing relics in the altar is of such a nature that the consecration of the altar without the relics is invalid.[36] When the relics are removed from the altar it is considered as desecrated, and must be consecrated again before Mass can lawfully be celebrated on it.[37]

An apostolic indult is required if an altar without relics is to be consecrated validly, or if Mass is to be said licitly upon an altar which does not contain relics. Although this indult is very rarely and only with difficulty obtained, nevertheless examples are not wanting, as the Congregation for the Propagation of the Faith has granted to missionaries under its jurisdiction the faculty of celebrating Mass on altars without relics in extraordinary circumstances, such as times of persecution, or under other similar hardships when no other altars were at hand.[38]

(*c*) *The Ceremonies of Consecration*

The consecration of a fixed altar must be performed according to the liturgical rite contained in the *Roman Pontifical*.[39] The difference between the consecration of a fixed altar and of a portable altar consists essentially in this that in the consecration of the portable altar only the surface of the altar stone is anointed, whereas in the

[34] Can. 1198, § 4. "Tum in altari immobili tum in petra sacra sit, ad normam legum liturgicarum, sepulcrum continens reliquias Sanctorum, lapide clausum."

[35] Can. 2.

[36] Gasparri, *De Sanctissima Eucharistia,* I, n. 324; Many, *Praelectiones de Locis Sacris,* n. 119; Augustine, *A Commentary,* VI 90; Coronata, *De Locis et Temporibus Sacris,* n. 103.

[37] Can. 1200, § 2, 2°; *Pontificale Romanum,* C. I, X, *De consecratione ecclesiae vel altaris,* III, 40.

[38] S. C. S. Off., 14 maii 1681; S. C. de Prop. Fide, 14 ian. 1802; S. C. de Prop. Fide, 8 iul. 1838—*Coll. S. C. de Prop. Fide,* I, nn. 223, 660, 869.

[39] *Pontificale Romanum,* II, *De ecclesiae dedicatione seu consecratione, De altaris consecratione quae fit sine ecclesiae dedicatione.*

consecration of the fixed altar another special unction is made at the four corners at which the table of the altar is joined and connected with the base, so that not the one stone but the whole altar is considered consecrated. Hence a fixed altar may not be consecrated with the rites of a portable altar, or vice versa, although the consecration of a portable altar with the rites which by law are employed for the consecration of a fixed altar would certainly be valid.[40] Therefore the rites prescribed in the *Roman Pontifical* must be used and strictly observed. No deviations from these rites are tolerated, though some of the employed ceremonies and prayers are not required for validity.[41]

Article 5. The Desecration of a Fixed Altar

The desecration of an altar means the total loss of its consecration. A desecrated altar is the same as an unconsecrated altar, hence, since it is unlawful to say Mass upon an altar that is not consecrated, so also it is unlawful to celebrate on a desecrated altar. Thus a desecrated altar must be consecrated anew before Mass may be celebrated upon it. The causes which give rise to the desecration of altars are enumerated in canon 1200.

> **"§ 1. Altare immobile amittit consecrationem, si tabula seu mensa a stipite, etiam per temporis momentum, separetur; quo in casu Ordinarius potest permittere ut presbyter altaris consecrationem rursus perficiat ritu formulaque breviore.**
>
> **§ 2. Tum altare immobile tum petra sacra amittunt consecrationem:**
>
> **1°. Si frangantur enormiter sive ratione quantitatis fractionis sive ratione loci unctionis;**
>
> **2°. Si amoveantur reliquiae aut frangatur vel amoveatur sepulcri operculum, excepto casu quo ipse Episcopus vel eius delegatus operculum amoveat ad illud firmandum vel reparandum vel subrogandum, aut ad visitandas reliquias.**

[40] Gasparri, *De Sanctissima Eucharistia,* I, n. 314.
[41] Bliley, *Altars,* pp. 86, 87.

§ 3. Levis fractio operculi non inducit execrationem et quilibet sacerdos potest rimulam cemento firmare.

§ 4. Execratio ecclesiae non secumfert execrationem altarium sive immobilium sive mobilium; et viceversa."

1. The fixed altar is desecrated or loses its consecration by the separation of the table from its support, even if this separation is only momentary.[42] In order to render a fixed altar desecrated, it is not postulated that the table be altogether separated from the support or base and placed in another position; it suffices that the table be raised from the base, no matter for what reason, to cause the desecration of the altar.[43]

Most of the authors hold that the fixed altar is not desecrated if the whole structure, that is, the table and the support as a unit, is moved from one place to another, provided that the table and the support do not become separated in the removal.[44] Woywod, however, holds the opposite opinion, based on a decision of the Congregation of Sacred Rites, February 20, 1874, which required that an altar which had been moved only a few feet from its old location had to be consecrated again.[45] Since there is no mention about the manner of the removal or whether the table and support were separated, this decision can be interpreted as referring to an altar which had been taken apart and set up anew. Hence it seems

[42] Can. 1200, § 1, Cf. Bliley, *Altars*, p. 89.

[43] Gasparri, *De Sanctissima Eucharistia*, I, n. 334; Many, *Praelectiones de Locis Sacris*, n. 121; Coronata, *De Locis et Temporibus Sacris*, n. 113; S. R. C., *Senogallien.*, 15 maii 1819—*Fontes*, n. 5836; S. R. C., *Brixien.*, 15 apr. 1869—*Fontes*, n. 6028; S. R. C., *Neopolitana*, 23 febr. 1884, ad VII—*Fontes*, n. 6156.

[44] Gasparri, *op. cit.*, I, n. 337; Many, *op. cit.*, n. 121; Vermeersch-Creusen, *Epitome Iuris Canonici*, II, n. 507; Coronata, *op. cit.*, n. 114; St. Alphonsus, *Theologia Moralis*, Lib. VI, n. 369; Prümmer, *Manuale Iuris Canonici* (3 ed., Friburgi Brisgoviae: B. Herder, 1922), p. 442.

[45] Woywod, "The Law of the Code on Altars"—*The Homiletic and Pastoral Review* (New York, 1900—), XXVI (1925), 269. Cf. S. R. C., *Marianopolitana*, 20 febr. 1874—*Decr. Auth.*, n. 3326.

safe to follow the authors who maintain that the altar is not desecrated if it be moved without the separation of the table and the support.

If the fixed altar is desecrated by the separation of the table from the support, the entire altar is considered desecrated, so that it is not lawful to celebrate Mass on any part of it or to use the table as a portable altar.[46] The reason is that the consecration of a fixed altar is something indivisible and adheres to the two parts joined together as one. Hence, when the consecration is lost by the separation of the table from the base, it is lost not only to the entire altar but also to each of its parts.[47]

When the fixed altar is desecrated by the removal of the table from the support, the ordinary can delegate a priest to consecrate it anew with the short formula prescribed by the Holy See.[48]

2. The fixed altar is desecrated through a fracture which is regarded as considerable by reason either of the break itself or the position of the break, whether of an anointed place or not.[49]

3. The removal of the relics causes the desecration of the fixed altar.[50] No matter what may be the reason or the pretext for the removal of the relics, whether by chance or by design, the altar is thereby desecrated, except in the case in which the bishop or his delegate removes the cover in order to fasten it more securely, to repair it, or to substitute another cover, or to inspect the relics.[51] In this case the removal of the relics is allowed for a short duration only. If the removal endures for some time either through error or for some other reason, the altar is considered desecrated.[52]

4. The fixed altar is desecrated if the stone or cover which seals the sepulcher is broken. A slight break does not entail desecration,

[46] S. R. C., *Brixien.*, 15 apr. 1869—*Fontes*, n. 6028.

[47] Many, *Praelectiones de Locis Sacris*, n. 121, 3; Coronata, *De Locis et Temporibus Sacris*, n. 113.

[48] S. R. C., decr., 9 sept. 1920—*AAS*, XII (1920), 449; *Rituale Romanum*, appendix, tit. *De consecratione altarium execratorum*, n. 1.

[49] Can. 1200, § 2, 1°; cf. Gasparri, *De Sanctissima Eucharistia*, I, n. 340; Bliley, *Altars*, pp. 92, 93.

[50] Can. 1200, § 2, 2°.

[51] Can. 1200, § 2, 2°; Woywod, *A Practical Commentary*, II, 27.

[52] Coronata, *Institutiones Iuris Canonici*, II, n. 783; Bliley, *Altars*, p. 94.

and any priest may repair the break with cement, provided that he does not remove the stone or cover.[53]

5. Finally, the fixed altar is desecrated through the removal of the stone cover of the sepulcher or cavity for the relics, except in the case wherein the bishop or his delegate removes it for the purpose of fastening, repairing, or replacing it, or for the purpose of inspecting the relics.[54]

The desecration of a church does not entail the desecration of the immovable or portable altars of the church, or vice versa.[55] There is no special violation or profanation of an altar, distinct from the violation of a church. However, when the church is violated, the celebration of Mass is forbidden anywhere in that church until it is reconciled, and thus indirectly there is a violation of the altar.[56]

Article 6. The Portable Altar

The portable or movable altar consists of a stone, usually small in size, which alone is consecrated; or also of the stone with its support when the latter is not consecrated with the stone.[57] The portable altar must be of natural stone sufficiently hard to resist easy fracture. The stone itself must contain the same qualities as the table of the fixed altar.[58] A single entire stone without any breaks or cavities is required. Only the sepulcher for the relics and the five small crosses, where the unctions are made, may be cut in it. Thus a portable altar composed of two or more stones cemented together cannot be validly consecrated.[59]

The necessity of the consecration of the portable altar as a prerequisite for the celebration of Mass is identical with that of the

[53] Can. 1200, § 2, 2°; can. 1200, § 3.

[54] Can. 1200, § 2, 2°; Woywod, *A Practical Commentary,* II, 27.

[55] Can. 1200, § 4; Woywod, *op. cit.,* II, 27.

[56] Many, *Praelectiones de Locis Sacris,* n. 125; Coronata, *De Locis et Temporibus Sacris,* nn. 27, 118.

[57] Cf. *supra,* Chapter VIII, p. 132; Woywod, *op. cit.,* II, 25.

[58] Cf. *supra,* Chapter VIII, p. 133; can. 1198, § 1.

[59] S. R. C., decr., 8 iun. 1896, ad III—*Fontes,* n. 6262; cf. Bliley, *Altars,* pp. 98 ff.

fixed altar, hence it is not necessary to repeat the details.[60] With regard to the ceremonies of the consecration of a portable altar there is prescribed a rite different from that used in the consecration of the fixed altar.[61] For the valid consecration of the portable altar there must be a sepulcher or cavity made in the stone into which are inserted the relics of saints or martyrs.[62]

Article 7. The Desecration of the Portable Altar

The portable altar is desecrated or loses its consecration in the same manner as the fixed altar, except as regards the separation of the table from the base or support, which is applicable from its very nature only to the fixed altar. Before Mass may be celebrated on a desecrated portable altar, it must be consecrated again, unless the desecration is of such a nature that the stone could not be reconsecrated. In accordance with the regulations of canon 1200, § 2, 2°-4°, the portable altar becomes desecrated in the following ways:

1. The portable altar becomes desecrated through a notable fracture by reason either of the size of the piece broken or of the inclusion in the fracture of the place anointed.[63]

2. It also becomes desecrated through the removal of the relics for any reason, except in the case in which the bishop or his delegate undertakes a very temporary removal of the relics for the purpose of fastening, repairing, or substituting the stone cover of the sepulcher, or for the purpose of inspecting the relics themselves.

3. The portable altar is desecrated if the stone which covers the sepulcher of the relics is broken. A slight break, however, does not entail the desecration of the altar, and any priest may fill the break with cement, provided that he does not remove the stone cover.[64]

4. Lastly, the removal of the stone cover of the sepulcher of the

[60] Cf. *supra,* Chapter VIII, p. 135.

[61] *Pontificale Romanum,* II, tit, *De Altaris Portatilis Consecratione;* cf. *supra,* Chapter VIII, p. 137.

[62] Cf. *supra,* Chapter VIII, p. 136; Bliley, *Altars,* p. 104.

[63] Can. 1200, § 2, 1°, Cf. Bliley, *Altars,* p. 108; S. R. C., *Sancti Hippolyti,* 31 aug. 1867, ad III—*Fontes,* n. 6018; Many, *Praelectiones de Locis Sacris,* n. 133; Gasparri, *De Sanctissima Eucharistia,* I, n. 340.

[64] Can. 1200, § 2, 2°; § 3.

relics causes the desecration of the portable altar, except in the case when the bishop or his delegate removes it for the purpose of fastening, repairing, or substituting it, or for the purpose of inspecting the relics.[65] The desecration of the church does not entail the desecration of the portable altars in the church, or vice versa.[66]

Article 8. Liturgical Requirements of the Altar

Before Mass may be celebrated on an altar which has been duly constructed and consecrated according to law, the following liturgical requirements also have to be fulfilled. The Roman Missal in the introductory general rubrics states these requirements: (1) the antependium; (2) the crucifix; (3) the candlesticks; (4) the candles; (5) the Missal stand and altar cards; (6) the credence table with altar bell, cruets, and Communion paten; (7) the altar cloths.

(1) The antependium is a long decorative panel, usually of cloth, prescribed by the liturgy as a covering for the entire front of the altar from the mensa to the floor or platform of the altar.[67] The custom of using an antependium which covers only a small portion of the front of the altar has been condemned.[68]

The material is not prescribed. It may be gold, silver, or any other precious fabric, such as cloth of gold or silver, silk, velvet, or damask. It may be ornamented with jewels, rich embroidery or braid. A monogram may also be added, or a scene pertaining to the life or Passion of Christ, or to the Holy Eucharist. The Sacred Heart of Jesus or of Mary without the Person may not be represented for public devotion.[69]

The color of the antependium should correspond to that of the feast or of the Office, if possible. Gold and silver may be used for

65 Can. 1200, § 2, 2°; Cf. S. R. C., decr. 9 sept. 1920—*AAS,* XII (1920), 450. This short formula for the reconsecration of desecrated portable altars is also contained in the *Rituale Romanum,* appendix, tit. *De consecratione altarium execratorum,* n. 2.

66 Can. 1200, § 4; Woywod, *A Practical Commentary,* II, 27.

67 *Missale Ramanum,* Rubricae generales, XX; cf. O'Connell, *The Book of Ceremonies* (Milwaukee: The Bruce Publishing Co., 1944), p. 565.

68 S. R. C., *Mexicana,* 10 sept. 1898—*Fontes,* n. 6286.

69 S. R. C., *Marianopolitana,* 5 apr. 1879—*Decr. Auth.,* n. 3492.

all colors except black and violet, and may also be used on any of more solemn feasts.[70] For Requiem Masses black is used when the Blessed Sacrament is not reserved in the tabernacle of the altar; violet, when the Blessed Sacrament is reserved. However, the Congregation of Sacred Rites tolerates the use of black.[71]

(2) The Crucifix.

This is one of the most important liturgical requirements in connection with an altar destined for the celebration of Mass, but it is not required when Mass is said before the Blessed Sacrament exposed, or when a statue of the Crucifixion is on the altar.[72] The position of the crucifix should be in the middle of the altar between the candlesticks.[73]

Generally it should be placed on the table (*mensa*) of the altar, but when the tabernacle already occupies this position on the *mensa*, the crucifix may be set on a stand or be supported by a shaft attached to the back of *mensa*.[74] It cannot be placed on the altar table in front of the door of the tabernacle, nor on the throne on which the Blessed Sacrament is customarily exposed.[75] The base of the crucifix should be as high as the top of the two candlesticks nearest it, and thus the entire crucifix itself should stand higher than the candlesticks.[76] The crucifix does not require a blessing, but if it is blessed privately the formula *Solemnis Benedictio Imaginis* of the *Roman Ritual* is used.[77]

(3) The Candlesticks.

The candlesticks required on the altar for the celebration of Mass

[70] *Caeremoniale Episcoporum*, tit. I, c. xii, n. 11.

[71] S. R. C., *Montis Regalis*, 20 mart. 1869—*Fontes*, n. 6027.

[72] *Missale Romanum*, Rubricae generales, tit. XX; S. R. C., *Aquin.*, 2 sept. 1741, ad I—*Decr. Auth.*, n. 2365; S. R. C., *Rossanen.*, 16 iun. 1663, ad II—*Decr. Auth.*, n. 1270.

[73] *Missale Romanum*, Rubricae generales, tit. XX; *Decr. Auth.*, n. 4136; S. R. C., *Ordinis FF. Minorum Provinciae Portugalliae*, 11 iun. 1904, ad II—*Fontes*, n. 6331.

[74] *Missale Romanum*, Rubricae generales, c. XX.

[75] S. R. C., *Ordinis FF. Minorum Provinciae Portugalliae*, 11 iun. 1904, ad II—*Fontes*, n. 6331; *Decr. Auth.*, n. 4136.

[76] *Caeremoniale Episcoporum*, tit. I, c. xii, n. 11.

[77] S. R. C., *Urbis*, 12 iul. 1704—*Decr. Auth.*, n. 2143; *Rituale Romanum*. tit. VIII, c. 25; O'Connell, *The Book of Ceremonies*, p. 10.

must be single ones. Candelabra with more than one candle, and brackets attached to the wall, are not permitted.[78] The Code of Canon Law demands that they be constructed according to the traditional form,[79] which should consist of a base, a stem with its node, a candleholder.[80]

The proper position of the candlesticks on the altar is on the *mensa*,[81] but the Congregation of Sacred Rites tolerates the custom of placing them on the elevated step towards the rear of the *mensa*.[82] Two candlesticks with candles are required on every altar for low Mass;[83] on the main altar there should be always six, in constant preparation for the celebration of High Masses.[84]

The material of the candlesticks can be silver, brass, copper, or wood. On feast days or other solemn occasions the candlesticks ought to be of better material and greater height than on ordinary days.[85]

(4) The Candles.

The Congregation of Sacred Rites has issued many decrees regulating the quality of the candles to be used in the celebration of Mass. The only candle permitted to be used on the altar is the *beeswax* candle. No other material by way of substitution is tolerated.[86] For a Low Mass which is strictly private and celebrated by any priest of lesser rank than that of a bishop, two lighted candles are required.[87] But if it is a conventual or parochial Mass on Sundays or holydays of obligation, or on some solemn occasion,

[78] S. R. C., *Cameracen.*, 16 sept. 1865, ad I—*Decr. Auth.*, n. 3137.

[79] Can. 1296, § 3.

[80] O'Connell, *The Book of Ceremonies*, p. 10.

[81] *Missale Romanum*, Rubricae generales, tit. XX.

[82] S. R. C., *Lucana.*, 5 dec. 1891, ad II—*Decr. Auth.*, n. 3759.

[83] *Missale Romanum*, Rubricae generales, tit. XX.

[84] *Caeremoniale Episcoporum*, tit. I, c. xii, n. 11.

[85] *Caeremoniale Episcoporum*, tit. I, c. xii, n. 11.

[86] S. R. C., *Carolinopolitana*, 10 dec. 1857—*Decr. Auth.*, n. 3063; S. R. C., decr., 4 iun. 1895—*Decr. Auth.*, n. 3859; S. R. C., *Natcheten.*, 16 maii 1902—*Decr. Auth.*, n. 4097; S. R. C. *Declaratio Decretorum Luce Electrica*, 22 nov., 1907—*Decr. Auth.*, n. 4206; S. R. C., *Dubium*, 28 iul. 1911—*Decr. Auth.*, n. 4275.

[87] *Missale Romanum*, Rubricae generales, tit. XX.

more than two candles can be lighted.[88] For a High Mass (*Missa cantata*) at least four, but generally six, are used.[89] For a solemn Mass on Sundays and feast days, six candles are required;[90] four will suffice on other days, except on simple feasts and lesser ferias, when it is lawful to use only two.[91]

(5) The Missal stand and altar cards.

The proper stand or support for the Missal on the altar is a cushion,[92] but by common usage a metal or wooden stand is acceptable.[93] The custom of covering the stand with a cloth corresponding to the color of the vestments is a commendable one, except for a Requiem Mass, when it is preferable not to use a cover.[94]

The rubrics prescribe only one altar card containing the "secret" prayers of the Mass, but the custom of using three has become acceptable.[95]

(6) The credence table with bell, cruets, and Communion paten.

The credence table is used for the celebration of Mass, and occupies its position on the Epistle side of the altar. On it are placed the cruets, the bell, the Communion paten and other necessities. On the feasts of greater solemnity the credence table should be covered with a white linen cloth extending to the ground on all sides. On the less solemn feasts the cloth should not extend fully to the ground, and on simple feasts the top only should be covered.[96]

The bell used at Mass should be a small hand-bell with one tongue (*parva campanula seu tintinnabulum*). Gongs are forbidden, but chiming bells are tolerated, though they do not conform fully

[88] S. R. C., *Northantonien.*, 6 febr. 1858—*Fontes*, n. 5987; *Decr. Auth.*, n. 3065.

[89] S. R. C., *Nullius Dioecesis Piscien.*, 6 maii 1673, ad II—*Decr. Auth.*, n. 1470; S. R. C., *Briacen.*, 12 aug. 1854, ad VII—*Decr. Auth.*, n. 3029; S. R. C., *Baionen.*, 25 sept. 1875, ad I—*Decr. Auth.*, n. 3377.

[90] *Caeremoniale Episcoporum*, tit. I, c. xii, n. 11.

[91] *Caeremoniale Episcoporum*, *loc. cit.* Cf. O'Connell, *The Book of Ceremonies*, p. 12; Cappello, *De Sacramentis*, I, n. 727.

[92] *Missale Romanum*, loc. cit.

[93] Cappello, *De Sacramentis*, I, n. 730; O'Connell, *The Book of Ceremonies*, p. 17.

[94] O'Connell, *loc. cit.*

[95] Cf. Cappello, *op. cit.*, I, n. 729; O'Connell, *loc. cit.*

[96] *Caeremoniale Episcoporum*, tit. I, c. xii, n. II; cf. O'Connell, *loc. cit.*

to the rubrics.[97] The Congregation of Sacred Rites has required that the bell be always rung at Mass, even in strictly private Masses.[98] At Masses said during the exposition of the Blessed Sacrament the bell must not be rung.[99]

Cruets made of clear crystal or glass must be used for Mass, but cruets of gold, silver or other material are also tolerated.[100] A small bowl or basin also made of glass is required for the *Lavabo,* which for greater convenience should be oval shaped,[101] and a small towel is necessary to dry the priest's fingers.[102]

The Communion paten is placed on the credence table and must be used for the distribution of Holy Communion. It should be made of silver or gold, at least the inner surface of the receptacle should be gold plated and entirely smooth.[103]

(7) The Altar Cloths.

On the altar for the celebration of Mass three clean cloths made of linen or hemp are required.[104] The top cloth should cover completely the surface of the *mensa,* and should reach to the ground on both sides.[105] The other two may be shorter, or may be one cloth doubled, but should cover the entire surface of the table of the altar in length and width, whether it be a fixed or a portable altar.[106]

It is not prescribed that the upper cloth hang down in front, especially if an *antependium* is used. The Congregation of Sacred

[97] S. R. C., *Mexicana,* 10 sept. 1898—*Fontes,* n. 6286.

[98] S. R. C., *Marianopolitana,* 18 iul. 1885, ad III—*Decr. Auth.,* n. 3638.

[99] S. R. C., *Societatis Jesu,* 11 maii 1878, ad II—*Decr. Auth.,* n. 3448; S. R. C., *Mechlinien.,* 31 aug. 1867, ad X—*Decr. Auth.,* n. 3157.

[100] *Missale Romanum,* tit. XX; S. R. C., *Sancti Jacobi de Cile,* 28 apr. 1866—*Decr. Auth.,* n. 3149.

[101] S. R. C., *Baltimoren.,* 6 febr. 1858—*Decr. Auth.,* n. 3064.

[102] O'Connell, *op. cit.,* p. 18.

[103] O'Connell, *op. cit.,* p. 18; S. C. de Sacramentis, instr. 26 mart. 1929, III, 5—*AAS,* XXI (1929), 638. Cf. Bouscaren, *The Canon Law Digest,* II, 193-194.

[104] S. R. C., *Decretum generale,* 18 maii 1819—*Decr. Auth.,* n. 2600; S. R. C., *Placentina in Hispania,* 13 aug. 1895, ad II—*Fontes,* n. 6246; *Decr. Auth.,* n. 3868.

[105] S. R. C., *Resolutionis dubiorum,* 9 iun. 1899, ad I—*Decr. Auth.,* n. 4029. Cf. Cappello, *De Sacramentis,* I, n. 724.

[106] O'Connell, *The Book of Ceremonies,* p. 20.

Rites, however, has declared that the edges of the altar cloth at the front and at the two ends can be ornamented with linen or hempen lace. Such symbols as the cross, the chalice, the host, or other similar representations may be woven into this lace.[107] The practice of attaching a lace border to the front edge of the altar without in any way attaching it to the altar cloth is also tolerated.[108]

Before the altar cloths may be used for the celebration of Mass, they should first be blessed by the parish priest or the rector of the church.[109]

[107] S. R. C., *Syren.*, 5 dec. 1868, ad V—*Fontes*, n. 6024; *Decr. Auth.*, n. 3191.

[108] O'Connell, *op. cit.*, p. 20.

[109] Cappello, *De Sacramentis*, I, n. 724.

CHAPTER IX

THE PRIVILEGE OF A PORTABLE ALTAR

ARTICLE 1. NATURE AND EXTENT OF THE PRIVILEGE

THE present law in canon 822, § 1, requires that the Mass be celebrated on a consecrated altar, and in a church or oratory consecrated or blessed according to law. However, the same canon also mentions the privilege of a portable altar.

Canon 822, § 2. "Privilegium *altaris portatilis* vel iure vel indulto Sedis tantum Apostolicae conceditur.

§ 3. Hoc privilegium ita intelligendum est, ut secumferat facultatem ubique celebrandi honesto tamen ac decenti loco et super petram sacram, non autem in mari."

The privilege of the portable altar is conceded either by law or by an indult obtainable only from the Holy See. It is to be understood in such a sense that it bestows the faculty to say Mass on a consecrated altar stone anywhere in a decent and respectable place, but not at sea.[1] The privilege of a portable altar, therefore, consists precisely in this that one is permitted to say Mass outside of a church and public or semi-public oratory consecrated or blessed for divine worship. Besides the celebration of Mass on the sea, Gasparri also excluded from the privilege the celebration of Mass in the open air or below the earth, as these places, even though properly fitted and clean, were not considered respectable and safe under the former legislation.[2]

Since the publication of the Code these limitations seem to apply only to cases in which these places are expressly excluded by the

[1] Woywod, *A Practical Commentary,* I, 338.

[2] Gasparri, *De Sanctissima Eucharistia,* I, n. 272; cf. Ojetti, *Synopsis Rerum Moralium,* I, n. 337.

indult, for the Code does not except these places by a positive law; hence, only in cases wherein the open air or subterranean places cease to be respectable or decent would the privilege of the portable altar be excluded. There is no evident reason why in themselves the open air and subterranean places are not respectable and safe.[3]

The privilege of a portable altar, whether granted by law or by a special apostolic indult, is always personal, and is limited to the person to whom it is granted according to the words of the indult. Hence, if the indult is granted to a lay person, no priest may celebrate Mass in virtue of that privilege except in the presence of the lay person to whom it was granted; but if the privileged one is present, any priest may celebrate Mass in virtue of the privilege of the portable altar. Unless otherwise expressly mentioned in the indult, only one Mass each day is permitted in the concession of the privilege of a portable altar.[4] Cardinals and bishops, however, enjoy special privileges in this regard, which will be treated later.[5]

Furthermore, it may be noted here that the privilege of a portable altar differs from that of a private or domestic oratory. Although both privileges have much in common, they are not one and the same. The privilege of a private oratory refers primarily to the right of possessing or having a particular place reserved for divine services, whereas the privilege of a portable altar does not mean the right of possessing or having a portable altar, but bestows the faculty of celebrating Mass in any suitable and becoming place, on a consecrated altar stone, mainly outside of a church or oratory consecrated or blessed for divine worship. Thus, the principal differences between the privilege of the portable altar and that of the private oratory may be summarized as follows:

1. The privilege of a portable altar includes the faculty of celebrating Mass not only in an unconsecrated or in an unblessed place, but also in a place not destined for divine worship; in the privilege

[3] Cappello, *De Sacramentis,* I, n. 718; Coronat, *De Locis et Temporibus Sacris,* n. 123; Augustine, *A Commentary,* IV, 172.

[4] Cappello, *op. cit.,* I, n. 718.

[5] Cf. Gasparri, *De Sanctissima Eucharistia,* I, n. 272; Coronata, *De Locis et Temporibus Sacris,* n. 124.

of a private oratory, the place must be set aside for divine worship only, and must not be used for profane purposes.[6]

2. The privilege of a private oratory absolutely excludes the faculty of saying Mass in a bedroom.[7] The privilege of a portable altar, it seems, does not exclude this faculty, unless the celebration of Mass in a bedroom is expressly forbidden in the indult granted by the Holy See.[8] The clause forbidding the celebration of Mass in a bedroom, as mentioned in the Code,[9] refers to the permission granted by the bishop *per modum actus* to celebrate Mass on a portable altar outside of a church or oratory. This matter will be further treated later, in the section dealing with the celebration of Mass in a bedroom.

3. The private oratory must be inspected and approved as a fitting place for the celebration of Mass before the privilege can be used. This visitation must be made by the ordinary or his delegate. Such a visitation, however, is not required for the use of the privilege of a portable altar.[10]

4. It is very probable that all who assist at the Mass celebrated by a priest having the privilege of a portable altar fulfill their obligation of hearing Mass on Sundays and holydays of obligation. But those who hear Mass in private oratories do not fulfill their obligation unless this privilege is specifically granted by the Holy See.[11]

Article 2. Those Who Enjoy the Privilege of a Portable Altar

The privilege of a portable altar is granted by law, or by an indult obtainable only from the Holy See.[12] In the period before the Council of Trent (1545-1563) the Holy See was very generous in granting the privilege of the portable altar. Abuses, however,

[6] Can. 822, § 3; can. 1196.

[7] Can. 1196; cf. Coronata, *op. cit.*, nn. 78, i; 91b; 123.

[8] Cf. Regatillo, *Ius Sacramentarium,* I, n. 219.

[9] Can. 822, § 4.

[10] Cf. can. 1195, § 1; Gasparri, *De Sanctissima Eucharistia,* I, n. 272; Coronata, *De Locis et Temporibus Sacris,* n. 123.

[11] Can. 1249; Coronata, *op. cit.*, p. 124.

[12] Can. 822, § 2; Woywod, *A Practical Commentary,* I, 388.

arose with regard to the use of this privilege, so that the Council of Trent made strict regulations governing the celebration of Mass outside a church or oratory. These regulations indirectly caused the revocation of the privileges of a portable altar which theretofore had been granted. From this general revocation the privileges of cardinals and bishops were excepted.[13] After the Council of Trent the Holy See granted the privilege more sparingly, and the present law contains the discipline which has been observed since, although in the Code the privilege is extended to many local ordinaries.

The privilege of a portable altar is granted by law to the following:

(a) All cardinals enjoy the privilege from the time of their promotion in the consistory; they also have the faculty of permitting another Mass to be celebrated on a portable altar in their presence.[14] Furthermore they have the privilege of celebrating Mass on the sea under the proper precautions.[15] In order that a priest may celebrate the second Mass allowed by the above noted privilege, the presence of the cardinal himself is required since the favor is personal and has reference to the person of the cardinal.[16]

(b) All bishops, whether residential or titular, from the moment of the reception of the official notification of their canonical appointment have the privilege of a portable altar, with the additional faculty of permitting that another Mass be celebrated in their presence.[17] They also enjoy the privilege of saying Mass on board ship, provided all the necessary precautions are taken for the avoidance of all the dangers of irreverence. Thus the sea must be sufficiently calm, and the place of celebration decent and clean. Bishops may exercise the privilege of a portable altar outside their dioceses without the permission of the ordinary of the place. According to the Code, in virtue of this privilege a bishop can allow only one

[13] Cf. *supra,* Chapter IV p. 56; Benedictus XIV, *De Missae Sacrificio,* Lib. III, c. 6, nn. 1-5; Benedictus XIV, ep. encycl. *Magno cum,* 2 iun. 1751—*Fontes,* n. 413.

[14] Can. 239, § 1, 7°.

[15] Can. 239, § 1, 8°.

[16] Coronata, *De Locis et Temporibus Sacris,* n. 124; Gasparri, *De Sanctissima Eucharistia,* I, nn. 263-267.

[17] Can. 349, § 1, 1°.

priest to say Mass after he has celebrated, and he must be present at the Mass thus celebrated.[18] All those who hear the Mass celebrated in virtue of the privilege of a portable altar, whether said by the bishop or by a priest with the bishop present, fulfill their obligation to hear Mass on Sundays and feasts of precept, since the present law in canon 1249 does not exclude the fulfillment of the precept in these circumstances. The Congregation of Sacred Rites has declared that the faithful fulfill the precept,[19] and it seems that this concession is not abrogated by the Code.[20]

Cardinals and bishops are granted the privilege of the portable altar for their convenience, especially during illness, when they can permit a priest to celebrate Mass on a portable altar next to their bedroom (*iuxta cubiculum suum*), provided the place be suitable and duly respectable.[21]

(c) Vicars and prefects apostolic also enjoy the privilege of a portable altar. However, if they have not the episcopal character, they enjoy the privilege only during their term of office and within the limits of their territory.[22]

18 Cf. can. 349, § 1, 1° can. 239, § 1, 70.

19 S. R. C., *Dubia de Episcopis Titularibus,* 25 aug. 1818, ad 3—*Fontes,* n. 5835; *Decr. Auth.,* 2585; S. R. C., *Urbis et Orbis,* 8 iun. 1896—*Fontes,* n. 6261; *Decr. Auth.,* n. 3906.

20 Cf. Cappello, *De Sacramentis,* I, n. 718, 5.

21 S. R. C., *Tarvisina,* 12 mart. 1836—*Fontes,* n. 5879; *Decr. Auth.,* n. 2739.

22 Can. 308. Cf. Coronata (*De Locis et Temporibus Sacris,* n. 124) states that vicars and prefects apostolic have this privilege in virtue of canon 294, § 1. This seems inaccurate, since vicars and prefects who are not also bishops do not enjoy the privilege of a portable altar in virtue of canon 294, § 1, but in consequence of the ruling contained in canon 308, which entitles them to the privileges of protonotaries apostolic *de numero participantium.* Cappello states that abbots and prelates *nullius* also enjoy the privilege of a portable altar by law in view of canon 323. Although this canon grants them the same powers and obligation as bishops, it does not entitle them to the privileges that presuppose the possession of the episcopal character. The Code otherwise does not grant them an extension of privileges which include the privilege of a portable altar, hence it must be concluded that at least the matter remains in doubt—*De Sacramentis,* I, n. 718. Most of the authors do not include them in the list of those who enjoy the privilege by law. Cf. Vermeersch-Creusen, *Epitome Iuris Canonici,* II, n. 99; Coronata, *loc. cit.* Woywod, *A Practical Commentary,* I, 389; Augustine, *A Commentary,* IV, 170.

(d) Apostolic administrators by law enjoy the privilege of a portable altar, unless the contrary is expressly stated in the letter of appointment. If the apostolic administrator is not a bishop, he enjoys the privilege only as long as his term of office lasts and also only within the limits of his territory.[23]

(e) Protonotaries apostolic *de numero participantium* are also granted the privilege.[24]

(f) Auditors of the Holy Roman Rota have the privilege of the portable altar by virtue of which Mass may be celebrated in places suitable and becoming for this purpose, provided the rights of others are safeguarded.[25]

To all others the privilege of a portable altar is granted by a special indult from the Holy See. Those who enjoy the privilege by personal concession must observe all the conditions specified in the indult. Generally the celebration of Mass by only one priest is permitted. With regard to the days on which Mass may be said, the last three days of Holy Week are usually the only exceptions; hence the privilege may be used on all days except Holy Thursday, Good Friday and Holy Saturday. Thus, with these exceptions, Mass can be said on the portable altar even on those days when its celebration is prohibited in private oratories.[26]

The privilege of a portable altar is generally granted to priests in missionary territories, but with some restrictions. The privilege is obtained either directly from the Holy See or indirectly from the ordinaries of these territories. The Sacred Congregation for the Propagation of the Faith is accustomed to grant to local ordinaries in missionary countries the faculty of communicating this privilege to their missionaries. Generally it is not granted unconditionally, for according to the faculty the missionary priest may

[23] Can. 314; can. 315.

[24] Pius X, motu propr, *Inter multiplices,* 21 febr. 1905, nn. 2, 22—*Fontes,* n. 665; Cappello, *De Sacramentis,* I, n. 718; Pius XI, const. *Ad incrementum decoris,* 15 aug. 1934, n. XLVI—*AAS,* XXVI (1934), 507.

[25] Cappello, *op. cit.,* I, n. 718; Coronata, *De Locis et Temporibus Sacris,* n. 124; Gasparri, *De Sanctissima Eucharistia,* I, n. 271; Wernz, *Ius Decretalium,* V, n. 85; Pius XI, const. *Ad incrementum decoris,* 15 aug. 1934, nn. LXXIV, CVIII, CXXVII—*AAS,* XXVI (1934), 511, 515, 518.

[26] Cappello, *op. cit.,* I, n. 718.

use the privilege only in case of necessity, or in cases when he cannot otherwise say Mass.[27]

Regulars enjoyed the privilege of the portable altar either by direct concession from the Holy See, or indirectly through the intercommunication of privileges, that is, by sharing in the privileges that had been granted to religious orders until the Council of Trent.[28] In the XXII Session of the Council the privilege was revoked, so that a renewal had to be sought from the Holy See after the Council of Trent.[29] However many religious orders had the privilege renewed in the subsequent years, as, for example, the Canons Regular of the Lateran, who received it from Pope Pius IV in March, 1565; the Fathers of the Society of Jesus for their missions, with some restrictions, from Pope Gregory XIII on October 1, 1579; and the Dominican Order for the province of Poland, from Pope Gregory XIII on June 20, 1580.[30]

Finally, any lay person may obtain the privilege of a portable altar by special concession, in which case the privilege implies the permission of hearing Mass celebrated by any priest on a portable altar in a decent and becoming place chosen by the one having the indult.[31]

Article 3. The Celebration of Mass Outside a Church or Oratory Without the Privilege of a Portable Altar

According to the discipline handed down from the earliest times, the proper place for the celebration of Holy Mass is the church. Confirmed by many papal and conciliar decreès, this traditional

[27] Cf. Vermeersch-Creusen, *Epitome Iuris Canonici,* I, n. 873; Vermeersch, "Commentaria de Formulis quas S. C. de Propaganda Fide concedere solet."—*Periodica de Re Morali, Canonica,* XI (1922), 33.

[28] Gattico, *De Oratoriis Domesticis,* Pars II, c. VIII, n. 1; Many, *Praelectiones de Missa,* n. 8; Gasparri, *De Sanctissima Eucharistia,* I, n. 262.

[29] Conc. Trident., sess. XXII, *de observandis et evitandis in celebratione Missae*—Schroeder, *Canons and Decrees of the Council of Trent,* pp. 151-152, 423-424; cf. Gasparri, *op. cit.,* I, n. 262; Many, *op. cit.,* n. 8.

[30] Cf. Gattico, *op. cit.,* Pars II, c. XIII, n. 13, Gasparri, *loc. cit.;* Many, *op. cit.,* n. 9.

[31] Can. 63, § 1; can. 36, § 1.

discipline has received further confirmation in the Code of Canon Law.[32] Without relinquishing the long-standing trend in the matter, the Church in present legislation allows some exceptions. The privilege of the portable altar, as has already been shown in the preceding articles, is a limited concession, and enjoyed only by those who are entitled to it by law, and by those who have received it by way of special concession which can be granted only by the Holy See. Aware of the fact that there is a certain tendency and inclination among the faithful to withdraw the most sacred ceremonies of the Church from sacred places, the Holy See wisely reserves to itself the faculty of granting permission to say Mass outside a church or oratory on a portable altar. However, another exception is made in canon 822, § 4, but only with strict limitations, which curtail its use.

> **Canon 822, § 4. "Loci Ordinarius aut, si agatur de domo religionis exemptae, Superior maior, licentiam celebrandi extra ecclesiam et oratorium super petram sacram et decenti loco, nunquam autem in cubiculo, concedere potest iusta tantum ac rationabili de causa, in aliquo extraordinario casu et per modum actus."** [33]

The local ordinary, or in the case of an exempt religious house, the major superior, may grant the permission to say Mass outside a church or oratory, under the conditions stated in the canon. The term local ordinary is taken in the usual sense as it is contained in canon 198, § 1, and the major superiors, who also may grant the permission, are those who are mentioned in canon 488, 8°. A major superior of exempt religious, however, can give the permission in question only with regard to a house of his own religious

[32] Can. 822.

[33] "The local Ordinary—or, in the case of an exempt religious house, the major superior—can give permission for a just and reasonable cause to celebrate Mass outside a church or oratory on a consecrated altar-stone in a decent place, but never in a bedroom. This permission can be given only in an extraordinary case and in individual cases (*per modum actus*), not habitually"—Woywod, *A Practical Commentary,* I, 388, 389.

institute. Hence, without a special indult he cannot permit his subjects to say Mass in a strange place which is not owned or controlled by his religious institute. Thus while the religious is on a journey the competent ordinary to grant this permission in the ordinary of the place where the religious wishes to say Mass.[34]

(a) The Power of the Ordinary and the Conditions Required for the Granting of This Permission

The Council of Trent, as already shown, took away from bishops the previously enjoyed faculty of permitting Mass in private houses or outside a church or oratory.[35] This revocation, however, was commonly interpreted by the authors as applying only to the power of permitting the celebration of Mass outside a church or oratory perpetually (*per modum habitus*), but not to the individual case (*per modum actus*). These authors based their mild interpretation on the words of the Council, and held that the words *"Neve patiantur Episcopi . . ."* did not absolutely abolish the power of bishops. They contended that, if the Council had intended the total withdrawal of the faculty, it would have used more severe and definite terminology. Hence, they claimed that local ordinaries, even after the Council of Trent, enjoyed the faculty of permitting the celebration of Mass outside churches and oratories *per modum actus* in cases of grave necessity.[36]

This opinion of the authors prior to the Code was confirmed by the Holy See, which in many replies recognized the power of bishops to permit the celebration of Mass outside a church or oratory for a grave cause and *per modum actus*.[37] Thus it can be concluded

[34] S. C. de Prop. Fide, 18 nov. 1765—*Coll. S. C. de Prop. Fide,* n. 461, *Fontes,* n. 4547.

[35] Conc. Trident., sess. XXII, *de observandis et evitandis in celebratione missae; supra,* Chapter IV, p. 62.

[36] Lehmkuhl, *Theologia Moralis,* II, 167; Many, *Praelectiones de Missa,* n. 5; Gasparri, *De Sanctissima Eucharistia,* I, n. 275; Wernz, *Ius Decretalium,* III, 457; Alphonsus, *Theologia Moralis,* Lib. VI, n. 359.

[37] S. C. de Sacramentis, *Meliten.,* 22 mart. 1915, ad I—*Fontes,* n. 2110; S. C. de Sacramentis, *Romana et aliarum,* 23 dec. 1912, ad I,—*Fontes,* n. 2107; S. C. de Prop. Fide, decr. 18 nov. 1765—*Fontes,* n. 4547.

that even after the Council of Trent bishops had the faculty to permit Mass to be said outside a church or oratory *per modum actus* in cases of grave necessity.

The present law as contained in canon 822, § 4, adopts the pre-Code discipline. There were some who thought that a change was introduced in the Code, since the earlier law required a grave cause to justify the granting of the permission, and the new law demands only a just and reasonable cause. This opinion no longer holds, for the Holy See itself, in a letter to the bishops of Italy, has clearly stated that canon 822, § 4, confirms the traditional discipline concerning this matter.[38] Furthermore the secretary of the Sacred Congregation of the Sacraments in the annotations concerning a reply of May 3, 1926, stated:

> ". . . From this obligation [that of celebrating Mass in a church or oratory], according to the ancient practice, there was but one excuse, namely, a *great* (c. 1, D. I, *de consecr.*) or *supreme necessity* (c. 11, D. I, cit.). . . . Has the Code introduced a change? Some think so, and seem to be influenced by the fact that the Code requires a *just and reasonable cause;* from which they conclude that the cause need not be a grave one.
>
> But if one considers that not only the reason for the permission must be just and reasonable, but besides that the permission must be given only by way of act, and only in an extraordinary case, it can reasonably be inferred that there is no change in this respect. For the gravity of the cause, or necessity, is to be taken in moral estimation; and since c. 822, § 4, requires that not only the cause be just and reasonable, but that the permission be granted by the Ordinary only by way of act and in some extraordinary case, surely we have then a case of moral necessity. And therefore no change has been introduced in the old law and jurisprudence."[39]

Thus, there can be little doubt that canon 822, § 4, as regards the cause necessary for the granting of the permission in question, has confirmed the regulations as they existed before the Code.

[38] S. C. de Sacramentis, litt. ad Revmos. Ordinarios Italiae, 26 iul. 1924—*AAS,* XVI (1924), 370-371.

[39] S. C. de Sacramentis, *Romana et aliarum,* 3 maii 1926, *adnotationes,* ad I—*AAS,* XVIII (1926), 389-390; translation by Bouscaren, *The Canon Law Digest,* I, 388.

(b) The Just and Reasonable Cause

The cause required for the exercise of the faculty must be just and reasonable. Such a cause must be intimately connected with divine worship or with the spiritual good of the faithful.[40] Profane celebrations, political gatherings and other such meetings, which have no bearing whatsoever on divine worship or the spiritual welfare of the faithful, are excluded by the Holy See as inadequate reasons for the granting of the permission.[41] Much less can any purpose, occasion, or gathering, which has a superstitious import, be regarded as a just and reasonable cause. In these cases, if the petitioner insists that the permission be given for special considerations, by reason of a person, place, or time, the ordinary may not give the permission, but must refer the matter to the Holy See.[42]

Authors before the Code, in dealing with the cause required for the legitimate use of this faculty of ordinaries, invariably mentioned the necessity of the faithful to fulfill the precept of hearing Mass. In furnishing examples of this necessity there was common agreement that the need of a great number of the faithful to fulfill the precept constituted the required cause. Thus, they held that the ordinary can permit the use of a portable altar, for example, when the church was destroyed; when it was too small to accommodate the faithful on a solemn feast; when in time of pestilence the faithful cannot hear Mass in a church, because of the danger of contagion; when a large number of the faithful on a journey cannot go to a church, etc.[43] In general, this necessity was regarded as present when there was no church or oratory, or when the church or oratory could not be attended, or attended only with grave inconvenience, and the precept of hearing Mass could not otherwise be fulfilled on the part of a great number of the faithful.[44]

[40] Coronata, *De Sacramentis,* I, n. 258.

[41] S. C. de Sacramentis, 26 iul. 1924—*AAS,* XVI (1924), 370.

[42] *AAS,* XVI (1924), 370; Coronata, *op. cit.,* I, n. 258.

[43] Cf. Gasparri, *De Sanctissima Eucharistia,* I, n. 276; Many, *Praelectiones de Missa,* n. 6; Cappello, *De Sacramentis,* I, n. 710; Coronata, *De Sacramentis,* I, n. 258.

[44] Gasparri, *op. cit.,* I, n. 274.

Since the necessity of fulfilling the precept on the part of a great number of the faithful was regarded in the law before the Code as a sufficient cause for the grant of permission to celebrate Mass outside a church or oratory, and since canon 822, § 4, as already seen, merely confirms the earlier law, it seems that a similar cause justifies local ordinaries and major superiors in granting the permission in question under the present law.[45]

Hence the necessity of fulfilling the precept of hearing Mass on the part of a large number of the faithful, occasion of certain celebrations, meetings, or conventions which have a religious import, and such other causes connected with divine worship or the spiritual welfare of the faithful, are regarded as just and reasonable.

(c) In An Extraordinary Case

In addition to the existence of a just and reasonable cause, to permit the ordinary to use his faculty there is required an extraordinary case, and then he may exercise it *per modum actus,* but never to permit Mass to be said in a bedroom.[46]

There is some difficulty in determining exactly the meaning of the words "in an extraordinary case." A case that is common in a certain territory cannot be regarded as extraordinary in that territory. A similar case in relation to another territory may be truly extraordinary. For example, it occurs commonly in the United States that parish churches cannot accommodate all the parishioners for Sunday Mass; hence, a case of this kind cannot be regarded as extraordinary in relation to the United States. But this case can be extraordinary in relation to other territories in which such cases are rare. In determining the meaning of "extraordinary case" as used in the canon one must decide whether the case is extraordinary in relation to the diocese or country of the one who grants the permission, or extraordinary only in relation to the entire Church or Christian world. Since the Code legislates for the universal

[45] Cf. Guiniven, *The Precept of Hearing Mass,* The Catholic University of America Canon Law Studies, n. 158 (Washington, D. C.: The Catholic University of America Press, 1942), p. 124.

[46] Can. 822, § 4.

Church, Guiniven, who treats the matter extensively, concludes that the extraordinary case as demanded in the canon need be extraordinary only in relation to the entire Church.[47]

Authors enumerate various cases which justify the ordinary to permit the celebration of Mass outside a church or oratory. Some are as follows: when the parish church cannot accommodate all the parishioners for the Sunday Mass in consequence of the rapid increase in its membership; when the people in country "missions" are too poor to erect a church; when in a non-sectarian institution an oratory cannot be erected, due to the civil law or opposition of the authorities in charge; when Catholic Action groups, Boy Scouts, etc., by their meetings, give rise to an emergency; if there is need for Mass when there is no oratory in army camps, etc.[48] In these cases local ordinaries and major superiors—the latter within the added restrictions already indicated—can exercise the faculty enjoyed by reason of canon 822, § 4.

(d) "Per Modum Actus"

There is no common agreement among the authors as regards the precise meaning of the phrase *"per modum actus."* [49] All, however, admit that the ordinary or major superior cannot grant permission for Mass to be celebrated perpetually outside a church or oratory in any given case. It is also certain that he cannot by one and the same act grant the permission in a case which will endure for an extended period of time, for such permission would not be granted *"per modum actus."*

[47] *The Precept of Hearing Mass,* p. 128.

[48] Guiniven, *The Precept of Hearing Mass,* pp. 126 ff; Vermeersch-Creusen, *Epitome Iuris Canonici,* II, n. 100; Noldin-Schmitt, *De Sacramentis,* III, n. 201; Coronata, *De Sacramentis,* I, n. 259; Cappello, *De Sacramentis,* I, n. 710; Bouscaren, "De Missa ex licentia Ordinarii celebrata"—*Periodica,* XXVIII (1939), 52-61; Regatillo, *Ius Sacramentarium,* I, n. 220.

[49] Lehmkuhl in commenting states: "non habitualiter, sed pro singulis vicibus seu una alterave vice"—*Theologia Moralis,* II, n. 167; Sabetti-Barrett explain the phrase thus: ". . . non necessario significat semel tantum, sed excludit habitualiter. Si aliqua transitoria ratio habetur, ea durante, concedi potest facultas"—*Compendium Theologiae Moralis* (34. ed. [8. ed. post Codicem], Neo-Eboraci: Frederick Pustet Co., 1939), n. 716.

Furthermore, it does not seem probable that he can grant permission for the celebration of Mass as long as the cause endures (*durante causa*) if the cause and the case resulting endure for more than a few weeks, as this would certainly seem to misrepresent the notion of the phrase "*per modum actus.*" Cappello claims that the permission to celebrate Mass could be extended to eight or ten times if the cause endures.[50]

The opinion that the phrase "*per modum actus*" means for each individual act seems to be the best representation of the mind of the legislator in relation to canon 822, § 4. Thus it means that the concession can be made for only one act, that is, that the ordinary can give permission for one celebration of Mass outside a church or oratory. This opinion is based on the reply of the Holy See with annotations officially published May 3, 1926, which stated that canon 822, § 4, must be interpreted strictly.[51]

However, in view of the fact that this strict interpretation is given only rarely by authors,[52] it seems safe in practice to hold that the ordinary can grant the permission once or twice, or even a few times.[53] This view seems to be substantiated by the response of May 3, 1926, cited above, which allows the ordinary, on the occasion of the death of certain distinguished persons, to permit one or two Masses in the funeral chamber, but not more than three.

If the case is one which will endure for only a short time, the local ordinary may grant the permission for Mass to be said outside a church or oratory for the duration of the cause, not however through one act, but rather by renewing the permission each individual time when it is required, or at least every two or three weeks.

If, however, the case which calls for the exercise of the faculty in question is such that it will last permanently, or for an extended period of time, it seems necessary that the ordinary apply

50 *De Sacramentis,* I, n. 709; cf. Cocchi, *Commentarium,* V, n. 32.

51 S. C. de Sacramentis, 3 maii 1926, *adnotationes—AAS,* XVIII (1926), 391.

52 Augustine, *A Commentary,* IV, 173.

53 Vermeersch-Creusen, *Epitome Iuris Canonici,* II, n. 552; Lehmkuhl, *Theologia Moralis,* II, n. 167.

to the Holy See for a special indult. While recourse to the Holy See is being made, the ordinary may exercise his faculty in the meantime.[54]

As the mind of the Church manifests, it does not seem probable that the concept "*per modum actus*" could be extended to cases which of their nature will endure permanently or for a long time. Hence a special indult from the Holy See seems to be required to meet such a situation, for the unlimited exercise of the faculty is neither justified by the Code nor favored by the Holy See.[55]

(e) In a Decent Place

The celebration of Mass is permitted outside a church or oratory on a portable altar only on condition that the place be respectable and decent. This decency or fitness is to be judged not only by the objective standard of neatness and adornment, but also in the light of the respect and reverence due to the most Holy Sacrifice. The present law makes no positive demands as regards specific requirements in the place. Authors regard a place as decent if in the common estimation it is respectable, becoming, and fitting, such as to insure that due reverence not only can be observed, but actually is observed, and that all danger of profanation can be and is precluded.[56]

It is evident, therefore, that the positive demands in this regard are not exacting, and create little difficulty in fulfillment. The following article treats of those places which are regarded as not legitimate for the celebration of Mass. This may help to determine more clearly the notion of a decent place.

[54] Cappello, *De Sacramentis,* I, n. 709.

[55] Cf. Commissio Interpretationis Codicis, 16 oct. 1919, ad XII—*AAS,* XI (1919), 478; S. C. de Sacramentis, decr. 3 maii 1926—*AAS,* XVIII (1926), 388-391; 26 iul. 1924—*AAS,* XVI (1924), 370; Pius XI, Litterae Apostolicae, 30 apr. 1929, n. 8—*AAS,* XXI (1929), 556. Guiniven, *The Precept of Hearing Mass,* pp. 129 ff.; Bastnagel, "Cases and Studies"—*The Jurist,* II (1942), 155-158.

[56] Coronata, *De Sacramentis,* I, n. 257; Gasparri, *De Sanctissima Eucharistia,* I, n. 272; Bliley, *Altars,* p. 117.

Article 4. Places Where the Celebration of Mass Is Not Permitted

(a) On Board Ship

The present law regards a ship at sea as an unsafe and not as a fitting place for the celebration of Mass.

> **Canon 822, § 3. "Hoc privilegium [altaris portatilis] ita intelligendum est, ut secumferat facultatem ubique celebrandi, honesto tamen ac decenti loco et super petram sacram, non autem in mari."**

The reason for this exception is the danger of irreverence which results from the possible upsetting of the chalice and spilling of the Precious Blood. Such a danger is always present in stormy seas and in small ships. Thus, unless a special faculty is granted by the Holy See to those who already enjoy the privilege of a portable altar, Mass is not permitted on board ship at sea. As already shown, cardinals and bishops have this privilege by law.[57] Neither the proper ordinary of the priest nor the ordinary of the port can give the permission.[58]

All, except cardinals and bishops, require a special indult to exercise the privilege of a portable altar at sea. The permission is usually given only on condition that the sea is so calm that there is no danger of upsetting the chalice and of spilling the Precious Blood. Furthermore, the assistance of another priest, if he is present, is required as an additional precaution against the danger of irreverence to the Sacred Species. If there is no regular chapel or oratory on the ship, the missionaries who enjoy this faculty must be careful that the place selected be suitable and becoming. The Holy See regards private cells or cabins of the passengers as unfit and unbecoming places for the celebration of the Holy Sacrifice.[59]

[57] *Supra,* Chapter IX, p. 151.

[58] S. R. C., *Vicen.,* 4 mart. 1901—*Fontes,* n. 6310; Gasparri, *De Sanctissima Eucharistia,* I, n. 277; Coronata, *De Sacramentis,* I, n. 257; Many, *Praelectiones de Missa,* n. 12.

[59] S. C. de Prop. Fide, 1 mart. 1902—*Coll. S. C. de Prop. Fide,* n. 2130.

The above cited decree was further explained by the Sacred Congregation for the Propagation of the Faith when it declared that it did not absolutely forbid the celebration of Mass in private cells on board ship. It was forbidden only if these places were not suitable or becoming. The same Congregation regarded these cells as decent and suitable if there was no danger of irreverence, and declared that priests who had the special privilege to say Mass at sea could celebrate in them.[60]

There is an opinion that in large ships which have a regular oratory or chapel with the right of reserving the Blessed Sacrament there any priest can celebrate Mass even without an apostolic indult.[61] The reason given in substantiation of this opinion is that in modern large transoceanic vessels there is no danger of irreverence arising from the spilling of the Precious Blood, since, it is claimed, this danger does not exist in large ships. Hence, the purpose of the law in canon 822, § 3, ceases in these cases. Cappello, furthermore, holds for the same reason that in the same large ships which do not have a chapel a priest who possesses the privilege of a portable altar can celebrate Mass, provided that the place selected be suitable and decent according to law.[62]

Though these opinions do not lack probability, they seem too liberal in the light of the prescription of canon 822, § 3. For even though in a particular case the reason for the law ceases, there seems to be insufficient justification for concluding that the law does not bind in all similar particular cases. Such a conclusion seems to be at variance with the ruling of canon 21.[63]

Hence, even though in particular cases there may not be a danger of irreverence in the celebration of Mass aboard ship, there is always the general danger in this matter. Thus a special indult over and above the privilege of a portable altar is required for the celebration

[60] S. C. de Prop. Fide, 13 aug. 1902—*Coll. S. C. de Prop. Fide,* n. 2153.

[61] Coronata, *De Sacramentis,* I, n. 257; Cappello, *De Sacramentis,* I, n. 712.

[62] *De Sacramentis,* I, n. 712; cf. Coronata, *De Sacramentis,* I, n. 257, footnote 5.

[63] Can. 21. Leges latae ad praecavendum periculum generale, urgent, etiamsi in casu peculiari periculum non adsit. Cf. also Hannan, "Cases and Studies"—*The Jurist,* VIII (1948), 69-70.

of Mass at sea. The Holy See alone grants this privilege. In the United States, however, the faculties of the Apostolic Delegate permit him to allow priests to celebrate Mass on board ship on a portable altar, provided that there be nothing unbecoming about the place where Mass is celebrated, and that there be no danger of the spilling of the Precious Blood.[64]

The faithful fulfill the precept of hearing Mass by assisting at the Mass celebrated aboard ship, provided it is said in the chapel used only for religious purposes.[65]

(*b*) *The Celebration of Mass in a Bedroom*

It is evident that the faculty of the local ordinary and of the major religious superior to grant the permission to say Mass on a portable altar does not include the permission to celebrate Mass in a bedroom as in a legitimate place.[66] There are some, however, who hold a probable opinion that those who enjoy the privilege of a portable altar by apostolic concession can exercise the privilege even in a bedroom.[67] They claim that the privilege of a portable altar obtained from the Holy See can be used everywhere, provided that the place be decent and respectable, and that the only exception is the celebration of Mass at sea.

This view seems to be against the prescription of the present law, as well as being at variance with the practice of the Church in this matter down through the ages. It is true that only one exception is made in canon 822, § 3, namely, the celebration of Mass at sea. But from this it cannot be concluded that the privilege can be used everywhere else, for the term *"ubique celebrandi"* is further limited by the condition which demands that the place be respectable and decent (*honesto tamen ac decenti loco.*) Hence the matter

[64] Bouscaren, *The Canon Law Digest,* I, 182.

[65] S. R. C., *Vicen.,* 4 mart. 1901, ad V—*Fontes,* n. 6310; Vermeersch-Creusen, *Epitome Iuris Canonici,* II, n. 563; Coronata, *Institutiones Iuris Canonici,* II, n. 824.

[66] Can. 822, § 4.

[67] Coronata, *De Locis et Temporibus* Sacris, n. 123; Barin, "Commentarium ad Canones Iuris Canonici sacram Liturgiam Spectantes,"—*Ephemerides Liturgicae* (Roma, Via Pompeo Magno, 21), XXXIV (1920), 353.

resolves itself into a determination of the question whether or not a bedroom is a suitable and becoming place for the celebration of Mass according to the present law.

In the law prior to the Code a bedroom was considered an unbecoming place for the celebration of the Holy Sacrifice. The Holy See granted the privilege of celebrating Mass in private houses, but rarely outside of a domestic oratory. The privilege was sometimes extended in favor of sick persons so that it was made allowable to celebrate Mass in an adjacent room, but never in the room in which the patient lay in bed. This extraordinary privilege was only granted to kings and most distinguished persons, and was of very rare occurrence.[68] The Sacred Congregation of the Sacraments on February 7, 1909 in explaining the privilege of a portable altar granted to sick persons, declared that Mass can be said in a room next to the bedroom or close to it, but not in the bedroom itself.[69]

Canon 822, § 3, states that the privilege of a portable altar granted through an indult from the Holy See can be used for the celebration of Mass anywhere in a respectable and decent place (*honesto tamen ac decenti loco*), but makes one exception, namely, that the privilege cannot be used to celebrate at sea. The canon does not list the places regarded as unsuitable or unbecoming, and mentions the sea because of the danger of irreverence arising from *insecurity*, but not because the sea is regarded as an unbecoming place. Hence, one must look outside of canon 822, § 3, for a determination of the places considered as unsuitable and unbecoming.

In canon 822, § 4, the bedroom is specifically mentioned as excluded from the category of a *"locus decens"* and indeed is excluded in the strongest terminology, so that the ordinary can *never* grant permission for the celebration of Mass there. Hence there seems to be no reason for holding that the bedroom is to be considered as unbecoming in canon 822, § 4, but is not to be considered as such in canon 822, § 3.

Furthermore, unless it is maintained that a bedroom is an un-

[68] Cf. Gattico, *De Oratoriis Domesticis*, Pars II, c. XIV, nn. 9, 10; c. XV, n. 12; Regatillo, *Ius Sacramentarium*, I, n. 219.

[69] S. C. de Sacramentis, *Romana et aliarum*, 23 dec. 1912—*AAS*, IV (1912), 725.

becoming place, it would otherwise be difficult to explain and give an adequate reason why the local ordinary can never grant permission for the celebration of Mass in a bedroom, not even "*per modum actus*," while all those who enjoy the privilege of a portable altar in virtue of an indult from the Holy See are allowed to do so. Hence it seems that there can be little doubt that the privilege of a portable altar cannot be used in a bedroom without a special indult obtainable only from the Holy See.[70]

(*c*) *The Celebration of Mass in the Churches of Heretics and Schismatics*

Canon 823, § 1. "Non licet Missam celebrare in templo haereticorum vel schismaticorum, etsi olim rite consecrato aut benedicto."

Masses may not be said in the churches of heretics or schismatics, even though they may have once been duly consecrated or blessed. Pope Benedict XIV in his epistle of May 12, 1756, furnished the attitude of the Church towards the temples of heretics and schismatics, and proved by examples dating back to the Arians in the sixth century that the temples which formerly had belonged to non-Catholic sects were sometimes reconsecrated. It was also shown that if the dedicating minister of the temple of heretics or schismatics did not possess the true episcopal character, or if the rite used in the dedication ceremony was not the one prescribed by the Catholic Church, the temple was certainly not consecrated or blessed.[71]

The present law does not change the older discipline, but prohibits the celebration of the Holy Sacrifice in the churches of those who profess a false religion. The decisions of the Roman Congregations all convey the uniform position that wherever possible, rather than to say Mass in a non-Catholic temple, a priest should either use a portable altar or celebrate Mass in a private house.[72] Associa-

[70] Regatillo, *Ius Sacramentarium*, I, n. 219; Cappello, *De Sacramentis*, I, n. 712.

[71] Benedictus XIV, ep. *Iam inde*, 12 maii 1756, §§ 3 sq—*Fontes*, n. 440.

[72] S. C. de Prop. Fide, 21 maii 1627; 13 febr. 1629; 7 maii 1631—*Coll. S. C. de Prop. Fide*, nn. 34, 47, 69; *Fontes*, n.n. 4436, 4442, 4447.

tion and communication with heretics or schismatics, especially with regard to things pertaining to divine worship, always entails the danger of scandal and perversion, for such intermingling can give the impression of the condonation and approval of the heresy or schism. Thus while the church building remains in the possession of the non-Catholic sect, Mass cannot be celebrated there.

Exceptions to this rule are few, and even then they obtain only in the case of necessity and under certain restrictive conditions. The Holy Office permitted the use of a schismatic church in a case of necessity, but insisted that a separate Catholic altar be set up therein, and that one part of the church be reserved exclusively for Catholics.[73] Another instance of a special concession in this matter was the permission to use a garrison or army camp chapel simultaneously used for Catholic and non-Catholic services, but the Holy Office in granting the permission required that petition be made to the civil government to build a separate chapel for Catholics, or, if this could not be done, that one be erected from the proceeds of alms.[74]

Pope Clement XI had permitted Mass to be said in the so-called "simultaneous churches" in Switzerland after the reformation.[75] These churches became thus characterized because they were used by Catholics and non-Catholics alike for services which were held at different hours.[76] Since these buildings were not completely in the possession of non-Catholic sects, but rather destined for the public in general, the danger of scandal or perversion in the existing case of necessity was remote, for the churches were neutral buildings rather than the churches of heretical sects.[77]

[73] S. C. S. Off. (Archiep. Antibaren.), 1 dec. 1757—*Coll. S. C. de Prop. Fide*, n. 408; *Fontes*, n. 809.

[74] S. C. S. Off. (ad. Vic. Ap. Malacen.), 5 iun. 1889—*Coll. S. C. de Prop. Fide*, n. 1707; *Fontes*, n. 1119.

[75] S. C. S. Off., 13 iun. 1634—*Coll. S. C. de Prop. Fide*, n. 75.

[76] Augustine, *A Commentary*, IV, 174.

[77] Cappello, *De Sacramentis*, I, n. 713.

(*d*) *The Celebration of Mass on an Altar of Another Rite*

As a general rule Oriental churches had only one altar, and upon this altar only one Mass was celebrated each day.[78] Due to the increase in the number of clergy, this restriction regarding the use of an altar often occasioned much difficulty. The problem was solved for the Oriental rites with the approbation of the practice of concelebration,[79] but priests of the Latin rite cannot concelebrate except at the Ordination Mass, and at the Mass of the consecration of a bishop.[80] To facilitate matters in order that more Masses might be said each day, chapels or oratories called *parecclesiae* were built to adjoin the church. Besides, there was often found in the Byzantine churches not only a Greek altar for the Greek priests, but also a Latin altar for the Latin priests.[81]

In spite of the fact that these facilities were allowed, the Church did not favor the indiscriminate use of a church building or of an altar of another rite. Pope Benedict XIV in no uncertain terms forbade priests of the Latin rite to say Mass in churches of the Greek rite, and upon the main altar of these churches, except in cases of necessity, namely, when there were no churches of the Latin rite in that place, and when there were no other altars in the church of the Greek rite. Furthermore, the Latin priest had to have the permission of the pastor of the Greek church, who however was not free in such circumstances to refuse this permission.[82]

On the other hand, the priests of the Greek rite were not allowed to celebrate in the churches of the Latin rite, unless they had permission from the Latin ordinary, or from his vicar general, who

[78] Benedictus XIV, const. *Etsi pastoralis,* 26 maii 1742, § VI, n. VIII—*Fontes,* n. 328; ep. encycl. *Demandatum,* 24 dec. 1743, § 8—*Fontes,* n. 338; ep. encycl. *Allatae sunt,* 26 iul. 1755, § 37—*Fontes,* n. 434; Gasparri, *De Sanctissima Eucharistia,* I, n. 287.

[79] Benedictus XIV, ep. encycl. *Demandatam,* § 9; *Allatae sunt,* § 38; Gasparri, *op. cit.,* I, n. 360.

[80] Can. 803.

[81] Benedictus XIV, ep. encycl. *Allatae sunt,* 26 iul. 1155, § 39—*Fontes,* n. 434.

[82] Const. *Etsi pastoralis,* § VI, n. VIII; § IX, n. XV—*Fontes,* n. 328.

could grant this permission even though no necessity existed as long as some spiritual good could be expected.[83]

Pope Benedict XIV stated also in his encyclical that the celebration of Mass in a church of another rite did not constitute a promiscuity of rites.[84] It was understood that a priest who celebrated Mass in a church of another rite or upon an altar of another rite had to follow the rubrics of his own rite. The use of the vestments and of the sacred vessels, as well as of the altar, was reserved to each rite, and could not be used by the priests of another rite.

However, Pope Benedict XIV confirmed the privilege granted by Pope Clement VIII (1592-1605) in 1602, which allowed Ruthenian priests to celebrate their Mass according to the Ruthenian rite in churches and upon altars and with the vestments and sacred vessels of the Latin rite. On the other hand, in virtue of the same privilege, priests of the Latin rite were permitted to say Mass in the Latin rite on the altars in Ruthenian churches, and to use the vestments and sacred vessels of the Ruthenian rite.[85]

The Code of Canon Law abrogated the former legislation concerning the prohibition against the celebration of Mass in the church of another rite and upon an altar of another rite. Canon 823, § 2, states the law which now obtains for priests of both rites:

> "Deficiente altari proprii ritus, sacredoti fas est ritu proprio celebrare in altari consecrato alius ritus catholici, non autem super Graecorum *antimensiis*."

Thus, in order to celebrate Mass lawfully on an altar of another rite, four conditions are required according to canon 823, § 2: (1) that an altar of the priest's own rite be not available; (2) that the celebrant say the Mass according to his own rite; (3) that the altar be consecrated; and (4) that the altar pertain

[83] Const. *Etsi pastoralis,* § IX, n. XVI—*Fontes,* n. 328; cf. also ep. encycl. *Allatae sunt,* § 35—*Fontes,* n. 434; const. *Imposito nobis,* 29 mart. 1751, § 7—*Fontes,* n. 410.

[84] Ep. encycl. *Allatae sunt,* 26 iul. 1755, § 35—*Fontes,* n. 343.

[85] Benedictus XIV, const. *Imposito nobis,* 29 mart. 1751, § 7: Pope Benedict XIV here quoted the decree of Pope Clement VIII—*Fontes,* n. 410.

to a Catholic rite. If a priest celebrated Mass on the altar of another rite, he would sin gravely if any one of these conditions were unfulfilled.[86] Thus, the present law does not prohibit the celebration of Mass in the church of another rite; it prohibits simply the use of an altar of another rite without any necessity.

The altar used must be consecrated. If it pertains to the Latin rite there is no difficulty, since all altars in that rite must be consecrated before Mass can be celebrated on them. However, the Oriental rite distinguishes two kinds of altars: (1) altars consecrated by a bishop, which are found only in consecrated churches, and are the same as the consecrated altars of the Latin rite, and (2) the *Antimension.* This second type of altar corresponds to the Latin corporal and altar stone. It is a square piece of linen doubled, in which are sewn relics anointed by the bishop with chrism. The *Antimension* is always consecrated by an Oriental bishop, and is used for the celebration of Mass in the Oriental rite on a consecrated altar as well as on an unconsecrated altar.[87]

A priest of the Latin rite cannot use the *Antimension,* since he must celebrate Mass on a consecrated altar. Only with an indult from the Holy See can priests of the Latin rite use the Greek *Antimension.*[88] The indult to use this altar is given to priests who enroll in the Catholic Near East Welfare Association. The indult was given at Rome on January 28, 1928, and granted enrolled priests the privilege of saying Mass in churches of the Oriental rite on the Greek corporal (*super antimensiis Graecorum*).[89]

It cannot be concluded that this indult abrogates the requirements of canon 823, § 2. Hence a priest with an indult by virtue of his enrollment in the Catholic Near East Welfare Association can celebrate Mass on a Greek *Antimension* only when it is impossible

[86] Cappello, *De Sacramentis,* I, 720.

[87] Henry, *The Mass and Holy Communion*: *Interritual Law,* The Catholic University of American Canon Law Studies, n. 235 (Washington, D. C.: The Catholic University of America Press, 1946), pp. 23, 24; cf. also Gulovich, "Mass and Communion according to the Oriental Rite in a Church of the Latin Rite"—*The Jurist,* II (1942), 48.

[88] Can. 823, § 2.

[89] The only record of this indult is the leaflet issued by the Catholic Near East Welfare Association, which lists all the privileges enjoyed by the members.

for him to celebrate on a consecrated altar of his own rite, whether portable or fixed, or upon an altar consecrated in another rite, whether portable or fixed.[90] Permission has also been granted to military chaplains serving at the front to offer Mass without an altar stone, and to use instead the *Antimension*.[91]

(*e*) *Papal Altars*

A papal altar is so called either because it was consecrated by the Pope or because he said Mass upon it or because he directly granted this special distinction to it.[92] With regard to these altars the Code of Canon Law retains the former legislation, and prescribes that no one is allowed to say Mass on papal altars without an apostolic indult.

Canon 823, § 3. "In altaribus papalibus nemo celebret sine apostolico indulto."

The reason for this rule is inherent in the consideration given to the dignity of the consecrator or grantor, who is the Roman Pontiff himself.[93]

The main papal altars are the following: the principal altars of St. John Lateran, of St. Peter (Vatican), of St. Paul Outside the Walls, and of St. Mary Major in Rome, the High Altar of the

[90] Henry, *The Mass and Holy Communion: Interritual Law*, p. 72.

[91] Bouscaren, *The Canon Law Digest*, II, 204; "Decrees and Decisions"—*The Jurist*, III (1943), 158.

[92] Benedictus XIV, ep. *Dilectus Filius*, 15 ian. 1745, § 1: "Equidem cum Nos ipsi sacraverimus hoc altare, et super ipso Deo operati Sacrum fuerimus, ob hanc causam pontificium altare appellandum est, nec ulli licet sacerdoti ad ipsum accedere, ut Missae sacrificium peragat, nisi antea facultas nostra intercesserit, iuxta morem, et institutum S. Romanae Ecclesiae, quae mater et magistra ceterarum Ecclesiarum habenda est. Id aperte demonstratur exemplo altarium, quae sunt in Ecclesiis Lateranensi, Vaticana, aliisque Patriarchalibus huius Urbis, in quibus aris solus Romanus Pontifex Sacrum facere potest, aut etiam Cardinalis aliquis certis temporibus, facta tamen prius a Pontifice potestate, quae per apostolicum diploma declaratur"—*Fontes*, n. 352.

[93] Cf. Augustine, *A Commentary*, IV, 174, 175.

Basilica of St. Francis at Assisi, and the altar sent to King John V (1706-1750) in Lisbon, Portugal.[94]

Before anyone other than the Holy Father may celebrate Mass on these altars, permission must be obtained from the Holy See on each individual occasion for use. However on the occasion of an extraordinary solemnity when the Pope himself cannot be present to say the Mass, permission is given to cardinals to say the Mass on the papal altar.[95]

[94] Cf. Benedictus XIV, ep. *Dilectus Filius,* 15 ian. 1745, § 1—*Fontes,* n. 352; allocut. *Postquam,* 30 sept. 1750, § 3—*Fontes,* n. 408; const. *Ad honorandum,* 27 mart. 1752, § 16—*Fontes,* n. 420; const. *Fidelis Dominus,* 25 mart. 1754, § 6—*Fontes,* n. 427; ep. *In postremo,* 20 oct. 1756, § 9—*Fontes,* n. 442.

[95] Coronata, *De Sacramentis,* I, n. 256.

Dates	0°	5°	10°	15°	20°	25°	30°	35°	40°	45°	50°	55°	60°	65°
	h.m.	h.m.	h.m.	h.m.	h.m.	h.m.	h.m.	h.m.	h.m.	h.m.	h.m.	h.m.	h.m.	h.m.
January 1	1.16	1.16	1.16	1.18	1.20	1.23	1.27	1.32	1.39	1.48	2.01	2.19	2.48	3.42
January 16	1.15	1.15	1.15	1.17	1.19	1.21	1.25	1.30	1.37	1.46	1.58	2.14	2.39	3.22
January 31	1.13	1.13	1.14	1.15	1.17	1.20	1.23	1.28	1.34	1.43	1.54	2.09	2.30	3.03
February 15	1.11	1.12	1.12	1.14	1.15	1.18	1.22	1.26	1.32	1.40	1.50	2.04	2.23	2.51
March 12	1.10	1.11	1.11	1.13	1.14	1.17	1.21	1.25	1.31	1.39	1.49	2.03	2.21	2.49
March 17	1.10	1.10	1.11	1.12	1.14	1.17	1.21	1.26	1.32	1.40	1.51	2.05	2.26	2.58
April 1	1.10	1.10	1.11	1.13	1.15	1.18	1.22	1.27	1.34	1.43	1.55	2.13	2.41	3.35
April 16	1.11	1.11	1.12	1.14	1.17	1.20	1.25	1.31	1.39	1.49	2.05	2.30	3.22	(1)
May 1	1.12	1.13	1.14	1.16	1.19	1.23	1.28	1.35	1.45	1.59	2.21	3.07	(1)	(1)
May 16	1.14	1.15	1.16	1.18	1.22	1.26	1.32	1.41	1.53	2.11	2.47	(1)	(1)	(1)
May 31	1.15	1.16	1.18	1.20	1.24	1.29	1.36	1.45	2.00	2.35	3.45	(1)	(1)	(1)
June 15	1.16	1.17	1.19	1.21	1.25	1.31	1.38	1.48	2.05	2.35	(1)	(1)	(1)	(1)
June 30	1.16	1.17	1.19	1.21	1.25	1.30	1.38	1.48	2.04	2.34	(1)	(1)	(1)	(1)
July 15	1.15	1.16	1.18	1.20	1.24	1.28	1.35	1.45	1.59	2.23	3.25	(1)	(1)	(1)
July 30	1.14	1.14	1.16	1.14	1.21	1.25	1.32	1.40	1.51	2.09	2.41	(1)	(1)	(1)
August 14	1.12	1.13	1.14	1.16	1.19	1.22	1.28	1.34	1.44	1.57	2.18	2.58	(1)	(1)
August 29	1.11	1.11	1.12	1.18	1.17	1.20	1.24	1.30	1.38	1.49	2.04	2.27	3.12	(1)
September 13	1.10	1.10	1.11	1.13	1.15	1.18	1.22	1.27	1.34	1.43	1.55	2.12	2.38	3.26
September 28	1.10	1.10	1.11	1.12	1.14	1.17	1.21	1.25	1.32	1.40	1.50	2.05	2.25	2.56
October 13	1.10	1.11	1.11	1.13	1.15	1.17	1.21	1.25	1.31	1.39	1.49	2.03	2.21	2.48
October 28	1.12	1.12	1.12	1.14	1.16	1.18	1.22	1.26	1.33	1.40	1.51	2.05	2.24	2.52
November 12	1.13	1.13	1.14	1.16	1.17	1.20	1.24	1.28	1.35	1.43	1.54	2.09	2.31	3.04
November 27	1.15	1.15	1.15	1.17	1.19	1.22	1.26	1.30	1.37	1.46	1.54	2.15	2.40	3.24
December 12	1.16	1.16	1.16	1.18	1.20	1.23	1.27	1.32	1.39	1.48	2.01	2.19	2.48	3.44
December 27	1.16	1.16	1.17	1.18	1.20	1.23	1.27	1.32	1.39	1.49	2.01	2.20	2.49	3.47

(1) The sun does not descend lower than 18 degrees below the horizon.

CONCLUSIONS

(1) There is not sufficient historical evidence to prove that Mass was offered daily during the first centuries, but after the Edict of Milan (313) daily solemn Mass became a common practice.

(2) Even up to the time of Gratian (ca. 1140) there was no legislation determining definitely the hours for the celebration especially of private Mass.

(3) There was never an offering of the Holy Sacrifice without an altar, but only after the last persecution (284-305) was legislation introduced against the celebration of Mass in private houses.

(4) Even though private low Masses were prohibited on the last three days of Holy Week, nevertheless it is evident from a study of the decrees of the Congregation of Sacred Rites and the opinions of the authors that the Church desires that both clergy and faithful be provided every opportunity of hearing Mass on Holy Thursday. Thus, for a reasonable cause which need not be a grave one, the bishop can permit a private low Mass on Holy Thursday.

(5) The expression *"in privata Missae celebratione"* in canon 33, § 1, must be taken in the juridic sense as any Mass, either a low Mass, a *Missa cantata,* or a solemn Mass, the celebration of which does not arise as a duty deriving from an official ecclesiastical obligation.

(6) The violation of the law which determines the time for the celebration of Mass is gravely sinful if without an excusing cause the celebrant anticipates or postpones the celebration for a period of one hour contrary to the prescriptions of the law. It seems that a more grave cause is required for the celebration of Mass earlier than one hour before dawn, than for its celebration after one o'clock in the afternoon.

(7) The bishop can for a just cause determine the schedule of Masses for the churches of the diocese, except for the churches of exempt religious. This exception holds only if in these churches sermons are preached and religious instructions are afforded to the faithful who are in attendance.

(8) In the face of the quite common occurrence in the United States that either there is no church in a given locality, or the church is too small to accommodate all, there exists an emergency which reflects the necessity of a great number of the faithful to hear Mass. These circumstances constitute an "extraordinary case" which seems to justify the bishop to exercise his faculty according to canon 822, § 4.

(9) The phrase *"per modum actus"* in reference to the faculty of the local ordinary to allow the celebration of Mass outside of a church or oratory cannot be extended to cases which endure either permanently or for a long period of time. In these cases a special indult is required from the Holy See.

(10) The opinion of Cappello, who claims that any priest even without the privilege of a portable altar may celebrate Mass on board ship, provided there is a chapel or oratory with the reservation of the Blessed Sacrament, seems to be at variance with the general law, and thus appears not to constitute a truly probable opinion.

(11) The view that the privilege of a portable altar can be exercised for the celebration of Mass in a bedroom is to be rejected as untenable.

BIBLIOGRAPHY

Sources

Acta Apostolicae Sedis, Commentarium Officiale, Romae, 1909—.

Acta et Decreta Concilii Plenarii Baltimorensis II, in Ecclesia Metropolitana Baltimorensi, a die VII ad diem XXI. Octobris A.D. MDCCCLXVI, Habiti et a Sede Apostolica Recogniti, editio altera mendis expurgata, Baltimore: John Murphy, 1894.

Acta et Decreta Concilii Plenarii Baltimorensis Tertii, A.D. MDCCCLXXXIV, Baltimore: John Murphy, 1886.

Acta Sanctae Sedis, 41 vols., Romae, 1865-1908.

Bouscaren, T. Lincoln, *The Canon Law Digest*, 2 vols., Milwaukee: The Bruce Publishing Company, Vol. I, 1934, and Vol. II, 1943.

Bullarium Romanum, a Leone I (440) ad Clementem XII (1740), 24 vols. cum appendice, ed. Taurinensis, 1857-1872.

Bullarii Romani Continuatio, 1740-1830, 14 vols., Prati, 1843-1867.

Caeremoniale Episcoporum, Clementis VIII, Innocentii X, et Benedicti XIII iussu editum, Benedicti XIV et Leonis XIII auctoritate recognitum, Mechliniae: H. Dessain, 1906.

Codex Iuris Canonici, Pii X Pontificis Maximi iussu digestus Benedicti Papae XV auctoritate promulgatus, ed. Petri Card. Gasparri, Civitate Vaticana: Typis Polyglottis Vaticanis, 1917. Reimpressio 1934.

Codicis Iuris Canonici Fontes, cura Emi Petri Card. Gasparri editi, 9 vols., Romae (postea Civitate Vaticana): Typis Polyglottis Vaticanis, 1923-1939. (Vols. VII, VIII, IX, ed. cura et studio Emi Iustiniani Card. Serédi).

Collectanea S. Congregationis de Propaganda Fide, 2 vols., Romae: Typographia Polyglotta S. C. de Propaganda Fide, 1907.

Concilii Tridentini Diariorum, Actorum, Epistularum, Tractatuum, Nova Collectio, edidit Societas Goerresiana, 13 vols. (incomplete), Friburgi Brisgoviae: Herder, 1901-1938. II, *Diariorum pars secunda* (ed. S. Markle, 1911).

Corpus Iuris Canonici, Editio Lipsiensis, 2 vols., ed. E. Friedberg, Lipsiae, 1879-1881 (Reimpressio 1922).

Corpus Iuris Civilis, 3 vols., Berolini: Weidmannos, 1928-1929; Vol. III, ed. stereotypa quinta, *Novellae*, quas recognovit Rudolphus Schoell; opus Schoellii morte interceptum absolvit Gulielmus Kroll, Berolini: Weidmannos, 1928.

Decreta Authentica Congregationis Sacrorum Rituum ex Actis eiusdem collecta eiusque auctoritate promulgata sub auspiciis SS. D. N. Leonis Papae XIII, 6 vols., Romae: 1898-1927.

Decretales D. Gregorii Papae IX suae integritati una cum glossis restitutae, cum privilegio Gregorii XIII, Pont. Max., et aliorum Principum, Romae, 1582.

Decretum Gratiani emendatum et notationibus illustratum una cum glossis, Gregorii XIII, Pont. Max. iussu editum, 2 vols., Romae, 1582.

Haddan, A. W., and Stubbs, W., *Councils and Ecclesiastical Documents relating to Great Britain and Ireland,* 3 vols. in 4, Oxford: Clarendon Press, 1869-1873.

Hardouin, Jean, *Acta Conciliorum et Epistolae Decretales ac Constitutiones Summorum Pontificum,* 12 vols., Parisiis, 1714-1715.

Jaffé, Phillipus, *Regesta Pontificum Romanorum ab condita Ecclesia ad annum post Christum natum MCXCVIII,* ed. 2 correctam et auctam auspiciis Gulielmi Wattenbach curaverunt S. Loewenfeld, F. Kaltenbrunner, P. Ewald, 2 vols. in 1, Lipsiae, 1885-1888.

Liber Sextus Decretalium D. Bonifatii Papae VIII, suae Integritati una cum Clementinis et Extravagantibus, earumque Glossis restitutus, cum privilegio Gregorii XIII, Pont. Max. et aliorum Principum, Romae, 1582.

Mansi, J. D., *Sacrorum Conciliorum Nova et Amplissima Collectio,* 53 vols. in 60, Parisiis, 1901-1927.

Missale Romanum ex Decreto Sacrosancti Concilii Tridentini restitutum, S. Pii V Pontificis Maximi iussu editum, aliorum Pontificum cura recognitum, a Pio X reformatum et Ssmi D. N. Benedicti XV auctoritate vulgatum, editio decima iuxta typicam, Turonibus: Typis Alfredi Mame et Filiorum, (1926).

Monumenta Germaniae Historia (188 vols., incomplete, Hannoverae, 1825—). *Gesta Pontificum Romanorum,* Vol. I, *Liber Pontificalis,* pars prior, ed. Theodorus Mommsen, Berolini, 1898.

Leges, in folio, 5 vols.; Vol. II, pars 2, *Capitula Spuria,* ed. G. H. Pertz, Hannoverae, 1837; Neudruck, 1925.

Leges, in 4°, Sectio II, *Capitularia Regum Francorum,* 2 vols., ed. A. Boretius et V. Krause, Hannoverae, 1883-1897.

Sectio III, *Concilia,* 3 vols., ed. F. Maassen, A. Werminghoff, H. Bastgen, Hannoverae, 1893-1924.

Epistolae, in 4°, 7 vols., Vol. VI, pars 2, fasc. 1.

Epistolae Karolini Aevi, ed. Ernestus Perels, Hannoverae, 1912.

Pallottini, Salvator, *Collectio omnium Conclusionum et Resolutionum quae in causis propositis apud Sacram Congregationem Cardinalium S. Concilii Tridentini Interpretum Prodierunt ab eius institutione anno MDLXIV ad annum MDCCCLX, distinctis titulis alphabetico ordine per materias digesta,* 18 vols., Romae, 1868-1895.

Pontificale Romanum, Summorum Pontificum iussu editum, a Benedicto XIV et Leone XIII, Pontificibus Maximis, recognitum et castigatum, tres partes cum Appendice in 4 vols., Cincinnati: Pustet, 1908.

Potthast, A., *Regesta Pontificum Romanorum inde ab anno post Christum natum MCXCVIII ad annum MCCCIV,* 2 vols., Berolini, 1874-1875.

Rituale Romanum Pauli V Pontificis Maximi iussu editum, aliorumque Pontificum cura recognitum, atque auctoritate Ssmi D. N. Pii Papae XI ad Normam Codicis Iuris Canonici Accommodatum, editio altera iuxta typicam, Ratisbonae: Sumptibus Typis Frederici Pustet, 1929.

Schroeder, H. J., *Canons and Decrees of the Council of Trent, Original Text with English Translation,* St. Louiis, Mo.: B. Herder Book Co., 1941.

Thesaurus Resolutionum Sacrae Congregationis Concilii, 167 vols., Romae, 1718-1908.

Wilson, H. A., *The Gelasian Sacramentary, Liber Sacramentorum Romanae Ecclesiae,* edited with introduction, critical notes and appendix, Oxford: Clarendon Press, 1894.

AUTHORS

Alphonsus Maria de Ligorio, St., *Theologia Moralis,* ed. nova cura et studio P. L. Gaudé, 4 vols., Romae: Typis Polyglottis Vaticanis, 1905-1912.

Aquinas, St. Thomas, *Summa Theologica,* editio XXII diligenter emendata, 6 vols., Taurini-Romae: Marietti, 1939.

———, *Commentaria in Quatuor Libros Sententiarum Petri Lombardi, emendata per Joannem Nicolai,* 4 vols. in 2, Parisiis, 1659.

Augustine, Charles, *A Commentary on the New Code of Canon Law,* 8 vols., Vol. IV, 3. ed., Vol. VI, 3. ed., St. Louis, Mo.: B. Herder & Co., 1925-31.

Ayrinhac, H. A., *Administrative Legislation in the New Code of Canon Law,* New York: Longmans, Green & Co., 1930.

Ballerini, A.—Palmieri, P., *Opus Theologicum Morale,* 7 vols., Prati, 1889-1893.

Benedictus XIV (Prosper Lambertini), *Commentarius de Sacrosancto Missae Sacrificio, cum appendicibus,* 2 vols., Lovanii: Typographia Academica, 1762.

———, *De Synodo Diocesana,* 13 books in 2 vols., Lovanii: Typographia Academica, 1736.

———, *Institutiones Ecclesiasticae,* Romae: Typis Sacrae Congregationis de Propaganda Fide, 1747.

Beste, Uldalricus, *Introductio In Codicem,* 2 ed., Collegeville, Minn.: St. John's Abbey Press, 1944.

Blat, Albertus, *Commentarium Textus Codicis Iuris Canonici,* 5 vols. in 7, Romae, 1919-1927; Lib. III, pars I, *De Sacramentis,* 2. ed., Romae, 1938.

Bliley, Nicholas M., *Altars According to the Code of Canon Law,* The Catholic University of America Canon Law Studies, n. 38, Washington, D. C.: The Catholic University of America, 1927.

Bona, Ioannes Card., *Rerum Liturgicarum Libri Duo,* 2 vols., Taurini, 1749.

Brehm, Franciscus, *Synopsis Additionum et Variationum in Editione Typica Missalis Romani,* Ratisbonae, 1920.

Cabrol, Fernand, *Liturgical Prayer, Its History and Spirit,* translated by a Benedictine of Stanbrook, London: Burns Oates and Washbourne Ltd., 1925.

Cappello, F. M., *Summa Iuris Canonici,* 3 vols., Vol. I, II, 4. ed., Vol. III, 2. ed., Romae: Universitas Gregoriana, 1938-1945.

———, *Tractatus Canonico-Moralis de Sacramentis,* 3 vols. in 6, Vol. I, 4. ed., Romae: Marietti, 1945.

Chardon, C. B., *Histoire des Sacrements,* 4 vols., Paris, 1745.

Cicognani, Amleto, *Canon Law,* translated by J. O'Hara and F. Brennan, Philadelphia: The Dolphin Press, 1934.

Cocchi, Guidus, *Commentarium in Codicem Iuris Canonici,* 8 vols. in 5, Vol. V, 4. ed., 1938; Vol. VII, 3. ed., 1940, Augustae Taurinorum: Marietti.

Coronata, Matthaeus Conte a, *De Locis et Temporibus Sacris,* Augustae Taurinorum: Marietti, 1922.

———, *Institutiones Iuris Canonici,* 5 vols., Vols. I, II, 2. ed., 1939; Vol. III, 2. ed., 1941; Vol. IV, 2. ed., 1945; Vol. V, 1936, Taurini, Romae: Marietti, 1936-1945.

———, *Tractatus Canonicus de Sacramentis,* 3 vols., Romae: Marietti, 1943-1946.

Davis, H., *Moral and Pastoral Theology,* 3. ed., 4 vols., London: Sheed and Ward, 1938.

De Herdt, J. B., *Sacrae Liturgiae Praxis iuxta Ritum Romanorum,* 3 vols., editio quarta revisa, Lovanii, 1863.

De Puniet, Jean, *The Mass, Its Origin and History,* translated by the Benedictines of Stanbrook, London: Burns Oates & Washbourne Ltd., 1931.

Devoti, Ioannes, *Institutionum Canonicarum Libri Quatuor,* 3 vols., Romae, 1785.

Dictionaire d'Archéologie Chrétienne et de Liturgie, 14 vols. in 27, Parisiis, 1907—.

Duchesne, Louis, *Christian Worship, Its Origin and Evolution,* translated from the third French edition, London: Society for Promoting Christian Knowledge, 1903.

Dubé, Arthur J., *The General Principles for the Reckoning of Time in Canon Law,* The Catholic University of America Canon Law Studies, n. 144. Washington, D. C.: The Catholic University of America Press, 1941.

Durantis, Gulielmus, *Rationale Divinorum Officiorum,* ed. 5. d'Avino, Neapoli: Apud Josephum Dura Bibliopolam, 1859.

Duranti, Ioannes Stephanus, *De Ritibus Ecclesiae Catholicae Libri Tres,* Romae, 1591.

Eisenhofer, L., *Handbuch der katholischen Liturgik,* 2 vols., Freiburg im Breisgau, 1932-1933.

Ellard, Gerald, *Men at Work and Worship,* New York: Longmans, Green & Co., 1940.

Eustace, Bartholomew, *Ritual for Small Churches,* translation of the *Memoriale Rituum* issued by Pope Benedict XIII and revised by authority of Pope Benedict XIV, New York: Joseph E. Wagner, Inc., 1935.

Feldhaus, Aloysius H., *Oratories,* The Catholic University of America Canon Law Studies, n. 42, Washington, D. C.: The Catholic University of America, 1927.

Ferraris, Lucius, *Prompta Bibliotheca Canonica, Iuridica, Moralis, Theologica, nec non Ascetica, Polemica, Rubricistica, Historica,* ed. novissima, 8 vols. cum indice, Romae: Ex Typographia Polyglotta Sacrae Congregationis de Propaganda Fide, 1885-1892.

Ferreres, Ioannes, *Compendium Theologiae Moralis,* 13. ed., Barcinone: E. Subirana, 1925.

———, *Historia del Missal Romano,* Barcinone: E. Subirana, 1929.

———, *Institutiones Canonicae,* ed. altera, 2 vols., Barcinone: E. Subirana, 1920.

Fortescue, Adrian, *The Mass, A Study of the Roman Liturgy,* with additions by Herbert Thurston, new edition, London: Longmans, Green & Co., 1937.

Funk, F. X., *A Manual of Church History,* second impression of the authorized translation from the fifth German edition by Luigi Cappadelta, 2 vols., St. Louis, Mo.: B. Herder Book Co., 1910.

Gasparri, P., *Tractatus Canonicus de Sanctissima Eucharistia,* 2 vols., Lugduni: Delhomme & Briguet, 1897.

Gattico, Ioannes B., *De Oratoriis Domesticis et de Usu Altaris Portatilis,* Romae, 1746.

Genicot, Eduardus—Salsmans, I., *Institutiones Theologiae Moralis,* 13 ed., 2 vols., Bruxellis: L'Edition Universelle, S. A., 1936.

Gesneri, J. M., *Epistolae,* 2 vols., Venetiis, 1786.

Gihr, Nicholas, *The Holy Sacrifice of the Mass,* translated from the sixth German edition, 12 ed., St. Louis, Mo.: B. Herder Book Co., 1937.

Gonzalez—Tellez, Emmanuel, *Commentaria Perpetua in Singulos Textus Quinque Librorum Decretalium Gregorii IX,* 5 vols. in 4, Lugduni, 1715.

Guiniven, John Joseph, *The Precept of Hearing Mass,* The Catholic University of America Canon Law Studies, n. 158, Washington, D. C.: The Catholic University of America Press, 1942.

Gulczynski, John T., *The Desecration and Violation of Churches,* The Catholic University of America Canon Law Studies, n. 159, Washington, D. C.: The Catholic University of America Press, 1942.

Henry, J. A., *The Mass and Holy Communion: Interritual Law,* The Catholic University of America Canon Law Studies, n. 235, Washington, D. C.: The Catholic University of America Press, 1946.

Hinschius, Paulus, *Decretales Pseudo-Isidorianae et Capitula Angilramni,* Lipsiae, 1863.

Krehbiel, E., *The Interdict, Its History and Operation,* Washington, D. C.: American Historical Association, 1909.

Lamy, T., *Hymni et Sermones St. Epraem,* 4 vols., Mechliniae, 1882-1902.

Lehmkuhl, Augustinus. *Theologia Moralis,* 4. ed., 2 vols., Friburgi Brisgoviae, 1887.

Magani, F., *L'Antica Liturgia Romana,* 3 vols., Milano, 1897-1899.

Many, S., *Praelectiones de Locis Sacris,* Parisiis, 1904.

———, *Praelectiones de Missa,* Parisiis, Letouzey et Ané, 1903.

Maroto, Phillipus, *Institutiones Iuris Canonici ad Normam Novi Codicis,* 2 vols., Vol. I, 3. ed., Romae: Apud Commentarium pro Religiosis, 1921.

Martène, Edmundus, *De Antiquis Ecclesiae Ritibus Libri Tres,* Editio Novissima, Venetiis, 1783.

Michel, Virgil, *The Liturgy of the Church,* New York: The MacMillan Co., 1939.

Michiels, G., *Normae Generales Iuris Canonici,* 2 vols., Lublin: Universitas Catholica, 1929.

Migne, J. P., *Patrologiae Cursus Completus, Series Latina,* 221 vols., Parisiis, 1844-1864.

———, *Patrologiae Cursus Completus, Series Graeca,* 161 vols., Parisiis, 1856-1866.

Mühlbauer, Wolfgang, *Decreta Authentica Congregationis Sacrorum Rituum et Instructio Clementina ex Actis eiusdem Collecta ab Aloisio Gardellini in usum Cleri Commodiorem ordine Alphabetico concinnata,* 3 vols. in 4, Monachii; Sumptibus Librariae J. J. Lentnerianae, 1863-1867.

Muratori, L., *Liturgia Romana Vetus,* 2 vols., Neapoli, 1776.

Navarrus, M. A., *Opera Omnia,* editio novissimo, 6 vols., Venetiis, 1618.

Newcomb—Holden, *Astronomy,* 3. ed., New York, 1887.

Noldin, H.—Schmitt, A., *Summa Theologiae Moralis,* 21. ed., 3 vols., Oeniponte: Typis et Sumptibus Fel. Rauch, 1932.

O'Connell, Laurence J., *The Book of Ceremonies,* Milwaukee: The Bruce Publishing Co., 1944.

O'Brien, John, *History of the Mass and Its Ceremonies,* 14. revised edition, New York: Catholic Publication Society Co., 1891.

Oesterle, Gerardus, *Praelectiones Iuris Canonici,* Vol. I, Romae: In Collegio S. Anselmi, 1931.

Ojetti, B., *Commentarium in Codicem Iuris Canonici,* 4 vols., Romae: Apud Aedes Universitatis Gregorianae, 1927-1931.

———, *Synopsis Rerum Moralium et Iuris Pontificii,* 3. ed., 4 vols., Romae, 1909-1914.

Petra, Vincentius, *Commentaria ad Constitutiones Apostolicas seu Bullas Singulas Summorum Pontificum,* 5 vols., in 2, Venetiis: Ex Typographia Balleoniana, 1729.

Prümmer, Dominicus, *Manuale Iuris Canonici,* 3. ed., Friburgi Brisgoviae: B. Herder, 1922.

———, *Manuale Theologiae Moralis,* 7. ed., 3 vols., Friburgi Brisgoviae: B. Herder, 1931.

Quasten, Johannes, *Monumenta Eucharistica et Liturgica Vetustissima,* Bonnae, 1935.

Ramsay, W. J., *The Church in the Roman Empire,* New York, 1893.

Regatillo, Eduardus F., *Ius Sacramentarium,* 2 vols., Santander: Sal Terrae, 1945-1946.

Reichel, Oswald J., *A Complete Manual of Canon Law*, Vol. I, *The Sacraments*, London: John Hodges, 1896.

Reiffenstuel, Anacletus, *Ius Canonicum Universum*, 4 vols., Venetiis, 1735.

Rufinus, *Summa Decretorum*, ed. Heinrich Singer, Paderborn, 1902.

Sabetti, A.,—Barrett, T., *Compendium Theologiae Moralis*, 34. ed., 8. ed. post Codicem, Neo-Eboraci: Frederick Pustet Co., 1939.

Schaefer, Timotheus, *Compendium de Religiosis ad normam Codicis Iuris Canonici*, 2. ed., Münster i. W.: Ex Officina Libraria Aschendorff, 1931.

Schmalzgrueber, Franciscus, *Ius Ecclesiasticum Universum*. 5 vols. in 12, Romae, 1843-1845.

Schroeder, H. J., *Disciplinary Decrees of the General Councils*, St. Louis: B. Herder, 1937.

Schuster, Ildefonso, *The Sacramentary*, translated from the Italian by Arthur Levilis-Marke, 5 vols., London: Burns Oates & Washbourne Ltd., 1924.

Scotùs, Joannes Duns, *Opera Omnia*, editio nova, 26 vols., Parisiis, 1891-1895.

Smith, S. B., *Compendium Iuris Canonici*, 4. ed., New York: Benziger Brothers, 1890.

Suarez, Franciscus, *Opera Omnia*, Editio nova a Carolo Berton, 28 vols., Parisiis: Apud Ludovicum Vivès, 1856-1878.

Thalhofer, V., *Theologische Bibliothek, Handbuch der katholischen Liturgik*, 2 vols., Freiburg: Herder, 1883.

Thomassinus, Ludovicus, *Vetus et Nova Ecclesiae Disciplina circa Beneficia et Beneficiarios*, 10 vols., Magontiaci, 1787.

Toso, Albertus, *Ad Codicem Iuris Canonici Commentaria Minora*, 5 vols., Romae: Marietti, 1920-1927.

Van de Burgt, H., *De Celebratione Missarum*, Ultrajecti, 1871.

Van Hove, A., *Commentarium Lovaniense in Codicem Iuris Canonici*, Vol. I, Tom. I, *Prolegomena*, 2. ed., Mechliniae-Romae: H. Dessain, 1945.

Vermeersch, Arthurus, *Theologiae Moralis, Principia-Responsa-Consilia*, 3. ed., 4 vols., Romae: Pont. Universitas Gregoriana, 1933-1937.

Vermeersch, A.—Creusen, J., *Epitome Iuris Canonici*, 3 vols., Vol. I, 6. ed., 1937; Vol. II, 6. ed., 1940; Vol. III, 5. ed., 1936, Mechliniae-Romae: H. Dessain.

Walsh, John, *The Mass and Vestments of the Catholic Church*, New York: Benziger Brothers, 1916.

Wernz, F., *Ius Decretalium*, 6 vols., Romae et Prati, 1898-1905.

Wernz, F.—Vidal, P., *Ius Canonicum ad normam Codicis exactum*, 7 vols. in 8, Vol. I, 1. ed., 1938, Romae: Apud Aedes Universitatis Gregorianae, 1923-1946.

Woywod, Stanislaus, *A Practical Commentary on the Code of Canon Law*, 9. ed., revised by Callistus Smith, 2 vols., New York: J. Wagner, 1945.

Ziolkowski, T. C., *The Consecration and Blessing of Churches*, The Catholic University of America Canon Law Studies, n. 187, Washington, D. C.: The Catholic University of America Press, 1943.

ARTICLES

Barin, Aloisius, "Commentarium ad Canones Iuris Canonici sacram Liturgiam Spectantes"—*Ephemerides Liturgicae* (Roma, Via Pompeo Magno, 21), XXXIV (1920), 353-356.

Bastnagel, C. V., "Cases and Studies"—*The Jurist,* II (1942), 155-158.

Bouscaren, T. L., "De Missa ex licentia Ordinarii celebrata"—*Periodica,* XXVIII (1939), 52-61.

Eidenschink, John A., "Dedication of Sacred Places in the Early Sources and in the Letters of Gregory the Great"—*The Jurist,* V (1945), 181-215; 323-358.

Hannan, J. D., "Cases and Studies"—*The Jurist,* VIII (1948), 69-70.

Gulovich, Stephen C., "Mass and Communion according to the Oriental Rite in a Church of the Latin Rite"—*The Jurist,* II (1942), 47-52.

Vermeersch, A., "Commentaria de Formulis quas S. C. de Propaganda Fide concedere solet"—*Periodica,* XI (1922), 33-36.

Vermeersch, A., "Ex audientia Sanctissimi"—*Periodica,* IV (1913), 311-313.

Woywod, S., "The Law of the Code on Altars"—*The Homiletic and Pastoral Review* (New York, 1900—), XXVI (1925), 269-272.

PERIODICALS

Ephemerides Liturgicae, Romae, Via Pompeo Magno, 21, 1887—.

Homiletic and Pastoral Review, The, New York, 1900—.

Jurist, The, Washington, D. C., 1941—.

Periodica de Re Morali, Canonica, Liturgica, Brugis, 1922-1936; Romae, 1937—.

ABBREVIATIONS

AAS—*Acta Apostolicae Sedis.*
ASS—*Acta Sanctae Sedis.*
Coll. S. C. P. F.—*Collectanea S. C. de Propaganda Fide,* ed. 1907.
Decr. Auth. S. R. C.—*Decreta Authentica Sacrorum Rituum Congregationis.*
Fontes—*Codicis Iuris Canonici Fontes cura . . . Gasparri editi.*
Hardouin—*Acta Conciliorum.*
Jaffé—*Regesta Pontificum Romanorum, ed. secunda.*
Mansi—*Sacrorum Conciliorum Nova et Amplissima Collectio* .
MGH—*Monumenta Germaniae Historica.*
MPG—Migne, *Patrologia Graeca.*
MPL—Migne, *Patrologia Latina.*
Pallottini—*Collectio Omnium Conclusionum . . . apud Sacram Congregationem Cardinalium quae in causis praepositis Concilio Tridentini Interpretum prodierunt . . .*
Potthast—*Regesta Pontificum Romanorum.*
Thesaurus—*Thesaurus Resolutionum Sacrae Congregationis Concilii.*

ALPHABETICAL INDEX

BIBLIOGRAPHICAL NOTE

JAMES GODLEY was born on February 14, 1915, in Ballyheigue, Co. Kerry, Ireland. He attended Glenderry National School, The Jeffers' Institute, Tralee, Co. Kerry, High School, and Mount Melleray Preparatory Seminary, Co. Waterford, from which he graduated in June, 1934. He studied Philosophy and Theology at St. Patrick's Seminary, Carlow, Ireland, where he was ordained for the Diocese of Cheyenne, Wyoming, on June 9, 1940.

In November of 1945 he was enrolled in the School of Canon Law of the Catholic University of America, from which he received the Baccalaureate in Canon Law in June, 1946, and the Licentiate in Canon Law in June, 1947.

CANON LAW STUDIES *

1. FRERIKS, REV. CELESTINE A., C.PP.S., J.C.D., Religious Congregations in Their External Relations, 121 pp., 1916.
2. GALLIHER, REV. DANIEL M., O.P., J.C.D., Canonical Elections, 117 pp., 1917.
3. BORKOWSKI, REV. AURELIUS L., O.F.M., J.C.D., De Confraternitatibus Ecclesiasticis, 136 pp., 1918.
4. CASTILLO, REV. CAYO, J.C.D., Disertacion Historico-Canonica sobre la Potestad del Cabildo en Sede Vacante o Impedida del Vicario Capitular, 99 pp., 1919 (1918).
5. KUBELBECK, REV. WILLIAM J., S.T.B., J.C.D., The Sacred Penitentiaria and Its Relation to Faculties of Ordinaries and Priests, 129 pp., 1918.
6. PETROVITS, REV. JOSEPH, J.C., S.T.D., J.C.D., The New Church Law on Matrimony, X-461 pp., 1919.
7. HICKEY, REV. JOHN J., S.T.B., J.C.D., Irregularities and Simple Impediments in the New Code of Canon Law, 100 pp., 1920.
8. KLEKOTKA, REV. PETER J., S.T.B., J.C.D., Diocesan Consultors, 179 pp., 1920.
9. WANENMACHER, REV. FRANCIS, J.C.D., The Evidence in Ecclesiastical Procedure Affecting the Marriage Bond, 1920 (Printed 1935).
10. GOLDEN, REV. HENRY FRANCIS, J.C.D., Parochial Benefices in the New Code, IV-119 pp., 1921 (Printed 1925).
11. KOUDELKA, REV. CHARLES J., J.C.D., Pastors, Their Rights and Duties According to the New Code of Canon Law, 211 pp., 1921.
12. MELO, REV. ANTONIUS, O.F.M., J.C.D., De Exemptione Regularium, X-188 pp., 1921.
13. SCHAAF, REV. VALENTINE THEODORE, O.F.M., S.T.B., J.C.D., The Cloister, X-180 pp., 1921.
14. BURKE, REV. THOMAS JOSEPH, S.T.D., J.C.D., Competence in Ecclesiastical Tribunals, IV-117 pp., 1922.
15. LEECH, REV. GEORGE LEO, J.C.D., A Comparative Study of the Constitution "Apostolicae Sedis" and the "Codex Juris Canonici," 179 pp., 1922.
16. MOTRY, REV. HUBERT LOUIS, S.T.D., J.C.D., Diocesan Faculties According to the Code of Canon Law, II-167 pp., 1922.
17. MURPHY, REV. GEORGE LAWRENCE, J.C.D., Delinquencies and Penalties in the Administration and the Reception of the Sacraments, IV-121 pp., 1923.
18. O'REILLY, REV. JOHN ANTHONY, S.T.B., J.C.D., Ecclesiastical Sepulture in the New Code of Canon Law, II-129 pp., 1923.

* All published numbers are available from the Catholic University of America Press, 620 Michigan Avenue, N.E., Washington 17, D. C., except the following: Nos. 1-114 inclusive, 115, 118, 120, 122, 123, 136, 153, 162, 182 and 198. But the following numbers, now reissuel, are obtainable from *The Jurist*, The Catholic University of America, Washington 17, D. C., namely: Nos. 5, 7, 11, 17, 18, 19, 26, 28, 30, 31, 34, 42, 44, 51, 52 and 61.

19. MICHALICKA, REV. WENCESLAS CYRILL, O.S.B., J.C.D., Judicial Procedure in Dismissal of Clerical Exempt Religious, 107 pp., 1923.
20. DARGIN, REV. EDWARD VINCENT, S.T.B., J.C.D., Reserved Cases According to the Code of Canon Law, IV-103 pp., 1924.
21. GODFREY, REV. JOHN A., S.T.B., J.C.D., The Right of Patronage According to the Code of Canon Law, 153 pp., 1924.
22. HAGEDORN, REV. FRANCIS EDWARD, J.C.D., General Legislation on Indulgences, II-154 pp., 1924.
23. KING, REV. JAMES IGNATIUS, J.C.D., The Administration of the Sacraments to Dying Non-Catholics, V-141 pp., 1924.
24. WINSLOW, REV. FRANCIS JOSEPH, O.F.M., J.C.D., Vicars and Prefects Apostolic, IV-149 pp., 1924.
25. CORREA, REV. JOSE SERVELION, S.T.L., J.C.D., La Potestad Legislativa de la Iglesia Catolica, IV-127 pp., 1925.
26. DUGAN, REV. HENRY FRANCIS, A.M., J.C.D., The Judiciary Department of the Diocesan Curia, 87 pp., 1925.
27. KELLER, REV. CHARLES FREDERICK, S.T.B., J.C.D., Mass Stipends, 167 pp., 1925.
28. PASCHANG, REV. JOHN LINUS, J.C.D., The Sacramentals According to the Code of Canon Law, 129 pp., 1925.
29. PIONTEK, REV. CYRILLUS, O.F.M., S.T.B., J.C.D., De Indulto Exclaustrationis necnon Saecularizationis, XIII-289 pp., 1925.
30. KEARNEY, REV. RICHARD JOSEPH, S.T.B., J.C.D., Sponsors at Baptism According to the Code of Canon Law, IV-127 pp., 1925.
31. BARTLETT, REV. CHESTER JOSEPH, A.M., LL.B., J.C.D., The Tenure of Parochial Property in the United States of America, V-108 pp., 1926.
32. KILKER, REV. ADRIAN JEROME, J.C.D., Extreme Unction, V-425 pp., 1926.
33. MCCORMICK, REV. ROBERT EMMETT, J.C.D., Confessors of Religious, VIII-266 pp., 1926.
34. MILLER, REV. NEWTON THOMAS, J.C.D., Founded Masses According to the Code of Canon Law, VII-93 pp., 1926.
35. ROELKER, REV. EDWARD G., S.T.D., J.C.D., Principles of Privilege According to the Code of Canon Law, XI-166 pp., 1926.
36. BAKALARCZYK, REV. RICHARDUS, M.I.C., J.U.D., De Novitiatu, VIII-208 pp., 1927.
37. PIZZUTI, REV. LAWRENCE, O.F.M., J.U.L., De Parochis Religiosis, 1927. (Not Printed.)
38. BLILEY, REV. NICHOLAS MARTIN, O.S.B., J.C.D., Altars According to the Code of Canon Law, XIX-132 pp., 1927.
39. BROWN, MR. BRENDAN FRANCIS, A.B., LL.M., J.U.D., The Canonical Juristic Personality with Special Reference to its Status in the United States of America, V-212 pp., 1927.
40. CAVANAUGH, REV. WILLIAM THOMAS, C.P., J.U.D., The Reservation of the Blessed Sacrament, VIII-101 pp., 1927.

41. Doheny, Rev. William J., C.S.C., A.B., J.C.D., Church Property: Modes of Acquisition, X-118 pp., 1927.
42. Feldhaus, Rev. Aloysius H., C.PP.S., J.C.D., Oratories, IX-141 pp., 1927.
43. Kelly, Rev. James Patrick, A.B., J.C.D., The Jurisdiction of the Simple Confessor, X-208 pp., 1927.
44. Neuberger, Rev. Nicholas J., J.C.D., Canon 6 or the Relation of the Codex Juris Canonici to the Preceding Legislation, V-95 pp., 1927.
45. O'Keefe, Rev. Gerald Michael, J.C.D., Matrimonial Dispensations, Powers of Bishops, Priests, and Confessors, VIII-232 pp., 1927.
46. Quigley, Rev. Joseph A. M., A.B., J.C.D., Condemned Societies, 139 pp., 1927.
47. Zaplotnik, Rev. Johannes Leo, J.C.D., De Vicariis Foraneis, X-142 pp., 1927.
48. Duskie, Rev. John Aloysius, A.B., J.C.D., The Canonical Status of the Orientals in the United States, VIII-196 pp., 1928.
49. Hyland, Rev. Francis Edward, J.C.D., Excommunication, Its Nature, Historical Development and Effects, VIII-181 pp., 1928.
50. Reinmann, Rev. Gerald Joseph, O.M.C., J.C.D., The Third Order Secular of Saint Francis, 201 pp., 1928.
51. Schenk, Rev. Francis J., J.C.D., The Matrimonial Impediments of Mixed Religion and Disparity of Cult, XVI-318 pp., 1929.
52. Coady, Rev. John Joseph, S.T.D., J.U.D., A.M., The Appointment of Pastors, VIII-150 pp., 1929.
53. Kay, Rev. Thomas Henry, J.C.D., Competence in Matrimonial Procedure, VIII-164 pp., 1929.
54. Turner, Rev. Sidney Joseph, C.P., J.U.D., The Vow of Poverty, XLIX-217 pp., 1929.
55. Kearney, Rev. Raymond A., A.B., S.T.D., J.C.D., The Principles of Delegation, VII-149 pp., 1929.
56. Conran, Rev. Edward James, A.B., J.C.D., The Interdict, V-163 pp., 1930.
57. O'Neill, Rev. William H., J.C.D., Papal Rescripts of Favor, VII-218 pp., 1930.
58. Bastnagel, Rev. Clement Vincent, J.U.D., The Appointment of Parochial Adjutants and Assistants, XV-257 pp., 1930.
59. Ferry, Rev. William A., A.B., J.C.D., Stole Fees, V-136 pp., 1930.
60. Costello, Rev. John Michael, A.B., J.C.D., Domicile and Quasi-Domicile, VII-201 pp., 1930.
61. Kremer, Rev. Michael Nicholas, A.B., S.T.B., J.C.D., Church Support in the United States, VI-136 pp., 1930.
62. Angulo, Rev. Luis, C.M., J.C.D., Legislation de la Iglesia sobre la intencion en la application de la Santa Misa, VII-104 pp., 1931.
63. Frey, Rev. Wolfgang Norbert, O.S.B., A.B., J.C.D., The Act of Religious Profession, VIII-174 pp., 1931.

64. Roberts, Rev. James Brendan, A.B., J.C.D., The Banns of Marriage, XIV-140 pp., 1931.
65. Ryder, Rev. Raymond Aloysius, A.B., J.C.D., Simony, IX-151 pp., 1931.
66. Campagna, Rev. Angelo, Ph.D., J.U.D., Il Vicario Generale del Vescovo, VII-205 pp., 1931.
67. Cox, Rev. Joseph Godfrey, A.B., J.C.D., The Administration of Seminaries, VI-124 pp., 1931.
68. Gregory, Rev. Donald J., J.U.D., The Pauline Privilege, XV-165 pp., 1931.
69. Donohue, Rev. John F., J.C.D., The Impediment of Crime, VII-110 pp., 1931.
70. Dooley, Rev. Eugene A., O.M.I., J.C.D., Church Law on Sacred Relics, IX-143 pp., 1931.
71. Orth, Rev. Clement Raymond, O.M.C., J.C.D., The Approbation of Religious Institutes, 171 pp., 1931.
72. Pernicone, Rev. Joseph M., A.B., J.C.D., The Ecclesiastical Prohibition of Books, XII-267 pp., 1932.
73. Clinton, Rev. Connell, A.B., J.C.D., The Paschal Precept, IX-108 pp., 1932.
74. Donnelly, Rev. Francis B., A.M., S.T.L., J.C.D., The Diocesan Synod, VIII-125 pp., 1932.
75. Torrente, Rev. Camilo, C.M.F., J.C.D., Las Procesiones Sagradas, V-145 pp., 1932.
76. Murphy, Rev. Edwin J., C.PP.S., J.C.D., Suspension Ex Informata Conscientia, XI-122 pp., 1932.
77. MacKenzie, Rev. Eric F., A.M., S.T.L., J.C.D., The Delict of Heresy in its Commission, Penalization, Absolution, VII-124 pp., 1932.
78. Lyons, Rev. Avitus E., S.T.B., J.C.D., The Collegiate Tribunal of First Instance, XI-147 pp., 1932.
79. Connolly, Rev. Thomas A., J.C.D., Appeals, XI-195, pp., 1932.
80. Sangmeister, Rev. Joseph V., A.B., J.C.D., Force and Fear as Precluding Matrimonial Consent, V-211 pp., 1932.
81. Jaeger, Rev. Leo A., A.B., J.C.D., The Administration of Vacant and Quasi-Vacant Episcopal Sees in the United States, IX-229 pp., 1932.
82. Rimlinger, Rev. Herbert T., J.C.D., Error Invalidating Matrimonial Consent, VII-79 pp., 1932.
83. Barrett, Rev. John D. M., S.S., J.C.D., A Comparative Study of the Councils of Baltimore and the Code of Canon Law, IX-223 pp., 1932.
84. Carberry, Rev. John J., Ph.D., S.T.D., J.C.D., The Juridical Form of Marriage, X-177 pp., 1934.
85. Dolan, Rev. John L., A.B., J.C.D., The Defensor Vinculi, XII-157 pp., 1934.
86. Hannan, Rev. Jerome D., A.M., S.T.D., LL.B., J.C.D., The Canon Law of Wills, IX-517 pp., 1934.

87. Lemieux, Rev. Delise A., A.M., J.C.D., The Sentence in Ecclesiastical Procedure, IX-131 pp., 1934.
88. O'Rourke, Rev. James J., A.B., J.C.D., Parish Registers, VII-109 pp., 1934.
89. Timlin, Rev. Bartholomew, O.F.M., A.M., J.C.D., Conditional Matrimonial Consent, X-381 pp., 1934.
90. Wahl, Rev. Francis X., A.B., J.C.D., The Matrimonial Impediments of Consanguinity and Affinity, VI-125 pp., 1934.
91. White, Rev. Robert J., A.B., LL.B., S.T.B., J.C.D., Canonical Ante-Nuptial Promises and the Civil Law, VI-152 pp., 1934.
92. Herrera, Rev. Antonio Parra, O.C.D., J.C.D., Legislacion Ecclesiastica sobra el Ayuno y la Abstinencia, XI-191 pp., 1935.
93. Kennedy, Rev. Edwin J., J.C.D., The Special Matrimonial Process in Cases of Evident Nullity, X-165 pp., 1935.
94. Manning, Rev. John J., A.B., J.C.D., Presumption of Law in Matrimonial Procedure, XI-111 pp., 1935.
95. Moeder, Rev. John M., J.C.D., The Proper Bishop for Ordination and Dismissorial Letters, VII-135 pp., 1935.
96. O'Mara, Rev. William A., A.B., J.C.D., Canonical Causes for Matrimonial Dispensations, IX-155 pp., 1935.
97. Reilly, Rev. Peter, J.C.D., Residence of Pastors, IX-81 pp., 1935.
98. Smith, Rev. Mariner T., O.P., S.T.Lr., J.C.D., The Penal Law for Religious, VIII-169 pp., 1935.
99. Whalen, Rev. Donald W., A.M., J.C.D., The Value of Testimonial Evidence in Matrimonial Procedure, XIII-297 pp., 1935.
100. Cleary, Rev. Joseph F., J.C.D., Canonical Limitations on the Alienation of Church Property, VIII-141 pp., 1936.
101. Glynn, Rev. John C., J.C.D., The Promoter of Justice, XX-337 pp., 1936.
102. Brennan, Rev. James H., S.S., M.A., S.T.B., J.C.D., The Simple Convalidation of Marriage, VI-135 pp., 1937.
103. Brunini, Rev. Joseph Bernard, J.C.D., The Clerical Obligations of Canons 139 and 142, X-121 pp., 1937.
104. Connor, Rev. Maurice, A.B., J.C.D., The Administrative Removal of Pastors, VIII-159 pp., 1937.
105. Guilfoyle, Rev. Merlin Joseph, J.C.D., Custom, XI-144 pp., 1937.
106. Hughes, Rev. James Austin, A.B., A.M., J.C.D., Witnesses in Criminal Trials of Clerics, IX-140 pp., 1937.
107. Jansen, Rev. Raymond J., A.B., S.T.L., J.C.D., Canonical Provisions for Catechetical Instruction, VII-153 pp., 1937.
108. Kealy, Rev. John James, A.B., J.C.D., The Introductory Libellus in Church Court Procedure, XI-121 pp., 1937.
109. McManus, Rev. James Edward, C.SS.R., J.C.D., The Administration of Temporal Goods in Religious Institutes, XVI-196 pp., 1937.

110. MORIARTY, REV. EUGENE JAMES, J.C.D., Oaths in Ecclesiastical Courts, X-115 pp., 1937.

111. RAINER, REV. ELIGIUS GEORGE, C.SS.R., J.C.D., Suspension of Clerics, XVII-249 pp., 1937.

112. REILLY, REV. THOMAS F., C.SS.R., J.C.D., Visitation of Religious, VI-195 pp., 1938.

113. MORIARTY, REV. FRANCIS E., C.SS.R., J.C.D., The Extraordinary Absolution from Censures, XV-334 pp., 1938.

114. CONNOLLY, REV. NICHOLAS P., J.C.D., The Canonical Erection of Parishes, X-132 pp., 1938.

115. DONOVAN, REV. JAMES JOSEPH, J.C.D., The Pastor's Obligation in Prenuptial Investigation, XII-322 pp., 1938.

116. HARRIGAN, REV. ROBERT J., M.A., S.T.B., J.C.D., The Radical Sanation of Invalid Marriages, VIII-208 pp., 1938.

117. BOFFA, REV. CONRAD HUMBERT, J.C.D., Canonical Provisions for Catholic Schools, VII-211 pp., 1939.

118. PARSONS, REV. ANSCAR JOHN, O.M.Cap., J.C.D., Canonical Elections, XII-236 pp., 1939.

119. REILLY, REV. EDWARD MICHAEL, A.B., J.C.D., The General Norms of Dispensation, XII-156 pp., 1939.

120. RYAN, REV. GERALD ALOYSIUS, A.B., J.C.D., Principles of Episcopal Jurisdiction, XII-172 pp., 1939.

121. BURTON, REV. FRANCIS JAMES, C.S.C., A.B., J.C.D., A Commentary on Canon 1125, X-222 pp., 1940.

122. MIASKIEWICZ, REV. FRANCIS SIGISMUND, J.C.D., Supplied Jurisdiction According to Canon 209, XII-340 pp., 1940.

123. RICE, REV. PATRICK WILLIAM, A.B., J.C.D., Proof of Death in Prenuptial Investigation, VIII-156 pp., 1940.

124. ANGLIN, REV. THOMAS FRANCIS, M.S., J.C.D., The Eucharistic Fast, VIII-183 pp., 1941.

125. COLEMAN, REV. JOHN JEROME, J.C.D., The Minister of Confirmation, VI-153 pp., 1941.

126. DOWNS, REV. JOHN EMMANUEL, A.B., J.C.D., The Concept of Clerical Immunity, XI-163 pp., 1941.

127. ESSWEIN, REV. ANTHONY ALBERT, J.C.D., Extrajudicial Penal Powers of Ecclesiastical Superiors, X-144 pp., 1941.

128. FARRELL, REV. BENJAMIN FRANCIS, M.A., S.T.L., J.C.D., The Rights and Duties of the Local Ordinary Regarding Congregations of Women Religious of Pontifical Approval, V-195 pp., 1941.

129. FEENEY, REV. THOMAS JOHN, A.B., S.T.L., J.C.D., Restitutio in Integrum, VI-169 pp., 1941.

130. FINDLAY, REV. STEPHEN WILLIAM, O.S.B., A.B., J.C.D., Canonical Norms Governing the Deposition and Degradation of Clerics, XVII-279 pp., 1941.

131. Goodwine, Rev. John, A.B., S.T.L., J.C.D., The Right of the Church to Acquire Property, VIII-119 pp., 1941.

132. Heston, Rev. Edward Louis, C.S.C., Ph.D., S.T.D., J.C.D., The Alienation of Church Property in the United States, XII-222 pp., 1941.

133. Hogan, Rev. James John, A.B., S.T.L., J.C.D., Judicial Advocates and Procurators, XIII-200 pp., 1941.

134. Kealy, Rev. Thomas M., A.B., Litt.B., J.C.D., Dowry of Women Religious, IX-152 pp., 1941.

135. Keene, Rev. Michael James, O.S.B., J.C.D., Religious Ordinaries and Canon 198, V-164 pp., 1941 (printed 1942).

136. Kerin, Rev. Charles A., S.S., M.A., S.T.B., J.C.D., The Privation of Christian Burial, XVI-279 pp., 1941.

137. Louis, Rev. William Francis, M.A., J.C.D., Diocesan Archives, X-101 pp., 1941.

138. McDevitt, Rev. Gilbert Joseph, A.B., J.C.D., Legitimacy and Legitimation, X-247 pp., 1941.

139. McDonough, Rev. Thomas Joseph, A.B., J.C.D., Apostolic Administrators, X-217 pp., 1941.

140. Meier, Rev. Carl Anthony, A.B., J.C.D., Penal Administrative Procedure Against Negligent Pastors, XI-240 pp., 1941.

141. Schmidt, Rev. John Rogg, A.B., J.C.D., The Principles of Authentic Interpretation in Canon 17 of the Code of Canon Law, XII-331 pp., 1941.

142. Slafkosky, Rev. Andrew Leonard, A.B., J.C.D., The Canonical Episcopal Visitation of the Diocese, X-197 pp., 1941.

143. Swoboda, Rev. Innocent Robert, O.F.M., J.C.D., Ignorance in Relation to the Imputability of Delicts, IX-271 pp., 1941.

144. Dubé, Rev. Arthur Joseph, A.B., J.C.D., The General Principles for the Reckoning of Time in Canon Law, VIII-299 pp., 1941.

145. McBride, Rev. James T., A.B., J.C.D., Incardination and Excardination of Seculars, XX-585 pp., 1941.

146. Król, Rev. John T., J.C.D., The Defendant in Ecclesiastical Trials, XII-207 pp., 1942.

147. Comyns, Rev. Joseph J., C.SS.R., A.B., J.C.D., Papal and Episcopal Administration of Church Property, XIV-155 pp., 1942.

148. Barry, Rev. Garrett Francis, O.M.I., J.C.D., Violation of the Cloister, XII-260 pp., 1942.

149. Bolduc, Rev. Gatien, C.S.V., A.B., S.T.L., J.C.D., Les Études dans les Religions Cléricales, VIII-155 pp., 1942.

150. Boyle, Rev. David John, M.A., J.C.D., The Juridic Effects of Moral Certitude on Pre-Nuptial Guarantees, XII-188 pp., 1942.

151. Canavan, Rev. Walter Joseph, M.A., Litt.D., J.C.D., The Profession of Faith, XII-143 pp., 1942.

152. Desrochers, Rev. Bruno, A.B., Ph.L., S.T.B., J.C.D., Le Premier Concile Plénier de Québec et le Code de Droit Canonique, XIV-186 pp., 1942.

153. Dillon, Rev. Robert Edward, A.B., J.C.D., Common Law Marriage, X-148 pp., 1942.

154. Dodwell, Rev. Edward John, Ph.D., S.T.B., J.C.D., The Time and Place for the Celebration of Marriage, X-156 pp., 1942.

155. Donnellan, Rev. Thomas Andrew, A.B., J.C.D., The Obligation of the Missa pro Populo, VII-131 pp., 1942.

156. Eltz, Rev. Louis Anthony, A.B., J.C.D., Cooperation in Crime, XII-208 pp., 1942.

157. Gass, Rev. Sylvester Francis, M.A., J.C.D., Ecclesiastical Pensions, XI-206 pp., 1942.

158. Guiniven, Rev. John Joseph, C.SS.R., J.C.D., The Precept of Hearing Mass, XIV-188 pp., 1942.

159. Gulczynski, Rev. John Theophilus, J.C.D., The Desecration and Violation of Churches, X-126 pp., 1942.

160. Hammill, Rev. John Leo, M.A., J.C.D., The Obligations of the Traveler According to Canon 14, VIII-204 pp., 1942.

161. Haydt, Rev. John Joseph, A.B., J.C.D., Reserved Benefices, XI-148 pp., 1942.

162. Huser, Rev. Roger John, O.F.M., A.B., J.C.D., The Crime of Abortion in Canon Law, XII-187 pp., 1942.

163. Kearney, Rev. Francis Patrick, A.B., S.T.L., J.C.D., The Principles of Canon 1127, X-162 pp., 1942.

164. Linahen, Rev. Leo James, S.T.L., J.C.D., De Absolutione Complicis in Peccato Turpi, V-114 pp., 1942.

165. McCloskey, Rev. Joseph Aloysius, A.B., J.C.D., The Subject of Ecclesiastical Law According to Canon 12, XVII-246 pp., 1942 (printed 1943).

166. O'Neill, Rev. Francis Joseph, C.SS.R., J.C.D., The Dismissal of Religious in Temporary Vows, XIII-220 pp., 1942.

167. Prince, Rev. John Edward, A.B., S.T.B., J.C.D., The Diocesan Chancellor, X-136 pp., 1942.

168. Riesner, Rev. Albert Joseph, C.SS.R., J.C.D., Apostates and Fugitives from Religious Institutes, IX-168 pp., 1942.

169. Stenger, Rev. Joseph Bernard, J.C.D., The Mortgaging of Church Property, 186 pp., 1942.

170. Waldron, Rev. Joseph Francis, A.B., J.C.D., The Minister of Baptism, XII-197 pp., 1942.

171. Willett, Rev. Robert Albert, J.C.D., The Probative Value of Documents in Ecclesiastical Trials, X-124 pp., 1942.

172. Woeber, Rev. Edward Martin, M.A., J.C.D., The Interpellations, XII-161 pp., 1942.

173. Benko, Rev. Matthew Aloysius, O.S.B., M.A., J.C.D., The Abbot *Nullius,* XVI-148 pp., 1943.

174. Christ, Rev. Joseph James, M.A., S.T.L., J.C.D., Dispensation from Vindicative Penalties, XIV-285 pp., 1943.

175. Clancy, Rev. Patrick M. J., O.P., A.B., S.T.Lr., J.C.D., The Local Religious Superior, X-229 pp., 1943.

176. Clarke, Rev. Thomas James, J.C.D., Parish Societies, XII-147 pp., 1943.

177. Connolly, Rev. John Patrick, S.T.L., J.C.D., Synodal Examiners and Parish Priest Consultors, X-223 pp., 1943.

178. Drumm, Rev. William Martin, A.B., J.C.D., Hospital Chaplains, XII-175 pp., 1943.

179. Flanagan, Rev. Bernard Joseph, A.B., S.T.L., J.C.D., The Canonical Erection of Religious Houses, X-147 pp., 1943.

180. Kelleher, Rev. Stephen Joseph, A.B., S.T.B., J.C.D., Discussions with Non-Catholics: Canonical Legislation, X-93 pp., 1943.

181. Lewis, Rev. Gordian, C.P., J.C.D., Chapters in Religious Institutes, XII-169 pp., 1943.

182. Marx, Rev. Adolph, J.C.D., The Declaration of Nullity of Marriages Contracted Outside the Church, X-151 pp., 1943.

183. Matulenas, Rev. Raymond Anthony, O.S.B., A.B., J.C.D., Communication, a Source of Privileges, XII-225 pp., 1943.

184. O'Leary, Rev. Charles Gerard, C.SS.R., J.C.D., Religious Dismissed After Perpetual Profession, X-213 pp., 1943.

185. Power, Rev. Cornelius Michael, J.C.D., The Blessing of Cemeteries, XII-231 pp., 1943.

186. Shuhler, Rev. Ralph Vincent, O.S.A., J.C.D., Privileges of Religious to Absolve and Dispense, XII-195 pp., 1943.

187. Ziolkowski, Rev. Thaddeus Stanislaus, A.B., J.C.D., The Consecration and Blessing of Churches, XII-151 pp., 1943.

188. Heneghan, Rev. John Joseph, S.T.D., J.C.D., The Marriages of Unworthy Catholics: Canons 1065 and 1066, XVI-213 pp., 1944.

189. Carroll, Rev. Coleman Francis, M.A., S.T.L., J.C.L., Charitable Institutions.

190. Ciesluk, Rev. Joseph Edward, Ph.B., S.T.L., J.C.D., National Parishes in the United States, VI-178 pp., 1944.

191. Coburn, Rev. Vincent Paul, A.B., J.C.D., Marriages of Conscience, XII-172 pp., 1944.

192. Connors, Rev. Charles Paul, C.S.Sp., A.B., J.C.D., Extra-Judicial Procurators in the Code of Canon Law, X-94 pp., 1944.

193. Coyle, Rev. Paul Raymond, A.B., J.C.D., Judicial Exceptions, X-142 pp., 1944.

194. Fair, Rev. Bartholomew Francis, A.B., S.T.L., J.C.D., The Impediment of Abduction, XII-122 pp., 1944.

195. Gallagher, Rev. Thomas Raphael, O.P., A.B., S.T.Lr., J.C.D., The Examination of the Qualities of the Ordinand, X-166 pp., 1944.

196. Gannon, Rev. John Mark, S.T.L., J.C.D., The Interstices Required for the Promotion to Orders, XII-100 pp., 1944.
197. Goldsmith, Rev. J. William, B.C.S., S.T.L., J.C.D., The Competence of Church and State Over Marriages—Disputed Points, X-128 pp., 1944.
198. Goodwine, Rev. Joseph Gerard, A.B., S.T.B., J.C.D., The Reception of Converts, XIV-326 pp., 1944.
199. Kowalski, Rev. Romuald Eugene, O.F.M., A.B., J.C.D., Sustenance of Religious Houses of Regulars, X-174 pp., 1944.
200. McCoy, Rev. Alan Edward, O.F.M., J.C.D., Force and Fear in Relation to Delictual Imputability and Penal Responsibility, XII-160 pp., 1944.
201. McDevitt, Rev. Vincent John, Ph.B., S.T.L., J.C.L., Perjury.
202. Martin, Rev. Thomas Owen, Ph.D., S.T.D., J.C.D., Adverse Possession, Prescription and Limitation of Actions: The Canonical "Praescriptio," XX-208 pp., 1944.
203. Miklosovic, Rev. Paul John, A.B., J.C.L., Attempted Marriages and Their Consequent Juridic Effects.
204. Mundy, Rev. Thomas Maurice, A.B., S.T.L., J.C.D., The Union of Parishes, X-164 pp., 1944.
205. O'Dea, Rev. John Coyle, A.B., J.C.D., The Matrimonial Impediment of Nonage, VIII-126 pp., 1944.
206. Olalia, Rev. Alexander Ayson, S.T.L., J.C.D., A Comparative Study of the Christian Constitution of States and the Constitution of the Philippine Commonwealth, XII-136 pp., 1944.
207. Poisson, Rev. Pierre-Marie, C.S.C., A.B., Ph.L., Th.L., J.C.L., Droits Patrimoniaux des Maisons et des Eglises Religieuses.
208. Stadalnikas, Rev. Casimir Joseph, M.I.C., J.C.D., Reservation of Censures, X-141 pp., 1944.
209. Sullivan, Rev. Eugene Henry, S.T.L., J.C.D., Proof of the Reception of the Sacraments, X-165 pp., 1944.
210. Vaughan, Rev. William Edward, J.C.D., Constitutions for Diocesan Courts, X-210 pp., 1944.
211. Paro, Rev. Gino, S.T.D., J.C.D., The Right of Papal Legation, X-221 pp., 1944 (printed 1947).
212. Balzer, Rev. Ralph Francis, C.P., J.C.D., The Computation of Time in a Canonical Novitiate, X-227 pp., 1945.
213. Dougherty, Rev. John Whelan, A.B., S.T.L., J.C.D., De Inquisitione Speciali, XII-195 pp., 1945.
214. Dziob, Rev. Michael Walter, J.C.D., The Sacred Congregation for the Oriental Church, XII-181 pp., 1945.
215. Eidenschink, Rev. John Albert, O.S.B., B.A., J.C.D., The Election of Bishops in the Letters of Pope Gregory the Great, VIII-200 pp., 1945.
216. Gill, Rev. Nicholas, C.P., J.C.D., The Spiritual Prefect in Clerical Religious Houses of Study, X-140 pp., 1945.

217. HYNES, REV. HARRY GERARD, S.T.L., J.C.D., The Privileges of Cardinals, XII-183 pp., 1945.

218. MCDEVITT, REV. GERALD VINCENT, S.T.L., J.C.D., The Renunciation of an Ecclesiastical Office, XIV-179 pp., 1945.

219. MANNING, REV. JOSEPH LEROY, J.C.D., The Free Conferral of Offices, VII-116 pp., 1945.

220. MEYER, REV. LOUIS G., O.S.B., A.B., S.T.B., J.C.D., Alms-gathering by Religious, XII-163 pp., 1945.

221. O'DONNELL, REV. CLETUS FRANCIS, M.A., J.C.D., The Marriage of Minors, XII-268 pp., 1945.

222. PRUNSKIS, REV. JOSEPH, J.C.D., Comparative Law, Ecclesiastical and Civil, in Lithuanian Concordat, X-161 pp., 1945.

223. SWEENEY, REV. FRANCIS PATRICK, C.SS.R., J.C.D., The Reduction of Clerics to the Lay State, X-199 pp., 1945.

224. VOGELPOHL, REV. HENRY JOHN, J.C.D., The Simple Impediments to Holy Orders, XVI-190 pp., 1945.

225. BROCKHAUS, REV. THOMAS AQUINAS, O.S.B., J.C.D., Religious who are known as *Conversi*, X-127 pp., 1945.

226. GRIESE, REV. ORVILLE NICHOLAS, S.T.D., J.C.D., The Marriage Contract and the Procreation of Offspring, XVI-224 pp., 1946.

227. BOUDREAUX, REV. WARREN LOUIS, J.C.D., The *"ab acatholicis nati"* of Canon 1099, § 2, XII-110 pp., 1946.

228. BOWE, REV. THOMAS JOSEPH, A.B., J.C.D., Religious Superioresses, VIII-206 pp., 1946.

229. DIEDERICHS, REV. MICHAEL FERDINAND, S.C.J., J.C.D., The Jurisdiction of the Latin Ordinaries over their Oriental Subjects, XIV-153 pp., 1946.

230. DINGMAN, REV. MAURICE JOHN, A.B., S.T.L., J.C.L., The Plaintiff in Contentious Trials.

231. FRISON, REV. BASIL, C.M.F., M.MUS., J.C.D., The Retroactivity of Law, X-221 pp., 1946.

232. GALVIN, REV. WILLIAM ANTHONY, M.A., J.C.D., The Administrative Transfer of Pastors, XII-288 pp., 1946.

233. GORACY, REV. JOSEPH C., J.C.L., The Diriment Matrimonial Impediment of Major Orders.

234. HALE, REV. JOSEPH FRANCIS, M.A., S.T.L., J.C.D., The Pastor of Burial, X-247 pp., 1946 (printed 1949).

235. HENRY, REV. JOSEPH ARTHUR, A.B., J.C.D., The Mass and Holy Communion: Interritual Law, XII-138 pp., 1946.

236. LINENBERGER, REV. HERBERT, C.PP.S., J.C.D., The False Denunciation of an Innocent Confessor, VIII-205 pp., 1946 (1949).

237. LOWRY, REV. JAMES MARTIN, A.B., J.C.D., Dispensation from Private Vows, XII-266 pp., 1946.

238. LYNCH, REV. GEORGE EDWARD, A.B., S.T.L., J.C.D., Coadjutors and Auxiliaries of Bishops, X-107 pp., 1946 (printed 1947).

239. Lynch, Rev. Timothy, M.S.SS.T., J.C.D., Contracts between Bishops and Religious Congregations, XIII-232 pp., 1946.

240. McClunn, Rev. Justin David, A.B., S.T.L., J.C.D., Administrative Recourse, VII-142 pp., 1946.

241. Lohmuller, Rev. Martin Nicholas, A.B., J.C.D., The Promulgation of Law, XII-140 pp., 1947.

242. McGrath, Rev. James, A.B., J.C.D., The Privilege of the Canon, XII-156 pp., 1946.

243. Marbach, Rev. Joseph Francis, A.B., J.C.D., Marriage Legislation for the Catholics of the Oriental Rites in the United States and Canada, XIV-314 pp., 1946.

244. Shimkus, Rev. Bernard Aloysius, A.B., J.C.L., The Determination and Transfer of Rite.

245. Smith, Rev. Vincent Michael, A.B., S.T.L., J.C.L., Ignorance Affecting Matrimonial Consent.

246. Wachtrle, Rev. Paul Anthony, A.B., J.C.L., The Baptism of the Children of Non-Catholics.

247. Crotty, Rev. Matthew Michael, J.C.D., The Recipient of First Holy Communion, X-142 pp., 1947.

248. Eagleton, Rev. George, J.C.D., The Quinquennial Faculties, Formula IV, XIV-199 pp., 1947 (printed 1948).

249. Gibbons, Rev. Marion Leo, C.M., J.C.L., Domicile of the Wife Unlawfully Separated from Her Husband, XIV-171 pp., 1947.

250. Kelly, Rev. Bernard M., S.T.L., J.C.D., The Functions Reserved to Pastors, XII-141 pp., 1947.

251. Kilcullen, Rev. Thomas J., LL.M., J.C.D., The Collegiate Moral Person as Party Litigant, X-150 pp., 1947.

252. Lafontaine, Rev. Germaine Joseph, W.F., J.C.D., Relations Canoniques entre le Missionaire et Ses Superieurs, X-117 pp., 1947.

253. Lane, Rev. Loras Thomas, A.B., S.T.L., J.C.D., Matrimonial Procedure in the Ordinary Court of Second Instance, XVI-184 pp., 1947.

254. Lover, Rev. James Francis, C.Ss.R., J.C.D., The Master of Novices, X-168 pp., 1947.

255. McNicholas, Rev. Timothy Joseph, J.C.L., The *Septimae Manus* Witness.

256. Marositz, Rev. Joseph John, M.S.C., J.C.D., Obligations and Privileges of Religious Promoted to the Episcopal or Cardinalitial Dignities, XII-180 pp., 1947.

257. Murphy, Rev. Francis Joseph, J.C.D., Legislative Powers of the Provincial Council, XII-158 pp., 1947.

258. O'Brien, Rev. Romaeus William, O.Carm., J.C.D., The Provincial Superior in Religious Orders of Men, X-294 pp., 1947.

259. Pfaller, Rev. Benedict Anthony, O.S.B., J.C.D., *The ipso facto* Effected Dismissal of Religious, XII-225 pp., 1947.

260. Popek, Rev. Alphonse Sylvester, J.C.D., The Rights and Obligations of Metropolitans, XX-460 pp., 1947.
261. Ristuccia, Rev. Bernard Joseph, C.M., J.C.D., Quasi-Religious, XVI-318 pp., 1947 (printed 1949).
262. Sonntag, Rev. Nathaniel Louis, O.F.M.Cap., J.C.D., Censorship of Special Classes of Books, XII-147 pp., 1947.
263. Stadler, Rev. Joseph Nicholas, J.C.D., Frequent Holy Communion, X-158 pp., 1947.
264. Szal, Rev. Ignatius Joseph, J.C.D., The Communication of Catholics with Schismatics, XII-217 pp., 1947.
265. Wagner, Rev. Urban S., O.F.M. Conv., J.C.D., Parochial Substitute Vicars and Supplying Priests, IX-126 pp., 1947.
266. Quinn, Rev. Joseph, M.A., J.C.D., Documents Required for the Reception of Orders, XIV-207 pp., 1948.
267. Bennington, Rev. James Clement, A.B., J.C.L., The Recipient of Confirmation.
268. Blaher, Rev. Damian Joseph, O.F.M., A.B., J.C.L., The Ordinary Processes in Causes of Beatification and Canonization.
269. Clune, Rev. Robert Bell, B.A., J.C.L., The Judicial Interrogation of the Parties.
270. Courtemanche, Rev. Basil F., B.A., J.C.L., The Total Simulation of Matrimonial Consent.
271. Dlouhy, Rev. Maur John, O.S.B., A.B., J.C.L., The Ordination of Exempt Religious.
272. Donovan, Rev. John Thomas, Ph.B., S.T.L., J.C.D., The Clerical Obligation of Canons 138 and 140, XII-209 pp., 1948.
273. Freking, Rev. Frederick W., A.B., S.T.B., J.C.L., The Canonical Installation of Pastors.
274. Fulton, Rev. Thomas B., J.C.L., Prenuptial Investigation.
275. Godley, Rev. James P., J.C.L., Time and Place for the Celebration of Mass.
276. Kane, Rev. Thomas A., A.B., B.S., J.C.D., Jurisdiction of the Patriarchs of the Major Sees, XII-153 pp., 1948 (printed 1949).
277. Kennedy, Rev. Andrew A., J.C.L., The Annual Pastoral Report to the Local Ordinary.
278. Konrad, Rev. Joseph George, J.C.L., Transfer of Religious.
279. Kress, Rev. Alphonse, J.C.L., Contumacy in Ecclesiastical Trials.
280. McCartney, Rev. Marcellus Anthony, O.F.M., M.A., J.C.L., Faculties of Regular Confessors.
281. McCaslin, Rev. Edward Patrick, M.A., S.T.L., J.C.L., The Division of Parishes.
282. McElroy, Rev. Francis J., A.B., J.C.L., The Privileges of Bishops.

www.ingramcontent.com/pod-product-compliance
Lightning Source LLC
LaVergne TN
LVHW050240080826
844660LV00012B/569

* 9 7 8 0 8 1 3 2 2 4 5 3 4 *